Heinemann ECONOMICS A2 for Edexcel

Heinemann
ECONOMICS A2
for Edexcel

BY

Sue Grant *and* Chris Vidler

with Andrew Ellams

heinemann.co.uk
✓ Free online support
✓ Useful weblinks
✓ 24 hour online ordering

01865 888058

Inspiring generations

Heinemann Educational Publishers
Halley Court, Jordan Hill, Oxford OX2 8EJ
Part of Harcourt Education

Heinemann is the registered trademark of
Harcourt Education Limited

First published 2003

08 07 06 05 04 03
10 9 8 7 6 5 4 3 2 1

British Library Cataloguing in Publication Data is
available from the British Library on request.

ISBN 0 435 33083 7

Designed by Artistix

Typeset by Hardlines Ltd, Charlbury, Oxford

Original illustrations © Harcourt Education Limited, 2003

Illustrated by Hardlines Ltd, Charlbury, Oxford

Cover design by Matt Buckley

Printed in the UK by Scotprint

Picture research by Sally Cole

Acknowledgements
The publishers would like to thank the following for
permission to use photographs: p.18 Alamy/Sean Potter;
p.45 P.A. Photos/Sean Dempsy; p.55 P.A. Photos/John
Stillwell; p.58 P.A. Photos/EPA; p.59 Milepost 92
half/Virgin; p.89 Richard Jackson; p.97 Photofusion/Paula
Glassman; p.107 Science Photo Library/John Cole; p.129
Panos Pictures/Fernando Moleres; p.136 Corbis/Bettmann;
p.144 Panos Pictures/Howard Davies; p.151 Alamy/Holt
Studios International Ltd.; p.186 Gareth Boden; p.200
Rex/Action Press; p.210 Alamy/Image State.
pp.137,139 and 143 maps from *Modern School Atlas*, 93rd
edn. by George Philip Limited (2000), redrawn by
permission of Philip's.

Every effort has been made to contact copyright holders
of material reproduced in this book. Any omissions will
be rectified in subsequent printings if notice is given to
the publishers.

Tel: 01865 888058 www.heinemann.co.uk

Websites

There are links to relevant websites in this book. In
order to ensure that the links are up-to-date, that the
links work, and that the sites are not inadvertently
linked to sites that could be considered offensive, we
have made the links available on the Heinemann
website at www.heinemann.co.uk/hotlinks. When you
access the Heinemann website, enter the express code
0837P, and this will take you to the links you want.

Contents

General introduction

Welcome to *Heinemann Economics A2 for Edexcel*. This book has been specially written for students taking the Edexcel course. This means that it:

■ follows the Edexcel specification closely

■ has been written to ensure that all concepts are clearly explained in terms which students taking this subject for the first time will understand

■ includes plenty of advice from examiners to help you get the best possible grade.

The introduction is divided into three parts. Firstly the links to your AS are made clear. This is followed by a more formal description of how the A2 part of your course is organised and finally you will be introduced to the special features of this book which have been designed to help you get the grade you deserve.

Your AS experience

How was it for you? We hope you got the grade you deserved. If you didn't, think about a retake. Even if you scored well for AS, it may be worthwhile taking units again. It is easier to score marks for AS than it is for A2 and as the second year of your course involves more in-depth consideration of many of the topics you took in the first year you should get better and better at economics.

If things have gone reasonably well, you should be:

■ reasonably familiar with the special technical language associated with economics

■ used to using graphical analysis to show that you can predict the outcomes of changes in economic and other variables

■ developing skills of analysis and evaluation.

Your AS programme consisted of two sets of learning. You probably devoted up to two thirds of your time to the first two microeconomics modules on how markets work and why they might fail. The rest of your time would have been spent getting your head around macroeconomics and dealing with national issues like economic growth and inflation.

This structure is reflected in the A2 course. Module 4 is advanced microeconomics, Module 6 is advanced macroeconomics with a greater emphasis on international trade and related topics and Module 5 (not very logical in terms of numbering) involves choosing between an option in the economics of development or one on the labour market. At this stage, you need to think about your preferred option (more about this later), sort out any retakes and try to plan out your programme for study to spread pressure points over the whole year. You can sit 'Industrial economics' in both January and June but the two options and the UK and the global economy are only available in June. It is probably advisable to tackle Module 4 in January, leaving the summer session for your preferred option, Module 6 and, heaven forbid, any retakes you think you need. There are, of course, other ways of dividing up your course and your school/college may not allow you to take exams in January. Whatever the constraints, it pays to plan ahead, especially when it will reduce pressure on you next May and June.

The main thing to remember is that examiners can ask questions based on both the AS and A2 parts of your course. This particularly applies to Module 6, which is worth 20 percent of the total marks for your A-level and is designated as being synoptic. Don't throw away your notes from last year and don't forget to revise basic stuff like elasticity and aggregate demand and supply for your A2 examinations.

Moving up a gear

This is what you have to do for A2. Most students find the second year of the course much more demanding than AS. You have to know more, questions are less straightforward and usually require longer more detailed answers. This is because a higher proportion of marks is awarded for showing that you have the higher order skills of analysis and evaluation. The good thing about economics is that once you have mastered a particular topic it should stick in your brain.

As has already been indicated, Module 4, 'Industrial economics', is essentially advanced microeconomics. To quote from the specification:

> This unit develops the content of units 1 and 2 and examines how the pricing of, and nature of competition between, firms is affected by the number and size of market participants. At the end of this unit, students should be able to analyse the pricing and output decisions of firms in different contexts. They should also be capable of making an appraisal of government intervention aimed at promoting competitive markets.

This means that you need to have a more detailed understanding of:
- different types of market structure
- the impact of this on competition
- the effectiveness of different forms of government intervention.

The theory of the firm involves a deeper understanding of revenue and costs faced by firms operating under different market conditions and this links directly into consideration of why markets might be considered to fail and possible strategies for government intervention which themselves might fail.

Module 6, 'The UK and the global economy', is essentially advanced macroeconomics and consists of four linked elements:
- globalisation
- trade policies
- exchange rates
- assessing the effectiveness of different government economic policies on both the domestic economy and international competitiveness.

Although you will have developed a basic grasp of different economic policies in relation to the domestic economy, much of the content of this module is likely to be new to you as it involves taking a global rather than a national perspective.

This paper is synoptic, which means that you can expect questions which draw upon your complete understanding of economics from both AS and A2.

As for Module 5, if you study labour markets, you have to have a good understanding of:
- the special features of markets for labour
- unemployment
- trade unions
- the distribution of wealth and income.

Development economics, meanwhile, focuses on:
- measuring development
- theories about development
- looking at development across the world
- assessing the effectiveness of policies to promote development

Finding your way

The text of *Heinemann Economics A2 for EDEXCEL* is set out in a similar fashion to the AS text. The major difference is that the individual sections are longer to give enough space to develop the more detailed treatments required for A2. At the end of each part, there are sections devoted to exam preparation. This consists of advice from examiners who work for EDEXCEL on good practice when it comes to exams. They can give you a feel for what examiners actually look for when it comes to marking your work. Finally, there are sample questions and answers as well as further examination style questions for you to develop the skills which will be tested at the end of your course.

Sample section

The typical layout of each section is illustrated below.

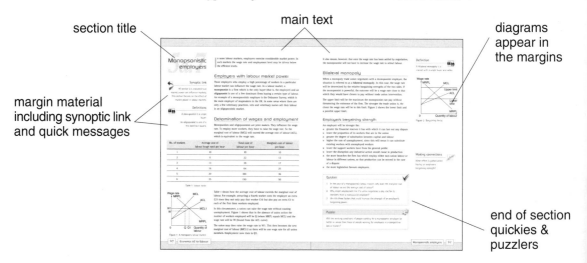

section title

main text

diagrams appear in the margins

margin material including synoptic link and quick messages

end of section quickies & puzzlers

The central body of text is designed to explain the key concept(s) featured in each section. This always ends with quick questions (quickies) to test your understanding. The margins of each section will contain a different selection of quick messages designed to assist your learning. Where relevant there are links to the work that you did for AS (synoptic links). Other hints relate to further research, weblinks, and controversial issues (hot potatoes). Each is associated with a symbol and these are explained in more detail below:

 Synoptic links – Links to AS and other areas of study which are relevant to your understanding of the current section.

 Hot potatoes – Controversial issues you might want to discuss or debate.

 Definitions – These define the key terms and vocabulary used in economics. You must know these and get into the habit of defining the main terms you use in all your exam answers.

 Research tasks – Suggestions for more in-depth exploration.

 Thinking like an economist – Questions and tasks that encourage you to apply economic analysis.

 Learning tips – Useful advice on how to learn effectively and efficiently.

 Making connections – Links between economics and life around us.

 Weblinks – Some useful websites to help consolidate your knowledge.

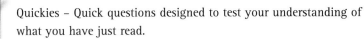 Exam hints – Little ideas that might make all the difference when it comes to the exam.

 Quickies – Quick questions designed to test your understanding of what you have just read.

Puzzler – Tricky stuff to get your head round.

Boost your grade – Tips designed to help you gain the highest grades.

Pitfalls to avoid – Common mistakes made by students.

PART 4

INDUSTRIAL
ECONOMICS

Introduction to industrial economics

Welcome to what, for most of you, will be the first module or unit that you tackle for A2.

Overview of module

Although the specification does not follow this pattern, it might be helpful to see this module as consisting of four different but overlapping sections.

- How and why firms grow – the size of firms has implications for the objectives they pursue and relates closely to the amount of power that they are able to exert in the market place which in turn impacts on economic effectiveness and efficiency.
- Theory of the firm - This includes detailed treatment of costs and revenue which you need to know to be able to predict how firms are likely to behave in relation to three key variables: price, output and profits. This will involve you becoming familiar with using graphical analysis to aid your understanding of how firms behave.
- Market structures – Follows on from theory of the firm and consists of four different models; perfect competition, imperfect competition, oligopoly and monopoly. Again the treatment is essentially graphical.
- Finally, an assessment of the impact of different forms of government intervention to promote competition and improve the efficient workings of markets. This involves a mixture of graphical and written analysis that you need to develop to show that you have reached the A2 standard.

Links with AS

You should quickly appreciate that much of the content of this module is similar to that which you learned for your AS 'Markets and market failure' module. For example, for AS you will have dealt with competitive and concentrated markets. For A2, a deeper theoretical understanding is required. Another way of seeing the differences is that for AS most of your treatment of markets was descriptive, whereas at A2 you are required to use graphs and be more precise in your analysis. Finally, government intervention in these markets builds and develops on the work that you did for AS in sections 2.3 and 2.12.

AS and A2

Students usually find this module and Module 6 on globalisation the hardest to do well on. There are a number of reasons for this.

- For AS, 60 per cent of your marks are for what some people think are the easier skills of knowledge, understanding and application. The other 40 per cent are for analysis and evaluation. The split for Modules 5 and 6 on the other hand is 50/50, which means that you have to give more longer answers in your exam.
- These longer answers will require you to have a better overall understanding of topics such that you can evaluate the usefulness of

particular microeconomic models. This means that you have to be able to step back from your work and see both the value and the limitations of these models in helping us understand how businesses and labour markets work in the real world.

- Synopticity – in other words you must show that you can see links between the different topics studied for AS and A2.
- Exam pressure is greater since you have to do much more in a relatively short period of time. Weaker students who work more slowly often have less time to devote to the high mark questions which tend to come up at the end of the paper.

Maximizing your grade

Obviously, knowing you stuff is the essential prerequisite for doing well but there are issues which you and your teachers need to consider, and these relate mainly to the sequencing or scheduling of your learning. It was suggested earlier that you might want to sit the examination for this module in January giving you a chance to have a second go in June. This means that the bulk of the autumn term of year 2 can be devoted to Module 4. If you choose the labour market option you will find that there are many links between these two units. Alternatively, there are also synergies between studying development economics and globalisation. However, the point its that it pays to devote as long a period as possible to this module. There is a lot to learn and the exam is challenging. But stick to it and you will win through.

The exam

This unit is very similar in style to AS in that you have to answer ten 'supported' choice questions and one data response question from a choice of two. It is likely, however, to have more high mark questions requiring longer, more detailed answers than was the case for AS. More detailed advice on exam preparation is given in section 4.17.

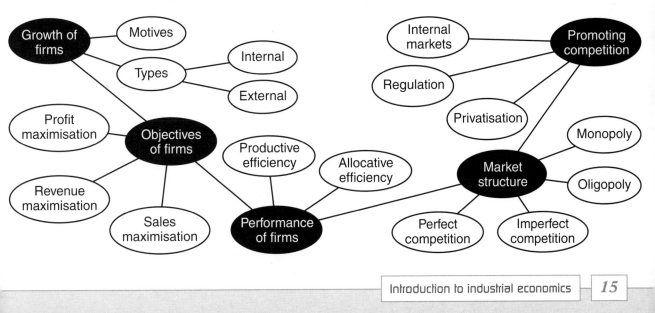

Industrial economics

4.2

Synoptic links

This unit builds directly on the work that you did for AS units 1 and 2 on how markets work and how they fail. The focus is on developing an understanding of how firms are likely to behave in different types of markets. This first section is devoted to understanding how firms grow and the motives behind such growth.

There are no hard and fast rules which apply to the birth and growth of firms. New firms emerge in two ways:
- innovation led birth
- organisation led birth.

Innovation led birth

Innovation is the technical term used to describe turning an invention into a product or services for which there is a demand. This is the classic 'rags to riches' story which can be typified by a 'eureka' moment of discovery of a cheaper way of making things, the development of a new service, or the invention of something completely new.

Examples of innovation include Woolworths, which was established in the 1880s to provide a different shopping experience – one in which customers could buy a wider range of products than was the case before, at rock bottom prices. Starting Easyjet and similar low-cost airlines involved a totally different approach to selling airline tickets. The development of mobile phone technology led to the creation of a completely new product which, prior to the 1980s, was unknown.

Organisation led birth

The organisation led birth and growth of firms is often more organic and developmental, especially when it arises out of the expansion of particular economic sectors. The Eden Project in Cornwall has led to the development of a range of businesses and services catering for the growing number of tourists. In this situation, new businesses grow in response to new demands. This kind of growth is therefore said to be demand rather than producer led.

Early stages of growth

Newly established firms are usually faced with similar challenges. These include:
- cash flow
- employment issues
- ownership and control
- competition.

New businesses often underestimate the amount of money needed to keep going and they often find it difficult to survive if they are faced with some unexpected bill or loss of business. Banks and other creditors often seem unsympathetic to the difficulties facing newly-established firms, and it may be difficult for small businesses to borrow.

Taking on additional labour can also present big challenges to small firms, especially in terms of whether or not there is enough additional business to finance a big addition to labour costs.

As businesses grow and expand, they are often faced with a difficult stage of transition. When small, it is easy for owners to exert day-to-day control and be at the centre of a web of informal relationships, which can make working for a small business friendlier. However, if businesses grow rapidly, such informal day-to-day control is difficult to sustain and some entrepreneurs deliberately limit the growth of the businesses to ensure that they remain firmly in charge.

Finally, competition is an ever-present threat, especially if barriers of entry are low. Other businesses may be established and existing larger businesses may adopt strategies designed to drive newcomers out of the market.

Survival

Clearly survival is the prime objective of a new business and one way of tackling this is by growth. This can:

- make it easier to raise additional funds
- help establish a more permanent place in a given market
- eliminate some of the risks arising from competition.

Growth

Firms can get bigger in two different ways. They can grow by:
- internal expansion
- external growth.

Internal expansion

Firms grow in size by increasing total sales or turnover. This can be achieved by out-competing rivals and gaining greater market share or by being part of an expanding market. Both approaches require development of greater productive capacity. These growth strategies can, to some degree, become self-financing, as retained profits can be used to provide the finance for expansion. Internal growth can lead to economies of scale and lower long-term costs of production, which in turn can provide greater competitive advantage and therefore help further growth.

Firms that successfully pursue such policies will also usually find it easier to raise additional funds either from banks or from the stock market. Most **oligopolistic firms** are **public limited companies (plcs)**, but this also makes expanding companies liable to take over, especially if they are competing in the same market as larger better-resourced firms.

Definitions

Oligopolistic firms are those operating in an industry with few competitors.

Public limited companies (plcs) are companies that have limited liability and sell shares to the general public.

Definitions

Conglomerate merger means taking over or merging with firms from different industries, for example, banks and building societies.

Horizontal integration means taking over or merging with businesses at similar stages of the distribution cycle, for example, supermarket retailers.

Monopoly theoretically means when one firm produces the whole output of a given industry.

Vertical integration means taking over or merging with businesses at different stages of the distribution cycle, for example, manufacturers and distributors.

Lloyds Bank's takeover of Cheltenham and Gloucester Building Society is an example of a conglomerate merger

External growth (mergers and takeovers)

Firms can also grow in size and economic power by merger when two businesses agree to collaborate to form one. More commonly, one business takes over another, either by outright purchase or by the accumulation of a controlling interest of shares. Both external forms of growth are usually referred to as mergers. These take three forms:

■ **vertical integration** – by which one firm merges with another involved in different stages of the production chain (for example, electricity supply companies buying into electricity generation)

■ **horizontal integration** – when mergers take place between companies at the same stage of the production chain (for example, Wal-Mart and Asda)

■ **conglomerate merger** – where firms from different industries merge (for example, Lloyds Bank take over of Cheltenham and Gloucester Building Society).

Merger activity provides a rapid means of building up market share. It helps to protect firms from competition and to ensure greater control over the productive process. However, it can also reduce customer choice and increase **monopoly** power.

Merger activity tends to be greatest towards the peak of the economic cycle. Successful companies generate profits, which can then be used to part-finance further acquisitions.

Global rank	Corporation	Country	Revenues year 2000 (US millions)
1	ExxonMobil	US	210,392
2	Wal-Mart Stores	US	193,295
3	General Motors	US	184,632
4	Ford Motors	US	180,598
5	DaimlerChrysler	US	150,069
6	Royal Dutch/Shell Group	UK/Netherlands	149,146
7	British Petroleum	UK	148,062
8	General Electric	US	129,853
9	Mitsubishi	Japan	126,579
10	Toyota Motor	Japan	121,416

Table 1 The ten largest multinationals

Multinationals

The process of growth and expansion has, especially over the last 100 years, resulted in the creation of multinational or transnational firms, who are able to exercise monopoly power on a global scale. The role and impact of such companies as Royal Dutch Shell, Unilever and General Motors is widely underestimated by the general public but some idea of their power can be gained from looking at Table 1.

Economists differ in their assessments of the impact of such large firms but have developed further theories and techniques to help measure market power and advise governments of possible intervention strategies.

Demergers

Contrary to the developments outlined on pages 17–18, there has been an increase in demergers over the last decade. Increasing competition and globalisation can leave large conglomerates at a disadvantage to firms more clearly focused on a particular economic activity.

Improvements in technology (especially ICT), the further development of subcontracting, multi-skilling of workers and the development of flatter, more customer-focused organisations are all combining to reduce the cost advantages enjoyed by conglomerates.

The fashion in business is increasingly to 'concentrate' on core activities. Selling off non-core activities is another way of financing further growth and development focused on particular activities. An example of this process is the restructuring of GEC. Its defence-related business was sold off to British Aerospace, and the company has been renamed Marconi to concentrate on the growth of the ICT sector.

Summary

Owning and running a business involves a mixture of chance, luck, innovation and inventiveness. If things work out, profits can be made but such activity is never without risk. Only one out of every two businesses survives the first year of trading. There are clearly pressures on businesses to minimise risks, and one of the most effective ways is to strive to gain monopolistic or oligopolistic power. Economic theory demonstrates that firms which are monopolies or oligopolies have considerable market power to set prices, determine customer choice, limit competition and prevent new market entrants. Such market leaders can be very large firms, commanding turnovers greater than most countries in the world, and able to use their economic power to influence the behaviour of governments. However, dominating a local or niche market can also give similar powers to set prices and minimise the risks of competition.

Research task

Choose a local firm and find out when it was first established and how it has grown. Present your findings to the rest of the class. What conclusions can you reach?

Hot potato

The interests of business are fundamentally at odds with those of consumers. How far do you agree?

Objectives of firms
4.3

Synoptic links

This section builds on several sections of the AS part of your course. Before you go any further make sure that you know about:

- monopolies (AS section 2.5)
- economies of scale (AS section 2.4)
- supply-side policies (AS section 3.22).

Definition

Sales maximisation refers to the firm selling as much output as it can to maximise its market share, subject to the constraint of not making a loss. Thus the firm can lower its price to increase the quantity demanded, up to the point that the price (AR) is just equal to the AC.

Section 4.3 is devoted to increasing your knowledge of how the objectives of firms are likely to affect the ways in which firms behave. This is a key element in helping you to develop your understanding of what is called 'industrial economics'. Most firms probably pursue a variety of objectives. These include:

- survival
- profit maximisation
- **sales maximisation**
- social and community objectives
- building shareholder value
- growth and expansion.

Survival

The survival rate of newly established businesses is not very high and many struggle to stay afloat. Competition is often intense and new businesses are often under-capitalised, which means they often have insufficient financial backing to survive unforeseen events.

Getting through the first year of trading is a difficult objective, and one that is likely to dominate the owners of small businesses. However, it is not just small and new businesses that have to fight to survive. Established UK companies like Marconi and Cable and Wireless are currently struggling to survive and, like their smaller counterparts, are doing everything they can to stay in businesses. If companies such as these don't try to ensure that they minimise any losses and don't strive to make as big a profit as possible, they probably won't survive.

Profit maximisation

Ensuring that a firm earns as much profit as possible is a similar objective to survival. It means that a business is as prepared to cut production as it is to expand, and it means that chasing profits is more important than any other objective. A firm that wishes to maximise profits will go on expanding production and sales until the last unit sold adds as much to its revenue as it does to its costs. In this way, a profit-maximising firm will always ensure that its profits are as large as possible.

Sales maximisation

This is a similar concept and applies to those firms that sell as much as they can while still covering their costs. A sales-maximising firm will go on producing and selling until the price that it receives for the last unit sold is the same as its cost of production.

Social and community objectives

Profit and sales are not always the most important objectives for some organisations. Schools, for instance, may set out to get the best examination results, but they are rarely run to make as big a profit as possible or to attract increasing numbers of students.

Other examples are local councils who will probably say that they strive to meet the needs of the local community and many voluntary organisations who will have similar social directed objectives. Many companies in the private sector also claim to have wider objectives than merely the pursuit of sales or profit. Ethical traders like Fairtrade are becoming more and more significant.

Building shareholder value

This and similar sounding terms are often used in the UK by plcs whose shares are publicly traded on the stock exchange. The value refers to the return that shareholders receive from owning shares. This can be boosted by larger dividends and, most importantly, by higher share prices. The determination of share prices is a complex and, some would argue, irrational process and large companies use a range of strategies to push up the price of their shares. In the USA in recent years this has included the use of dubious and illegal accounting practices.

Growth and expansion

This is almost the opposite of survival, and many medium-size and large firms strive to grow and dominate the industry in which they operate. This is often described as gaining market share – that is, the proportion of sales in a given market going to one particular firm – and can be achieved in two ways.

Firms can out-compete their competitors and build sales by selling at lower prices or by beating rivals in terms of quality. The same objectives can be achieved by merger and takeover of rivals or related businesses. Vodaphone, for instance, has become one of the three largest UK companies by the relentless acquisition of rivals.

Reconciling competing objectives

Few, if any, firms are simple, one-dimensional organisations. Most follow a clutch of different, potentially conflicting, objectives. Sorting out which is most important is often difficult. Firms themselves are not always very clear about how they prioritise their objectives. Economists are often forced to make generalisations. At a very basic level, no organisation can survive if it fails to ensure that revenue equals or exceeds costs.

Research task

Get hold of three different annual reports from plcs. What do they tell you about how large businesses prioritise objectives?

Small businesses probably need to go for profit at the expense of other objectives, and it is possible to argue that larger organisations are most likely to grow and build shareholder value. Some businesses set minimum levels of profit or market share, which allows them to pursue other objectives. This is called 'satisficing'.

Historical trends

Economists have undertaken extensive research into trying to establish what motivators or drivers are most important in determining how firms actually behave. There is a lot of evidence to suggest that business behaviour is heavily influenced by the culture of different societies. Thus, Japanese firms traditionally have put much more value on ensuring that a wide range of workers' needs are met – for example, health care, sport and recreation, child support and the like. US companies are often stereotyped as having a 'get up and go' attitude, in which growth and expansion are highly valued.

In his recent book, *The state We're In* (Vintage), Will Hutton argues that British businesses are too short-termist, and that quick returns and profits rather than long-term investment are the expectation. Economists have to be careful to avoid making sweeping generalisations, but it is clear that more and more business is being concentrated in the hands of fewer companies or corporations. These large transnational firms are often more powerful than all but the wealthiest countries, but understanding how major companies such as Ford, Sony, Exxon and Unilever work is a neglected area of research.

Ownership and control

The Canadian-born economist J.K. Galbraith argued that the growth of corporations in the US has led to a breakdown in the traditional relationship between ownership and control of firms. When businesses are small, their owners usually run them. Clearly, this is the case with sole proprietors and partnerships, and it is logical to argue that if people have put money into a business, they will run that business to ensure that they make reasonable profits. They are likely to be profit maximisers.

The growth of firms requires additional sources of finance. In countries such as the UK, the stock market is an important source of finance. Shares are sold to raise capital. Shareholders own plcs. Thus, Marks and Spencer is owned by thousands of individual shareholders. Galbraith argued that these shareholders did not actively participate in decision making. As long as they received what they considered to be a reasonable share of profits – their dividend – he argued that their role would be passive. Many decisions regarding company objectives would be left to senior managers.

Galbraith argued that this group of people were strongly motivated by status, and that status was earned in the US by being associated with a company that was growing and expanding. He suggested that such key managers would be more interested in boosting sales and achieving greater market share than they would be in chasing the highest possible profit. They would be foolish to totally ignore shareholders, but as long as they were happy with their returns, managers would be left to get on with running the company.

Evaluating Galbraith's arguments

Galbraith's arguments about the divorce between ownership and control of large corporations have had a significant impact on how economists deal with large companies. Clearly it is dangerous to automatically assume that all business are profit maximisers, but at the same time companies that ignore the pursuit of profit are likely to find it difficult to survive in the long term.

It is possible to argue that widespread share ownership leads to the conclusion that individual shareholders exert little power. However, shares are very rarely evenly distributed. They are not all owned by little old ladies living in Eastbourne. In the UK, it is very common for directors of plcs to also be major shareholders. Such people are likely to regard themselves as both owners and those in control.

The only way in which Galbraith's arguments and those of his critics can be properly evaluated is by undertaking empirical research of individual companies.

Quickie

Business objectives and their prioritisation will affect how firms behave, especially in terms of setting levels of output and/or price. Which of the following is likely to set the lowest prices?
(a) A profit maximiser.
(b) A sales maximiser.

Puzzler

Economists have to make simplifying assumptions. How valid is the assumption that profit maximisation is more important than any other objective?

Costs of production: 1

Synoptic links

This section builds on the work that you did for AS on supply curves (see AS sections 1.6–1.10). This may not be immediately obvious. But remember, you have already learned that supply curves almost always slope upwards from left to right. The detailed analysis on costs will provide you with an improved rationale as to why this is the case.

All firms, regardless of their mission statements, objectives, ownership and what they might say about themselves, have to make decisions about two key factors: costs and revenue. If firms are going to survive, they need to ensure that their revenues are, at the very least, the same as their costs. Most businesses strive to ensure that revenue exceeds costs. This positive difference is described by economists as profit. Should costs exceed revenue, a loss is made. The economic analysis contained in this section and in section 4.5 is based on this very simple reasoning.

Thus, examination of data about costs and revenue is important in helping you to develop a better understanding of the behaviour of firms. This applies just as much to organisations that are not primarily motivated to make profits – for example, government agencies and voluntary groups. This section is devoted to developing an understanding of how economists look at costs of production in the short run. Section 4.5 is devoted to long run costs. This is followed by consideration of those factors that affect the revenue firms can earn.

Short run costs of production

All payments made by a firm in the production of a good or provision of a service are called costs. Economists use of the convention followed by many businesses of distinguishing between overheads and running costs.

Overheads

Overheads are costs of production that businesses have to pay regardless of their level of output. Thus, a bookstore is likely to be faced with bills for rent, business rates and repayment of loans, which will remain the same regardless of how many books are sold. These expenditures are classified as fixed costs and the convention is that these do not change in the short run, which is defined as that period of time in which it is not possible to change the quantity of an input of a particular factor of production (usually called factor input).

Running costs

Running costs, such as payment of wages, stock purchases and the like, which will change as sales change in the short run, are classified as variable costs.

Classifying fixed and variable costs

In practice, it is not always easy to decide whether a particular cost should be classified as fixed or variable. For example, contracts and salaries might be agreed to cover a particular length of time, making them fixed, whereas maintenance costs might change considerably as output changes, making them variable.

Total costs

The addition of fixed to variable costs gives total costs, which include all the costs faced by a firm in the production of a good or the provision of a service.

Average costs

The total cost divided by the output of the business gives the short run average total cost, which is usually abbreviated to short run average cost, or even just average cost. This is probably the most useful of these measures, as it indicates the cost of producing each item or providing a service. The average cost is sometimes referred to as the unit cost.

Marginal costs

Finally, economists and business people make use of the concept of marginal cost, which is the additional cost of producing an extra unit of output of a particular good or service. Thus, if a clothing manufacturing company were to produce an extra suit, it would be faced with the costs of additional materials and labour, but would not have to pay out any more for design or machine-setting costs.

Short run costs

Economic analysis of the behaviour of firms focuses on either the short or the long run. In the short run, as has already been indicated, a firm can change only the input of variable factors such as labour. In the long run, it can change the inputs of any factor. This section is concerned with the analysis of changes in the short run, and a series of logical deductions can be made on the basis of this classification. The data contained in Table 1 is based on the actual costs of running a bookshop and illustrates how short run costs are likely to behave.

Table 1 shows it is easy to work out the monthly total costs (total fixed cost plus total variable cost) of running the bookshop. From this, it is possible to derive the average cost of selling convenient bundles of books. In this example, let us assume that 2,500 books were sold in March. If this figure is divided into the total costs of £8,850, the average cost of selling each book is £3.54.

Graphing average costs

If it were possible to continue to collect cost data relating to different levels of output or sales, it would be possible to construct graphs illustrating the relationship between costs and different levels of sales.

To take an agricultural example, farmers are likely to have a fair idea of the best number of livestock to keep given the acreage and quality of their

Thinking like an economist

John Maynard Keynes argued that we should focus on the short run because in the long run we are all dead. Do you agree?

Fixed costs	£
Rent	2000
Uniform business rate	1000
Bank loan repayment	750
Depreciation of computer and other equipment	50
Insurance	50
Wages	2000
Total fixed cost	5850
Variable costs	£
Purchase of new stock	2000
Postage	300
Telephone	200
Overtime	500
Total variable cost	3000
Total cost	8850

Table 1 Average monthly costs of Forest Bookshop (March 2002)

farmland. In Table 2, average costs of producing each lamb on a 250 acre farm are related to different 'outputs' of lambs.

Annual sales of lambs	Fixed costs (£)	Variable costs (£)	Total costs (£)	Average costs (£)
0	5000	0	5000	
50	5000	1000	6000	120
200	5000	4000	9000	45
500	5000	14,000	19,000	38
1000	5000	60,000	65,000	65
1500	5000	105,000	110,000	73

Table 2 Sales of lambs

Table 2 shows what a good farmer would know – that is, the most appropriate number of ewes to keep given the size of farm and cost of different factor inputs.

In this example, if no lambs were sold, the farmer would still be faced with certain fixed costs which will probably be dominated by fencing, rent and repayment of loans.

A small flock of around 30 ewes might be expected to produce 50 lambs. Variable costs for feed, veterinary treatment and the abattoir would be incurred. However, given the relatively high level of fixed costs, it would cost £120 to rear and slaughter each lamb. Production of 200 lambs would be more 'economic', as better use would be made of the available land. However, each lamb would still cost £45 to produce.

Increasing the flock size to around 300 ewes could produce 500 lambs and even better use would be made of the farm, giving an average cost of £38 per lamb. Continued expansion of the flock would, however, push up average costs to £65 a lamb when 1000 are produced and £73 if 1500 were raised. Breeding more and more lambs would put pressure on the available grass, lead to the purchase of more and more hay and concentrates, and probably lead to a greater incidence of disease.

In short, if this farmer wanted to be most efficient and keep short run costs to a minimum, he or she should produce around 500 lambs a year. The average cost data contained in the table is illustrated in Figure 1.

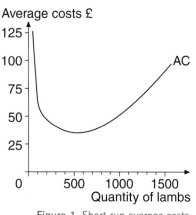

Figure 1 Short run average costs of sheep farmer

Output is measured on the horizontal axis and average costs of production on the vertical. This (short run) average cost curve is 'U' shaped. As output expands, efficiency increases and short run average costs fall. They reach a minimum, or 'optimum', point beyond which short run costs rise, indicating declining efficiency. Average costs are pushed down by falling marginal costs and then pulled up by rising marginal costs. When the use of a variable factor is increased while another factor input remains fixed, marginal costs may initially fall and then rise. The **law of diminishing marginal returns** applies when marginal costs start to rise.

Definition

Law of diminishing marginal returns applies to short run costs faced by a firm. It states that if a firm seeks to increase production in the short run, its marginal costs of production will first fall, then bottom out, then rise.

In Figure 1, more and more fodder and concentrates were purchased to feed an expanding flock of sheep, but the size of the farm remained the same. Similarly, if a factory manager wanted to increase production in the short run they would not be able to rapidly expand the size of the factory, nor buy new machines. Employees could be asked to work overtime and more workers could be taken on. If this process were to continue, a point would be reached when overcrowding and the sheer mass of workers would contribute to rising short run average costs.

Graphing marginal costs

Daily number of MoT tests costs (£)	Total daily costs (£)	Average costs (£)	Marginal costs (£)
0	150		
1	150	150.00	150
2	180	90.00	30
3	196	65.30	16
4	211	52.75	15
5	224	44.80	13
6	236	39.30	12
7	247	35.30	11
8	257	32.10	10
9	226	29.50	9
10	274	27.40	8
11	280	25.40	6
12	285	23.75	5
13	292	22.50	7
14	301	21.50	9
15	311	20.70	10
16	331	20.70	20
17	355	20.90	24
18	385	21.40	30
19	423	22.30	38
20	471	23.60	48

Table 3: Total daily costs incurred by garage specialising in MoTs

As indicated on page 25, any change in costs brought about by changing production by an additional unit is described as a marginal cost. These costs can be calculated by looking at how total costs change according to changes in output. Table 3 relates to total costs incurred on a daily basis by a garage specialising in undertaking MoTs.

In the example, the garage owner is faced with fixed costs of £150 a day – rent, business rates, wages, loan repayment and so forth. As more and more MoTs are carried out, resources are used more efficiently, which is reflected in both falling average and marginal costs.

As with the sheep farmer in Figure 1, the garage owner will find that costs will bottom out and then begin to increase. In this example, undertaking 16 rather than 15 MoTs causes a big rise in costs – perhaps because extra labour is required. As work increases, the garage becomes more crowded and congested, and both average and marginal costs rise.

The data contained in Table 3 is illustrated in Figure 2. Marginal costs are plotted against the midpoint of each unit change in output, and the marginal cost curve will cut the lowest point of the average cost curve.

What is important is, in the short run, average and marginal cost curves will always have the same relationship to each other. The application of the law of diminishing marginal returns means that any attempt to increase output by changing the use of one factor while the use of others remains fixed will initially lead to falling average and marginal costs. An optimum will then be reached where average costs are at a minimum and, thereafter, growing inefficiency will lead to rising average costs. This observation that short run average cost curves are 'U' shaped is one with which all students of economics should become familiar.

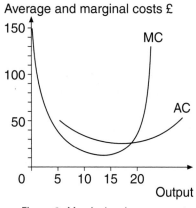

Figure 2 Marginal and average costs

As indicated on page 25,

Learning tip

Get used to drawing average and marginal cost curves. Draw the 'U' shaped average cost curve first, then the marginal cost curve. The upward final bit passes through the lowest point on the average cost curve. Finally, don't ever forget to label your axis – costs on the vertical and output on the horizontal.

Quickie

Assume the Forest Bookshop is able to sell twice as many books in April 2002 than it did March. Construct your own table of data reflecting these higher sales. What will be the effect on the following?
(a) Fixed costs.
(b) Variable costs.
(c) Average costs.
(d) And, by implication, potential profits.

H aving focused on short run costs in section 4.4, this section looks at long run costs. The long run is defined as that period of time in which it is possible for a firm to alter any or all of its factor inputs. Traditionally, economists have considered that the distinction between the long and the short term is very important in analysing costs and the behaviour of firms. There is now more debate about this approach, and at the end of this section there is an outline of alternative approaches. You need to understand both traditional and newer approaches to the analysis of costs.

Costs of production: 2

Traditional theory

This builds on the analysis in section 4.4. Thus, the long run is about the sheep farmer purchasing more land, the bookseller expanding its premises and the garage installing new car-testing machinery. The effect of expanding production on long run average costs is likely to depend on a number of factors. The following three scenarios apply to the sheep farmer doubling the size of their farm.

Scenario 1

Suppose the cost of a loan to purchase additional land is the same as was already being paid for the original 250 acres. Assume that there will be proportionately similar increases in costs for labour, winter feed, fencing and veterinary fees. In this situation, the average short run cost of producing each lamb would not be very different from the short run cost on the smaller farm.

This means that at the optimum level of output each lamb would cost about £38 to produce. However, the farmer can now produce 1,000 lambs a year whereas on the smaller farm diminishing returns occurred if more than 500 lambs were produced. This is illustrated by Figure 1, which shows unchanged average costs of production and a possible long run average cost curve.

Scenario 2

In this case, the cost of borrowing additional money might be greater and the newly acquired land might be less productive. Here, long run costs would be rising, as shown in Figure 2. At the farmer's optimum level of output, the short run average costs of producing each lamb would be greater than was the case with the optimum level on the smaller farm, giving a rising long run average cost curve.

Scenario 3

In contrast to the previous scenario, the newly acquired land might be cheaper and more productive. It may pay the farmer to transport their own livestock, and suppliers of winter feed might be prepared to supply larger orders at a discount. In this case, optimum short run costs of production would fall. This means that not only would the farmer be able to produce

Synoptic link

The central concept which you need to understand to analyse long run costs is that of economies of scale. Look back on your notes on market failure for AS (section 2.4) and make sure you understand what the following are and why they might occur:
- internal and external economies of scale
- internal and external diseconomies of scale.

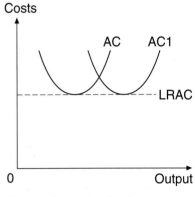

Figure 1 Economies of scale

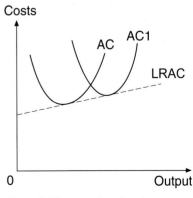

Figure 2 Diseconomies of scale

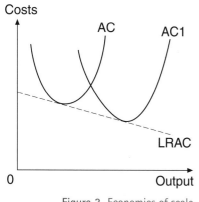

Figure 3 Economies of scale

more lambs, but also they would be able to produce each one more cheaply. In this case, Figure 3 clearly indicates that long run costs are falling.

Returns to scale

These three scenarios illustrate the concept of returns to scale, which is used to judge the impact on costs in the long run of changing any or all factor inputs. Scenario 1, where average costs of production remain the same, is described as an example of constant returns to scale. Scenario 2 involves rising long run costs, which can also be described as diseconomies of scale. Scenario 3 is about economies of scale which are falling long run costs.

Factors affecting returns to scale

Unlike short run costs, there is no law or certainty governing the shape of long run average cost curves. Some factors, such as more bureaucracy and paperwork, are likely to push up costs, whereas technical economies often contribute to falling long run costs. The following sources of economies and diseconomies of scale have to be balanced against each other.

Internal economies of scale relate to a growth in the size of the individual firm and include technical factors, organisational factors and market power.

Sources of external economies of scale include growth and concentration of particular industries in defined geographical areas which lead to greater efficiencies in the supply chain, local supplies of appropriately skilled labour and the benefit of positive externalities.

Internal diseconomies of scale are generally technical or organisational.

External diseconomies of scale usually result from the collapse of local economy and infra structure, poor communications or negative externalities.

Traditional approaches to long run costs

In traditional economic theory, there is no automatic formula that can be applied to the average costs of firms as the positives and negatives from the above factors have to be weighed up against each other. In some industries – for example, motorcar manufacture – potential economies of scale that benefit firms able to produce in large scale for a global market are enormous. In others, especially where more traditional methods of production are used, diseconomies of scale may be more significant.

Research task

Choose a business that you are confident you can find out more about. Identify its main fixed costs, variable costs, the length of time it takes to vary inputs of land, labour and capital, and the existence of significant economies or diseconomies of scale.

Exam hint

Sorting out the balance between economies and diseconomies of scale is a good lead in to an assess/discuss/evaluate question, and using technical and organisation factors provides a way of structuring your answer to such high scoring questions.

Modern approaches to costs

Some economists have questioned the wisdom of making a rigid distinction between short and long run costs, while others have researched the actual nature of costs faced by firms in different industries. This research has had two broad outcomes.

Outcome 1

In many modern businesses, flexible working and modern technological developments mean that the distinction between the short and the long run can become blurred. Modern technologies can link factories in one country to others in the world. If more machine parts are needed, it is not necessary to construct a new factory or plant; new orders can very easily be sub-contracted to other suppliers in most parts of the world. Similarly, improvements in the transportation of materials mean that individual components can be shipped around the world quickly and relatively cheaply.

Outcome 2

Many firms find that initial growth in output and sales is accompanied by dramatic cost savings – that is, economies of scale are significant. Thereafter, unit or average costs remain similar, regardless of output, until a point is reached at which average costs rise dramatically.

If these two sets of research findings are applied to traditional approaches of classifying costs, they have a significant effect on how the behaviour of firms is analysed. This is shown in Figure 4. There is no short run average cost or long run average cost, just an average cost 'curve' that might be 'trench' shaped.

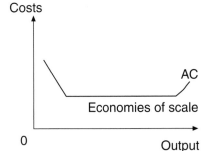

Figure 4 Modern approaches to average cost curves

Summary

This section has presented two different ways of treating costs faced by firms. Traditional economic analysis is based on a rigid distinction between the short and the long term, and this provides a rationale for the existence of the U-shaped average cost curve and the concept of returns to scale. Alternative treatments regard the distinction between short and long run as artificial, and consider that firms can be much more flexible and responsive in their reactions to changing market conditions.

Quickie

Draw a long run average cost curve that shows gradual economies of scale followed by both internal and external diseconomies of scale.

Research task

Using other texts and journal articles, research different approaches to modelling average costs. Is the modern approach outlined in this section more helpful to you in making sense of the behaviour of firms? Visit www.heinemann.co.uk/hotlinks and click on this section to locate suitable articles.

Total, average and marginal revenue

4.6

Synoptic link

Make sure you have re-read section 1.7 from your AS text. You should remember that if the price elasticity of demand for a product is relatively inelastic, any cut in price is likely to decrease total revenue, whereas if demand is relatively elastic, a cut in price will raise total revenue. You should also bear in mind spectrum of competition.

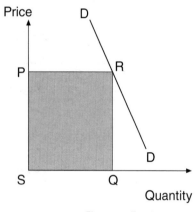

Figure 1 Total revenue

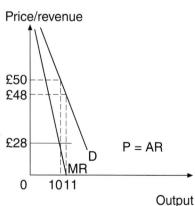

Figure 2 Derivation of marginal revenue

This section will help you to develop an understanding of different measures of revenue and how this appears in graphs. This is added to earlier work in A2 sections 4.3, 4.4 and 4.5 on business objectives and costs to provide an introduction to the Theory of the firm.

Revenue

'Revenue' is the term used by economists to describe those flows of money that are received by a firm. This is distinct from 'costs', which refers to those payments made by firms.

Calculating average revenue and total revenue

Calculating average revenue and total revenue is straightforward for those businesses that rely on the sales of a good or service. The demand curve shows the relationship between sales and different prices. In Figure 1, P is the price that will be paid if Q is sold. In other words, P is the average revenue. Total revenue is simply price multiplied by the number of items sold: P × Q. Therefore, the shaded area **PRQS** represents the total sales revenue earned.

Marginal revenue

Marginal revenue (MR) is defined as the change in revenue that occurs if sales are changed by one unit. In Figure 2, if sales are increased from 10 units to 11 units, revenue will rise by £28. (Ten units sold for £50 each, giving a total revenue of £500, but to sell 11 units the firm has to accept a lower price of £48 per unit, giving a new total revenue of £48 × 11 = £528.)

If sales are further increased, the marginal revenue will continue to decline. In other words if the demand curve is downward sloping to the right, more goods can only be sold at a lower price, which means that **MR** will always be less than **AR**. Thus, if the demand curve for a product or service is represented by a straight line, then the marginal revenue curve will bisect the angle formed by the average revenue (or demand) curve and the vertical axis as shown in Figure 2. Note that the marginal revenue is plotted against the mid points of sales represented on the horizontal axis.

Putting costs and revenue together

It should be clear that Figure 3 illustrates a business that would not be likely to survive. At any point on the diagram, average costs are above average revenue or price. This firm is clearly making a loss in the short run.

On the other hand, Figure 4 shows a range of outputs including average costs and less-than-average revenue. This means that between **Q** and **Q1** this business would be making some level of profit.

Profits

At this stage in the analysis of a firm's behaviour, it is important to clarify how economists define the term 'profit'. They use the term 'normal profit' to define the amount of additional return, once all other costs have been met, that is just sufficient to keep a business producing its current level of production. Anything above this is called 'supernormal' or 'abnormal' profit. If a firm is making less than normal profits, it is making a loss.

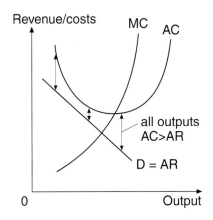

Figure 3 Loss maker

Business objectives

The work that you did in section 4.3 on business objectives needs to be brought into the analysis because understanding these is useful in helping to determine the level of output chosen by an individual firm.

To survive, a business must choose an output between **Q** and **Q2** (see Figure 4). If a business wanted to maximise on sales, it would produce **Q2**. The profit maximising output, meanwhile, is found by applying what is known as the profit maximising rule. This means choosing the output **Q1** at which MC (**marginal costs**) and MR (**marginal revenue**) are equal. At this output, the gap between average revenue (**AR**) and average costs (**AC**) is maximised. If a firm chooses this output, total profits equal to the shaded area **abcd** would be earned. As AR is greater than AC, these would be called supernormal or abnormal profits.

If the firm decided on an output to the right of **Q1**, marginal costs would exceed marginal revenue – in other words, expanding production beyond **Q1** would raise costs by a larger amount than any increase in revenue, reducing total profits. On the other hand, any point to the left of **Q1** would mean that marginal costs were less than marginal revenue, meaning that if output were expanded, revenue would grow by more than costs. Only at the point at which **MR** equals **MC** will profits be maximised.

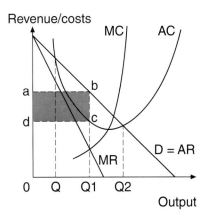

Figure 4 Profit maker

Definitions

Marginal cost is the change in cost brought about by changing production by one unit.

Marginal revenue is the addition to total revenue brought about by changing production by one unit.

Summary

The revenue earned by a firm will be determined by the interaction of price and the demand for its good or service. Data on revenue and costs can be put onto the same graph, and this can be used to predict the levels of output chosen by different types of firms according to their business objectives. This section provides an introduction to what is known as the Theory of the firm.

Exam hints

Understanding this section is absolutely vital. Read it through at least three times. Shut your text, then make your own summary of the main points – including the diagrams.

Never forget the following mantra: a firm seeking to maximise profits must ensure that marginal cost equals marginal revenue.

Quickie

Suppose a business is known to want to maximise profits. How will it change production if the following things happen?
(a) Demand increases.
(b) Variable costs increase.
(c) Fixed costs increase.

Productive and allocative efficiency

47

This section builds on the work that you did for AS by using diagrams to analyse the behaviour of firms acting under conditions of perfect competition. When you have done this, you should be able to show off your higher order skills by critically assessing the proposition that perfect competition could result in the optimum allocation of resources.

Synoptic links

To further develop your understanding of how, given certain assumptions, perfect competition can lead to an optimum allocation of resource, re-read sections 1.14 and 2.2 of your AS text on productive and allocative efficiency. The argument is that if we lived in a perfectly competitive economy, goods and services would be produced at the lowest possible price (productive efficiency) and in accordance with the demands of consumers (allocative efficiency).

Productive efficiency

The starting point for this analysis is to consider the equilibrium of the perfectly competitive firm and industry. This is illustrated in Figure 1, and it is important to note that, given the assumptions of perfect competition, the individual firm will be obliged to produce the output at which average costs are minimised. The profit-maximising rule of equating MC with MR has to applied if the firm is to avoid making a loss and that coincides with the lowest, or optimum, point on the average cost curve (AC).

Just suppose that the owner of one firm operating in this industry has a 'eureka' moment and discovers a new quicker, cheaper way of making whatever. If the new production technique is quicker and cheaper, the average cost curve will shift downwards to the right, dragging the marginal cost curve with it. The profit maximising firm will expand production from Q1 to Q2, and will now be making supernormal profits shown by the shaded area in Figure 2.

This situation will only persist in the short run, as all competitors have perfect knowledge of what is going on within the industry. They will find out how the innovating firm has been able to cut production costs and copy the more efficient means of production. New firms might also enter the industry.

This long run change will involve an increase in the industry-wide supply of the product. This rise in supply will force prices down from P to P1 and the firm that began the process with its 'eureka' moment will be back to earning normal profits, as shown in Figure 3.

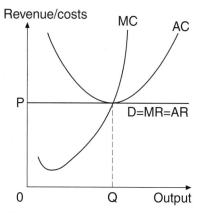

Figure 1 Perfectly competitive equilibrium

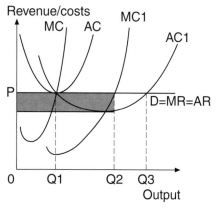

Figure 2 Perfectly competitive supernormal profit

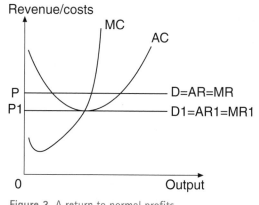
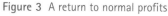

Figure 3 A return to normal profits

An added twist to this argument is that if particular firms are slow in copying the more efficient means of production, they will find themselves making losses as output in the industry increases. Loss-making firms will be forced out of the industry. This is illustrated in Figure 4 where costs exceed revenue at all outputs.

The logic of this analysis is that if the assumptions underpinning the perfectly competitive model were to be met, competition between large numbers of firms producing identical goods would ensure that there would be a continuous incentive to develop cheaper more efficient ways of producing goods and providing services.

The reward for this would be short-term supernormal profits. The sanction for not keeping up with competitors would be losses and business failure. The real beneficiaries would be the public, who would be assured of a constant stream to newer, better, more cost-effective products and services.

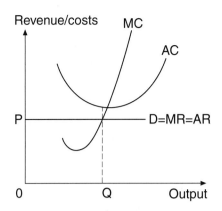

Figure 4 How a loss-making firm could be forced out of the industry

Allocative efficiency

This refers to consumer sovereignty. In a perfectly competitive market, it is consumers who ultimately determine which of the world's resources are used to produce what products and services. This can be analysed diagrammatically by considering what happens if consumers' tastes change for some reason.

Suppose there is an increase in demand for DVD players at the expense of VCRs. Two changes will take place: there will be a shift to the right in the demand curve for DVDs and there will be a shift to the left in the demand for VCRs. This will lead to a rise in price to P1 for DVDs and a fall in price to P1 for VCRs – as shown in Figure 5.

When translated into changes in demand facing the perfectly competitive producers of DVDs and VCRs, the former will be faced with supernormal profits and the latter potential losses. This is shown in Figures 6 and 7.

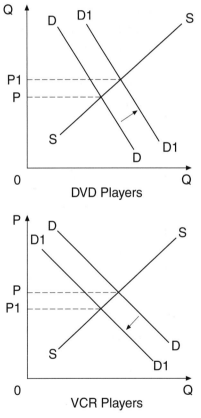

Figure 5 Shifting demand curves

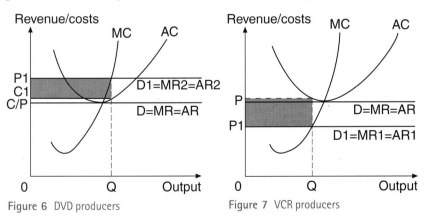

Figure 6 DVD producers

Figure 7 VCR producers

The long run response to this situation is that losses will force some firms to drop out of the VCR market while new firms will be attracted into the DVD market, and new long-term equilibriums will be reached in which both sets of firms earn normal profits but the industry output of DVDs will have increased while the production of VCRs will have been reduced.

The essence of the analysis is that if the assumptions are true, perfect competition will force businesses to adjust and change production decisions according to customer demands. If they fail to respond, they are likely to go out of business.

However, the analysis does not stop here. More successful companies will make larger short run profits. They will be able to pay more to attract scarce factors of production. Owners of these factors will sell their capital, land, labour or enterprise to the highest bidder and resources will be diverted to the production of goods that are most in demand.

Therefore, if all industries were perfectly competitive there would be an optimum allocation of resources. Consumers would determine what is produced, and these goods and services would be produced at the lowest possible cost.

Critically assessing the perfectly competitive model

When you critically assess the effects of each assumption on the perfectly competitive model, it is crucial to ask yourself the following two questions.

- Are the assumptions valid?
- What is the effect on the model if any of the assumptions are relaxed?

The assumptions used to develop this model are homogenous outputs, many firms, perfect consumer knowledge, perfect producer knowledge and freedom of entry and exit.

Homogenous outputs

Another way of testing this assumption is to ask whether a particular product or service can be identified with an individual producer. Clearly, branding is designed to ensure that we differentiate most consumer products from each other.

Companies use branding to build up brand loyalty, which ultimately means that customers are prepared to pay more for one brand than another. Take away the packaging or label, and goods become much more homogenous – one computer is much like another. Moreover, the closer we get to raw materials the harder it is to distinguish between the output of different producers.

Many firms

It is not hard to think of industries that are made up of many individual producers who are forced to accept the price set by the market. Most producers of agricultural products and those that can be simply produced using little capital or expertise probably fall into this category.

However, as shown in later sections of this module (section 4.8), the control of production in some industries is becoming increasingly concentrated in the hands of fewer producers.

Perfect consumer knowledge

This is not a very realistic assumption. It is argued that the average consumer knows only the likely price of fewer than 20 different items in a supermarket stocking 15,000 different products. Individually, we may be expert about some products and services. But collectively, the evidence is such that we might be nearer to perfect consumer ignorance than we are to perfect knowledge.

Perfect producer knowledge

This is harder to assess. Successful businesses need to have a good knowledge of developments within their industry. By the same token, it is in the interest of firms to keep things secret. Sometimes this is protected by law, as with patents. Although there are exceptions – such as the formula for making Coca-Cola – it is reasonably safe to assume that over a long period of time producers have relatively good knowledge of their industry.

Freedom of entry and exit

Some economists argue that this is the crucial assumption and there is no clear 'yes' or 'no' answer as to its validity. Three factors are likely to be important; the cost of entry or exit, attitudes of businesses within a given industry and the legislative framework.

Hot potato

Has the development of the Internet encouraged greater competition? Give reasons for your answer.

Thinking like an economist

Just because the assumptions underpinning perfect competition are very rarely met, it does not mean that the analysis in this section can be ignored.

Quickie ✔

Use diagrams to predict what will happen to short run supernormal profits of an individual firm if:
(a) new entrants are attracted to the industry
(b) demand for the product increases
(c) customer ignorance is reduced.

Puzzler

How perfect is 'perfect knowledge'?

Monopoly

This section develops the descriptive treatment of monopoly and competition looked at in section 2.5 of your AS book. Graphical analysis can be used to compare output, prices and profits under the two extremes of perfect competition and monopoly.

Monopoly

In order to understand the behaviour of monopolists, it is useful to understand how economists have built up a theoretical model of monopoly in a similar way to that of perfect competition. This model is based on two related simplifying assumptions:
- production of a whole industry is in the hands of one firm
- complete barriers prevent the entry and exits of firms.

These assumptions mean that the demand curve for the individual firm will be the same as that for the industry as a whole. Moreover, there is no distinction – as there is with perfect competition – between the short and the long run. If a monopoly is total, barriers to entry are absolute and this prevents other firms competing away excess profits. The monopolist will be able to set the price or quantity sold, and therefore has considerable freedom to pursue particular economic and social objectives.

Possible price, sales and output levels can be analysed graphically – as shown in Figure 1, where demand and average revenue are above average costs at outputs between Q and Q2. This means that a monopolistic firm could set a price anywhere between P and P2, and make more than normal profits.

In this case, a profit maximising monopolist would produce at Q1 and a sales maximiser at Q2. Barriers to entry would ensure that this short run situation was also the long run position.

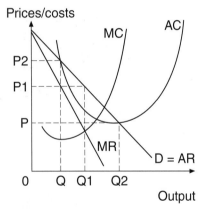

Figure 1 Demand and cost conditions facing a monopolistic firm

Changing market conditions

The analysis of increases or decreases in demand for average costs are quite straightforward, although the diagrams get a little complicated. Thus, if the demand for the output of a monopolist increases, the demand curve will shift to the right, dragging the MR curve with it. This is illustrated in Figure 2.

If the monopolist is a profit maximiser, MC meets the new MR curve at Q1. P1 will be charged for the product and abnormal profits will increase from *abcd* to *efgh*. In other words, an increase in demand will lead to an increase in sales, prices and profits.

If, on the other hand, the costs of raw materials were to rise, the average and marginal cost curves would move upwards to the left, resulting in lower sales, output and profit levels.

If markets exist which conform to this model:
- average costs of production are not necessarily minimised
- excessive profits could be earned in the long run

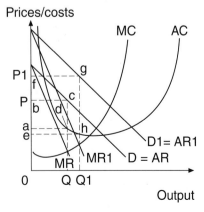

Figure 2 Increasing demand

- firms would not have to attempt to maximise profits
- firms would not necessarily have to respond to changes in demand
- there would be little incentive to innovate
- customer choice could be restricted.

Comparisons with perfect competition

Graphical analysis can be used to demonstrate that, in the short run, prices under monopoly will be higher than those if perfect competition were to apply and output would be lower. This is illustrated in Figure 3.

Under perfect competition, firms are forced by competitive pressures to produce where MC equals price. If this applied to a whole industry, perfectly competitive output would be at Q and price at P, whereas a profit maximising monopolist would charge P1 for an output of Q1.

This conclusion depends on one implicit assumption – that both monopolist and perfectly competitive firms would be faced with the same average and marginal cost conditions.

One argument used to justify the existence of monopolies is that they are able to enjoy the benefits of economies of scale that may arise in increasing size, which then leads to falling long run average costs. The effects of this possibility are illustrated in Figure 4, where AC1 and MC1 represent lower long run costs that might be generated by economies of scale enjoyed by the monopolist. In this case, the profit maximising monopolist will charge P1 for output Q1, compared to P and Q for the perfectly competitive industry.

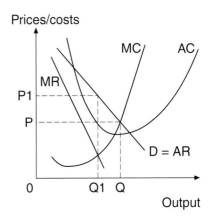

Figure 3 Monopoly and perfect competition compared

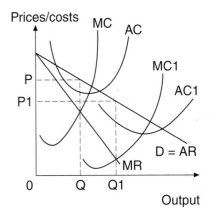

Figure 4 Monopolist benefiting from economies of scale

Summary

The use of graphical analysis indicates that prices might be lower and outputs higher under conditions of perfect competition than under monopoly. However, this simple comparison ignores the existence of economies of scale and the greater freedom that a monopolistic firm has to pursue differing objectives.

Hot potato

The monopolistic model is as much help as the perfectly competitive one in helping us understand how businesses operate in the 'real' world. Do you agree?

Thinking like an economist

Don't jump to conclusions based on the analysis in this section. In the real world it is hard to fine pure monopoly or perfect competition. However, you will find that firms behave in some of the ways that have been described in this section.

Quickie

Which of the following are closest to being monopolies?
(a) Microsoft.
(b) Network Rail
(c) Littledean Village Store.

Puzzler

How might a monopolist respond to an increase in fixed costs? This may require some detailed analysis and lots of logic.

Imperfect competition

Synoptic links

AS Unit 1 was devoted to how freely operating markets might work and in Unit 2 you will have learned about uncompetitive markets. Make sure you can recall the features that make a market:
- perfectly competitive
- monopolistic.

Also, make sure you know the arguments for and against the application of these models to the real world.

For AS you needed to be able to describe the main features of competitive and monopolistic markets and to begin to analyse the effects of these different market structures on the behaviour of firms. At A2 you need to extend and develop this treatment by considering imperfect and oligopolistic markets and using graphs make your analysis more sophisticated.

It is hard to find industries and firms to which it is possible to apply the assumptions that underpin the models of monopoly and perfect competition. Common sense tells us that most markets lie between these two extremes. This view is supported by the many economists who have sought to develop theories that are modelled more accurately on the characteristics of businesses operating in the 'real' world.

This unit is devoted to imperfect competition – a term used to describe market structures which lie between the theoretical extremes of perfect competition and monopoly.

Imperfect competition

In the 1930s, two economists, Joan Robinson and Edward Chamberlain, both developed similar models which they considered were more realistic than the extremes of monopoly and perfect competition. Chamberlain, an American, called his theory 'monopolistic competition'. Robinson, an English woman, preferred the term 'imperfect competition'. Although there are differences between these two approaches, for AS and A2 they can be treated as one. Edexcel prefer the term 'imperfect competition'.

The following underpinning assumptions, borrowed from the theories of perfect competition and monopoly, are used to build up this model.
- Freedom of entry and exit – as with perfect competition, it is assumed that there are no barriers preventing firms from joining or leaving the industry in question.
- Knowledge of profit levels being earned in the industry.
- Independent decision-making by firms – that is, individual firms decide about sales levels, product design and the like without reference to the behaviour of potential competitors. In this respect, firms are expected to behave in a similar way to perfectly competitive firms.
- Product differentiation – it is assumed that each firm operating under conditions of imperfect competition will seek to make its product or service different to that of its competitors. Such differences might be in packaging or branding, but could also include more fundamental differences in design or construction. This characteristic has more in common with monopoly that it does with perfect competition.

Equilibrium under conditions of imperfect competition

The third assumption above means that the demand curve facing the imperfectly competitive firm will slope downwards to the right (as with monopoly). This means that the marginal revenue curve will also slope downwards to the right (also like monopoly). In other words, a firm operating in these conditions is to some degree a price maker rather than a price taker. These features are both illustrated in Figure 1.

If market conditions are like those illustrated in Figure 1, there will be a range of profitable outputs between Q and Q2, and prices between P and P1 between which average costs would exceed average revenue. A profit maximising firm would choose to produce at Q1 where MC equals MR, and abnormal profits equivalent to the area **abcd** would exist.

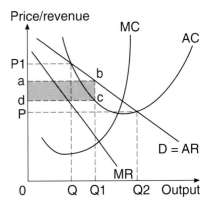

Figure 1 Short run equilibrium of a imperfectly competitive firm

Long run equilibrium of the firm under conditions of imperfect competition

In the long run, the situation will be determined by the application of the first two assumptions made in building up this model. Other firms will realise that abnormal profits can be made by copying the behaviour of the firm managing to produce with **AR>AC**. Existing firms will increase production and new firms will be attracted into the industry, leading to a long-term increase in supply, which will result in a decrease in the price. Prices will fall and the short run abnormal profits will be eroded until the situation shown in Figure 2 is reached.

The converse of this analysis also applies. If demand falls for the outputs of a firm operating in an imperfectly competitive industry, the demand and marginal revenue curves will shift to the left, resulting in losses irrespective of the chosen output.

In this case the least efficient and/or less well-resourced businesses will go out of business first, leaving the remaining firms to compete for shares in a larger market. The exit of some firms should result in the reestablishment of a long run equilibrium as shown in Figure 2.

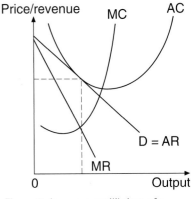

Figure 2 Long run equilibrium of a imperfectly competitive firm

Imperfectly competitive firms

If firms in an industry satisfy the assumptions of this model then it is likely that the following will be true.

- Supernormal profits can only be earned in the short run because low barriers to entry will attract new firms into the industry and encourage competitors to expand production.
- There is a constant incentive for firms to innovate and differentiate their product from that of competitors. In essence, imperfectly competitive firms will want to try to make the demand for their products or services more inelastic.

- Advertising and branding become important as these represent strategies aimed at both boosting demand and creating brand loyalty.
- In the long run, firms will not be maximising their efficiency, as they will not be producing at the lowest point on their average cost curve. In fact, output will be lower and an imperfectly competitive firm will have spare or excess capacity.
- If firms are to survive in the long run, they are obliged to maximise profits.

Critical evaluation

This is up to you. Is this model more realistic? Check out the original assumptions:
- numbers of firms
- slightly differentiated products
- advertising
- freedom of entry and exit.

Leading to the following predictions:
- long run normal profits
- lower levels of efficiency than in more competitive markets
- the importance of advertising.

What is your judgement?

Research task

Outline the principal features of imperfect competition. How useful is this model in explaining the behaviour of businesses in the real world?

Quickie

Which of the following industries comes closest to satisfying the assumption of imperfect competition?
(a) PC manufacture.
(b) Low cost airlines.
(c) Pubs selling food.

Oligopoly

4.10

O ligopoly literally means competition among the few. There are two principal assumptions that underpin this model. The first is the existence of barriers of entry to and from the industry. These will vary from industry to industry, but their existence makes the analysis of oligopoly more similar to that of monopoly. The second principle is the interdependence of decision-making. The assumption is unique to this model and means that individual firms make decisions about prices, marketing, product design and so on with reference to how they believe their competitors will respond. Each firm is affected by the actions of others.

Barriers to entry

The first assumption has special importance in understanding the likely behaviour of oligopolists. In theory, a monopolist's market dominance is secure. Barriers to the entry of other firms are absolute.

Perfectly competitive firms can, theoretically, try to maintain short run barriers. However, in the long run the assumption of perfect knowledge should ensure that any form of product differentiation could be copied.

Oligopolists, on the other hand, are protected by barriers and are likely to constantly erect new barriers in order to maintain long-term market share and profits. Barriers to entry and exit are likely to include the following.

- Capital costs – especially in capital and technology intensive industries such as Sony Music.
- High levels of sunk costs – that is, those fixed costs attributable to capital equipment that cannot be transferred to other uses (for example, the Channel Tunnel).
- National and global branding – Nike, Adidas and other leisureware firms have spent billions of pounds on promoting a global image that would be both costly and difficult for a newcomer to match.
- Patent and copyright – especially important in pharmaceuticals (for example, GlaxoSmithKline).
- Technological expertise – especially when backed up by large research and development expenditures (for example, Nokia).
- Takeover – dominant firms often respond to the threat of new entrants by taking them over (for example, Microsoft).

Interdependence

The second assumption is very significant because it makes it much more difficult for economists to model the behaviour of an oligopolistic firm. The behaviour of one firm will depend on its perceptions of how other firms will react to changes. The responses of other firms will depend on their perceptions of the responses of others. It is harder, therefore, to predict how oligopolistic firms are likely to behave.

Synoptic links

This is all new but builds on your understanding from AS of perfect competition and monopoly as well as using what you have learnt in A2 section 4.8 about graphical treatments of different market structures.

The models developed by economists to analyse perfectly competitive and monopolistic markets are of little use and different ways have been developed to aid our understanding of the behaviour of oligopolists. The crucial issue is that because pricing and output decisions can be interdependent, oligopolistic firms may choose to compete but it may well be in their interest to collude. This describes a situation in which firms find some way of agreeing with each other to avoid the risks associated with competition. Colluding firms may seek to set common prices or levels of output for each. This topic is dealt with in more detail in the next section.

Game theory

Predicting the outcomes of decision making by oligopolists is difficult. To take a current example which demonstrates this, Volkswagen needs to decide on the recommended selling price for its new Polo. It is currently selling a basic version of the Polo for £8999. However, some competitors, such as the Nissan Micra, are available more cheaply while others, such as the Vauxhall Corsa, are more expensive.

There are fears in the automobile industry that car prices are likely to fall. So what should Volkswagen do? If it cuts its price and competitors follow suit, it will end up with the same market share. If it cuts its prices and competitors fail to respond, its market share may increase. However, what if Vauxhall or Nissan make larger price cuts?

One approach used by economists to try to make sense of such competitive behaviour is game theory, first developed by psychologists when trying to predict human responses in a similarly unpredictable situation. At a simple level, this can be restricted to looking at the behaviour of one firm and the possible responses of another. This is illustrated in Figure 1.

■ To begin with, assume that the market for small cars is shared equally between Volkswagen and Nissan. They charge the same price of £8999 for cars with similar specifications, and they both share equally the total 'industry' profit of £200 million. This is depicted in box **A** of the matrix.

■ The outcomes of Volkswagen cutting £1000 from its recommended price will depend upon the response of Nissan. If Nissan keeps its original price, Volkswagen will gain a bigger market share and a larger proportion of the industry profit. This is illustrated in box **B**.

■ Alternatively, Nissan could copy Volkswagen, leaving both with an equal market share but reduced profits because of the price cut. This is shown in box **D**.

■ A fourth option is that Volkswagen maintains its price at £8999, but Nissan cuts its to £7999. In this case, both Volkswagen's market share and profits will be cut as shown in box **C**.

This approach to the analysis of the behaviour of oligopolists yields an important prediction. For Volkswagen, option B would give the best possible return, but it is also the most risky. It depends on Nissan ignoring an

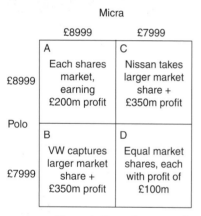

Figure 1 Game theory matrix

aggressive price cut. Option **C** is the worst outcome, while options **D** and **A** are the least risky. Logic dictates that Volkswagen ought to collude with Nissan.

Competitive oligopolists

If oligopolistic firms decide to pursue competitive strategies, they may well try to drive weaker competitors out of their market. Predatory pricing policies are sometimes used to achieve this objective. Those firms which are larger and better resourced may be prepared to sell output at a loss if this enables them to undercut the prices charged by competitors.

The attraction of this strategy is that competitors are faced with a stark choice. Cut their prices to retain market share or stick tight and hope that demand for their product is relatively inelastic. If the former response is preferred then there is every chance of a price war breaking out. This might not be attractive, as competitive price-cutting could result in losses which none of the firms in the industry could sustain.

Nonetheless, price wars do happen. Ryanair and Easyjet have used predatory pricing to not only gather major market shares but also to force competitors like Buzz and Go out of business.

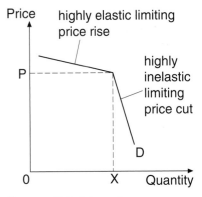

Low cost airlines - a winning strategy?

Kinked demand curves

An alternative theoretical treatment of the behaviour of oligopolists is that associated with the American economist Paul Sweezy. Sweezy observed that even if oligopolists were in competition with each other, prices in such markets tended to be stable. He used a simplified form of game theory by reasoning that as pricing decisions by oligopolists were interdependent, an individual firm would be very reluctant to raise its prices because it would fear that none of its competitors would follow suit.

On the other hand, he argued that an individual firm would be reluctant to cut its prices because this decision would be copied by competitors. In other words, the oligopolist would be faced with an elastic demand curve in terms of price rises and an inelastic curve for price cuts. This is illustrated in Figure 2. Although this theory provides a convincing argument as to why price stability can be a feature of oligopoly, Sweezy's theory has been attacked by a number of economists as lacking in any empirical evidence.

Figure 2 Kinked demand curve

Summary

Analysing the behaviour of oligopolists is far more complex than for firms operating in other market structures. Graphical analysis is less helpful, as outcomes in terms of pricing, output and profits are less predictable.

Particular industries may be characterised by high levels of competition, while in others tacit agreements result in high levels of price stability and little or no competition.

Some industries may alternate between periods of intense competition and periods of stability and collusion. However, a number of generalisations can be made about the behaviour of oligopolists.

- There will be strong incentives to collude.
- Price competition will generally be avoided, because non-price competition in terms of advertising and customer service is less risky.
- Agreements – whether overt or tacit – can easily be broken, leading to price wars and market instability.
- Oligopolistic firms will tend to maintain and strengthen barriers to entry into their industry.

Quickie

Which of the following industries comes closest to satisfying the assumptions of oligopolistic competition?
(a) Brewing.
(b) Airlines.
(c) Electricity generation.

Puzzler

Construct a matrix to predict possible outcomes of interdependent decision-making in an industry of your choice.

conomic theory demonstrates that firms that are monopolies or oligopolies have considerable market power to set prices, determine customer choice, limit competition and prevent new market entrants. These firms are also often very large, commanding turnovers greater than most countries in the world, and able to use their economic power to influence the behaviour of governments. Economists differ in their assessments of the impact of such large firms, but have developed further theories and techniques to help measure market power and advise governments of possible intervention strategies. This section is devoted to:

- price discrimination
- consumer and producer surplus
- contestable markets.

Market power

Synoptic links

This section develops the models of monopoly and oligopoly discussed in A2 sections 4.8 and 4.10 and shows how large firms exert power in the market place.

Price discrimination

One method of assessing the degree of power that any firm has in the marketplace is to establish the degree to which it is able to charge different customers different prices for the same product or service. This is called price discrimination, and is an aspect of market power used by firms to boost revenue and profits.

Most of us are used to being charged a range of different prices for particular goods or services. Airfares are a good example. Customers flying from London to New York can pay anywhere between £200 and £1000 for the same seat in the same aircraft. In order to benefit from price discrimination, airlines need to ensure that the following conditions are fulfilled.

- The firm must have some degree of market power and be a price maker.
- Demand for the good or service must be spread between different customers, each with differing price elasticities of demand for the product or service.
- These different market segments have to be separated from each other.
- The proportion of fixed to total costs must be high.

Market power

Only those firms that are facing a downward sloping overall demand curve for their products or services will be able to charge different prices to different customers. The more market power a firm enjoys, the more it can price discriminate. On the other hand, those firms that are closer to being perfectly competitive will have only a limited opportunity to charge different prices to different customers. Clearly, there is a limited number of airlines flying between London and New York. Those that offer the most flights will be able to set prices rather than having to accept the 'market' price.

Differing price elasticities of demand

A discriminating monopolist will wish to charge higher prices to some of its customers and will be prepared to sell the same product or service to others at a lower price as long as this boosts overall revenue.

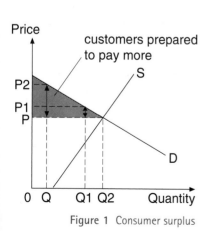

Research task

Collect three examples of price discrimination at work. Is anyone being 'ripped off'?

Airlines exploit this by charging much higher fares to those who have to fly at particular times or whose airfare is likely to be part of an expense account. Other market segments, such as young people travelling around the world, are likely to be much more price sensitive and will only be attracted by lower fares. Another important segment for some airlines is the holiday market. Holiday companies may make block bookings of seats but will expect significant discounts. Finally, seats that are hard to sell can be sold through 'bucket shops' and those travel agencies dealing in last-minute bookings.

Separation of markets

Elaborate strategies such as those outlined above will only work if it is impossible for one set of airline customers to sell on its cheaper tickets to passengers who would otherwise be prepared to pay higher fares. This is relatively easy for the airlines, because tickets can only be used by a named person. Other price discriminators use time to separate markets. Train tickets bought at different times of the day cost different amounts and can be used only on specified trains.

Relatively high fixed costs

The bulk of the costs of flying from London to New York are fuel, maintenance and debt repayment. Once committed to the flight, the airline has low levels of variable costs. Put another way, marginal costs of carrying additional passengers are low. It costs little more to carry 350 passengers than it does to carry 349. Hence, the airline will add to its profits once it has covered the costs of extra meals, ticketing and costs associated with the 350th passenger.

If variable costs are relatively more significant, marginal costs would be higher and a profit-seeking company would be more limited in its opportunities to discount.

Consumer and producer surpluses

Another way in which economists attempt to assess the impact of non-competitive behaviour by firms is by the use of two concepts:

- consumer surplus
- producer surplus.

Consumer surplus

This concept uses graphical analysis to illustrate the benefits that customers gain from consuming a particular product or service. Figure 1 illustrates consumer surplus and P represents an equilibrium price with the level of sales at Q2.

The last customer is prepared to pay the market price for the product, but all earlier customers would have been prepared to pay more. For instance, Q1 customers would have been prepared to pay P1, and Q customers would have been prepared to pay still more at P2. The vertical distances indicate how much more some customers would have been prepared to pay. Taken

Figure 1 Consumer surplus

together, the shaded area represents an additional benefit enjoyed by consumers of this product. This is referred to as consumer surplus.

Producer Surplus

A similar analytical approach can be made to gains made by producers of a good or service. In Figure 2, Q2 producers receive P2 for their total output, but some producers would have been prepared to supply the good or service for less. Q1 producers were prepared to supply for P1, whereas Q producers were prepared to accept even less at P. The shaded area, therefore, represents producers' surplus.

This concept is applied to understanding the impact of monopoly power. Figure 3 shows that a profit maximising oligopolist or monopolist will produce at Q and charge P1 for its output, whereas a perfectly competitive industry facing the same cost structure will produce at Q1 and charge P for its output.

Consumer surplus under monopolistic conditions will be the equivalent of area *a*, but under perfect competition it would be larger and equal to *a* + *b* + *c*.

Producer surplus, on the other hand, is bigger under monopoly, consisting of *d* + *b* compared with a perfectly competitive producer surplus of *d* + *e*. In other words, this graphical analysis shows that producers gain while consumers lose.

Overall, *c* + *e* represents losses under monopoly of both producer and consumer surpluses. This area is known as deadweight welfare loss of monopoly.

Summary

This section has been devoted to an explanation of some of the techniques economists use to measure the extent and possible effects of the exercise of monopoly power. The ability of firms to charge different prices to different sections of their markets was also considered. Graphical analysis has been used to indicate the possible harmful affects of monopoly power.

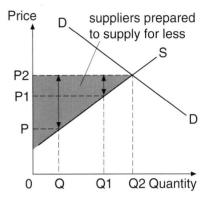

Figure 2 Producer surplus

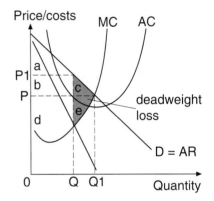

Figure 3 Deadweight welfare loss of monopoly

Exam hint

There is lots of scope in this section for questions that test your higher order skills. Be prepared to assess, evaluate or discuss the degree of competition in a given market. Remember to develop a number of arguments and make a clear conclusion.

Quickie

Which of the following operates the most comprehensive policies of price discrimination?
(a) Mobile phone providers.
(b) Package holiday suppliers.
(c) The railway operating companies.

Puzzler

How might consumer and producer surpluses be affected by the following?
(a) Reduction of barriers of entry in an industry.
(b) The establishment of a cartel in an industry.

Can oligopolists be competitive?

Synoptic link

This section builds on A2 section 4.10, looking once again at the implications of the game theory matrix and introducing the contestable market theory.

Definitions

A **cartel** is a group of producers who agree to fix price levels.

A **quota** is a limit on the quantity of a product that can be imported.

This section focuses on two contrasting aspects of oligopolistic theory and behaviour. Firstly, consideration is given to extending the game theory introduced in section 4.10. The game theory matrix on page 44 showed that it can be in the interests of oligopolistic firms to collude, that is, form agreements to reduce the risks attached to competition, especially price competition.

The remainder of this section is devoted to contestable market theory, which can be used to argue that firms in an industry dominated by a small number of firms may actually behave in a competitive rather than a collusive way.

Collusion

It may be in the interests of oligopolists to co-operate and work together rather than compete. Agreements to limit competition can take different forms, including:

- open or overt
- informal or covert
- tacit.

Open agreements

Open or overt agreements are publicly-made, formal, collective agreements. Those joining in such an agreement are called a **cartel** and they may enter into binding agreements to set agreed price levels and/or production **quotas**. This will, almost always, involve pushing up prices and cutting down on output.

If cartels are going to work, it is important that agreement is reached about both prices and outputs. If this is not done there is a great incentive for individual members of a cartel to secretly produce more and benefit from the higher agreed prices. There is a clear conflict of interest between the members of a cartel and consumers and, with some exceptions, cartels are illegal in the UK and in most other 'western' countries.

They are, however, more commonly agreed in the global trade of particular commodities. The most famous cartel is that of OPEC, a group of petroleum exporting countries, who have had varying degrees of success in regulating the world price of crude oil. It can be argued that countries who are heavily dependent on the export of commodities such as oil, sugar and coffee will suffer greatly if there are regular price fluctuations. Indeed, poverty in a number of developing nations is directly attributable to the low prices of crops like coffee and sugar. In this context, there is a clear conflict of interest between the producer countries and those in which the commodities are consumed.

Informal or covert agreements

These are naturally much more difficult to find out about. Informal agreements occur both nationally and internationally, and almost always involve illegal activities by which firms try to find ways of keeping prices high and competition low. As prices for many consumer goods are higher in the UK than in the rest of Europe and the USA, there is evidence that manufacturers in this country inflate prices and stop retailers from selling at discounted prices.

It is likely that firms in the UK have informal agreements, especially in the markets for electrical goods, cars and perfumery, but, as this form of activity might be the target of government investigation and intervention, it is hard to find evidence of secret agreements.

Tacit agreements

Tacit agreement characterises the behaviour of individual oligopolists, and means that they can arrive at common pricing and output policies without formal or informal agreements. This makes it much more difficult to demonstrate or prove that firms may be acting illegally. Some industries are dominated by a particular firm, and others will follow its pricing decisions. In the UK, ESSO are seen as leaders in terms of petrol prices, Kellogg for breakfast cereals, and Nike for trainers.

It was noted in sections 4.7–4.10 that common prices and other apparent collusion can arise when firms in industries follow common pricing formulas and pay similar amounts for factor inputs. Most pubs mark up the price of beers and lager by 100 per cent, local stores add 40 per cent to the cost price of confectionery and similar products, and restaurants add 500 per cent to the cost of ingredients to price their menus. This can lead to competitive firms charging similar prices for the same meals. The use of these cost-plus-pricing strategies is more likely to result in stable prices and greater importance being attached to non-price competition.

Another related pricing strategy which can be either tacit or overt is that of limit pricing, where oligopolists will try to set their prices at the highest possible level without leading to new entrants into the industry. Often, existing businesses have different forms of competitive advantage which might mean that new entrants are faced with relatively higher costs. Limit pricing is designed to reduce the incentive effect of excessive profits.

Collusion, though attractive to oligopolists as a means of reducing risks and safeguarding profits, has particular dangers. It may:
■ attract unwelcome government intervention
■ create a poor public image
■ lead to broken agreements and, in turn, to competitive advantage being gained by rival firms or countries.

Contestable market theory

Definition

A **contestable market** is one that may appear to act as if it were competitive, even though the structure is oligopolistic.

This is an alternative approach developed by economists in the 1970s and 1980s, which has had significant influence on government policies in the UK and USA towards monopolies and oligopolists. **Contestable market theory** can be seen as an adaptation of traditional theory to assess the degree of competition which may occur within an industry. It is based on the premise that firms will operate competitively if they fear competition in some way. There are a number of variants of this theory and it is argued that a firm with monopolistic power will behave like a competitive firm if:

- there is a fear of take-over
- there are zero entry and exit barriers
- industries are dynamic.

Fear of takeover

No plc is free from the fear of takeover, and senior managers of such firms have to compete with other businesses on the stock market. Rising share prices are associated with business success and will be fed by stock market perceptions of potential profits, levels of customer service, responsiveness to changes in demand and so on.

Monopolistic and oligopolistic firms that fail to pursue those and other objectives associated with competitive behaviour will, the theorists argue, be punished by the stock market and share prices will fall, making such firms more liable to takeover. It could be argued that this describes the position of Marks and Spencer in 2000/1 and the position of Safeway in 2002/3.

Zero cost entry and exit

A slightly different treatment of contestable markets is that which concentrates on entry and exit (as you will have studied for perfect competition). A market is said to be perfectly contestable if barriers to entry and exist are zero. If this were the case, other firms would be attracted to those industries in which supernormal profits are being made.

In order to prevent increased competition, firms operating in a contestable market will keep prices down, and ensure that profits are kept to normal levels. Exit barriers need also to be minimised. If sunk costs are significant, firms already in an industry will be deterred from leaving, as they cannot transfer such resources to other uses. Moreover, new entrants will be deterred if they are unable to transfer capital elsewhere.

Hot potato

Contestable market theory is just a fig leaf for big bad capitalists. Do you agree?

Although there must be a strong temptation for oligopolists to avoid unnecessary risks by colluding with each other, some businesses are likely to be more aggressive and confrontational. Stable relationships between oligopolist firms can be upset by:

- new technologies
- changes in ownership.

Dynamic industries

If technologies and the ownership of firms are relatively dynamic then these changes are likely to result in more competitive behaviour.

The ways in which goods and services are produced is constantly changing, and as this process is likely to occur unevenly across the firms making up an industry, some firms are likely to find themselves producing goods more cheaply than their competitors. For example, digital technologies are revolutionising the printing and media industries. Those businesses in the forefront of this change are likely to try to use their lower production costs to drive competitors out of the industry. But the fear of new technological change may encourage existing firms to act competitively.

As with technology, ownership, especially of plcs, in the UK is not always static. Changes at the top can lead to changes in business strategy, especially if the goal is to drive up shareholder value. The **hostile acquisition** of rivals and aggressive behaviour in building up market share are non-collusive strategies. In particular, some firms may start price wars by deliberately selling close to or below costs of production with a view to driving out competitors.

Definition

Hostile acquisition means a takeover not accepted or welcomed by the current owners of a company.

Summary

This section has been devoted to two different theoretical treatments of the behaviour of large firms. Firstly, evidence was provided to support the contention that oligopolists are likely to collude, either openly or in secret, to keep prices high and outputs lower than would be the case in more competitive markets. Contestable market theory provides a theoretical case for firms which have monopoly power to act competitively. The changing nature of some markets may have the same effect.

Exam hint

The two approaches to oligopoly contained in this section can often appear in questions where you are asked to 'assess', 'evaluate' or 'compare'. Make sure you understand the subtleties of these trigger words.

Quickies ✓

1   Which firms do you suspect of collusion?
2   What example can you give of a market which might be contestable?

Limiting monopoly power

Synoptic link

You should have covered of lot of the content required in this A2 section in the work that you did for AS section 2.11. Make sure you know about the Competition Commission, and various policies to promote competition, including:
- privatisation
- regulation
- creating internal markets
- encouraging enterprise.

Industrial sector	Five-firm concentration ratio
Tobacco	99.5%
Iron and steel	95.3%
Motor vehicles	82.9%
Cement	77.7%
Water supply	49.7%
Footwear	48.2%
Bread and biscuits	47.0%
Carpets	21.8%
Clothing	20.7%
Plastics processing	8.8%

Table 1 Competitiveness in key economic sectors

The following section is devoted to policies designed to promote competition. It deals with:
- ways of measuring market concentration
- different forms of non-competitive behaviour
- assessing the effectiveness of government intervention.

Measuring concentrated markets

Economists use a simple device to illustrate whether or not production in a given market is in the hands of a few or many firms. These are called concentration ratios and involve the calculation of the share of output of the leading firms in a given market.

Thus, a three-firm concentration ratio would involve adding together the market shares of the three largest firms. The Labour government (first elected in 1997) uses a five-firm ratio to produce a measure of competitiveness in key economic sectors, which provides the information outlined in Table 1.

Examination of these ratios reveals the possible existence of two inter-related influences determining levels of competitiveness:
- differing levels of economies of scale – for example, steel and cement
- differing extent of barriers of entry – for example, clothing and water supply.

However, national ratios such as these do not indicate the level of global competitiveness (for example, motor vehicle manufacture), nor do they account for the existence of local monopolies (for example, water supply).

The case for government intervention

The more detailed theoretical treatment of the significance of market structures in A2 sections 4.6–4.9 tends to indicate that, subject to crucial assumptions, customers and societies will be better off if markets are competitive rather than monopolistic. However, there is growing evidence that concentration ratios in key industries tend to be increasing and that many firms develop strategies to avoid competitive pressures. This divergence between what might be seen as socially desirable and the actual behaviour of an increasing number of larger firms provides a challenge both to economists and to governments. This section explores how governments have attempted to promote competition and limit the adverse effects of firms able to exercise monopoly power.

The case against monopolies is summarised in the 'Thinking like an economist' box on page 56. The economic arguments against the exercise of monopolistic power are not conclusive and they provide a particular challenge to governments in developing policies which guard against the potential excesses of monopolistic power, while trying to ensure that possible benefits are not lost.

UK government policies towards monopolies

The UK government has not always been suspicious of the motives and behaviour of firms perceived to have monopoly power. In the 1930s the government promoted development of larger and more powerful companies because it was considered that they would provide a more secure business environment. However, since the Monopolies and Restrictive Practices Act was passed in 1948, successive governments have looked more critically at the activities of large firms.

This Act, which has been amended and strengthened by additional powers, has provided the basis of government control that continues today. The Secretary of State for Trade and Industry is advised by the Office of Fair Trading. In particular, the Office of Fair Trading identifies cases of possible abuse of monopoly power which should be investigated more fully.

This function is carried out by the Competition Commission (formally known as the Monopolies and Mergers Commission). The Commission is a quasi-legal body that hears evidence before coming to a judgement about suspected abuses of monopoly power. Its findings are reported to the Trade and Industry Minister, who is then responsible for taking or not taking action. The Trade and Industry Minister therefore has the final say.

The law defines a monopoly as being any firm that has a 25 per cent or more share in a local or national market, or two or more firms supplying 25 per cent of the total market if it is suspected they are colluding informally. The 1980 Competition Act identified various types of uncompetitive behaviour, which included:

- price discrimination
- selective distribution, by which a firm may refuse to supply particular companies
- predatory pricing, when firms deliberately cut prices below costs in an attempt to force competitors from a market.

The job of the Competition Commission is establish whether or not uncompetitive behaviour is taking place. They must then balance this against possible benefits in order to make a judgement as to whether or not the firm in question is acting in the public interest.

The Commission and its predecessor have investigated many different possible instances of the abuse of monopoly power. These include the control of public houses by major breweries, high profit levels earned by the major supermarkets, selective distribution by Bird's Eye Walls, and retail-only agreements by Rank Xerox. Various recommendations have been made which have included:

- price cuts
- reduced expenditure on advertising
- reducing barriers of entry.

The current government Trade Minister, Patricia Hewitt

Web link

For commentaries on the effectiveness of competition policy visit www.heinemann.co.uk/hotlinks and click on this section.

Control over mergers

In 1965, Parliament enacted legislation that strengthened government controls over the potential abuse of monopoly power by compelling companies to give notice to the Office of Fair Trading of any proposed merger resulting in the creation of a monopoly as defined by the legislation.

The Office of Fair Trading can recommend to the Trade and Industry Minister that conditions may be attached to giving permission for the merger to take place or reference can be made to the Competition Commission to investigate the likely outcomes of the merger in terms of the framework developed for investigating the abuses of monopoly power. The Commission, having considered evidence, recommends to the Trade and Industry Minister whether or not the merger should proceed.

In practice, only a tiny minority of mergers have been referred to the Commission. Practically all of these proposals have been rejected by the Trade and Industry Minister or abandoned by the companies in question. This apparent contradiction may indicate that government policies towards mergers have lacked consistency. It is not clear on what basis referrals are made to the Trade and Industry Minister and analysis of the outcomes indicates that mergers tend not to be in the public interest.

In November 1999, the Labour government published a green paper on reforms to its policies towards mergers. It proposes to give greater powers and independence to the Office of Fair Trading. Its Director would be empowered to decide which mergers be investigated by the Competition Commission and it is also suggested that the Director General of the Office of Fair Trading should take responsibility from the Trade and Industry Minister in making the final decision as to whether or not a proposed merger should take place.

Control over monopolistic and oligopolistic abuses

The legal framework used to curb the abuse powers of monopolists and oligopolists is tougher than that relating to their existence and creation. Restrictive Trade Practices is the legal terminology used to describe various forms of collusion. All such agreements have to be registered with the Office of Fair Trading and are banned unless participants can prove that they are in the public interest.

The law recognises that collusion can bring benefits such as:
- protecting employment
- promoting exports
- ensuring safety standards are met.

But even if it is possible to prove the existence of such benefits before the Restrictive Practices Court, firms still have to demonstrate that possible benefits outweigh any harmful effects.

Thinking like an economist

Economic theorists have argued that monopoly power can result in:
- higher prices
- lower outputs
- less customer choice
- fewer innovations
- less efficient production both allocatively and productively.

On the other hand it can be argued that firms with large market shares:
- are able to exploit economies of scale
- can compete more effectively in the global market place
- have the resources to devote to research and development
- can be socially responsible.`

Similarly, a tough stance is taken on limiting the power of manufacturers to set and enforce minimum retail prices for their products. Over the years, formal price-fixing agreements have been ended and only currently exist for some medical products.

European Union legislation

The development of the single European market has meant that member states have been forced to adopt a common approach to competition policy, especially in respect of those firms that have monopoly power within the EU. There is no minimum market share that triggers investigation. Firms that behave unfairly towards consumers by their pricing policies or other activities can be referred to the European Court of Justice. If found 'guilty', they can be fined as well as being debarred from acting uncompetitively.

EU policies towards mergers and collusive behaviour are similar. The focus is on investigation of uncompetitive behaviour rather than the existence of monopolies and their market share.

Summary

Governments in most countries intervene to limit the power of monopolists and oligopolists. The existence of considerable numbers of laws, regulations, and a quasi-court structure indicate that this is a complex aspect of economic policy over which it is difficult to legislate. However, the legal framework in this country is designed to try to ensure that government intervention promotes the public interest. Whether or not governments have been successful is a big question.

Quickies

1   Why is control over monopolies so difficult?
2   Which policies are likely to be most effective in limiting monopoly power?

Puzzler

Large multinational companies are more powerful than many governments. Do you agree?

Research task

Use this section in addition to other sources to plan and research an essay in which you assess the effectiveness of government attempts to limit the harmful economic effects of the abuse of monopoly power.

Promoting competition

Synoptic link

This section differs from the previous section in that the focus is on government policy to promote competition. You will see that there are also direct links between government policy and the theory of contestable markets developed in A2 section 4.12.

Industrial relations, production and the international competitiveness of the UK economy in the late 1970s were seen to be poor. Conservative Prime Minister Margaret Thatcher came to power in 1979 with the slogan 'Getting Britain back to work'. She was strongly influenced by 'right wing' economists, who argued that the performance of UK economy would improve if:

- monetarist polices were followed (AS sections 3.20–3.21)
- trade union power was reduced (AS section 3.19)
- some publicly owned organisations were privatised
- organisations remaining in public ownership should be made more competitive.

This section is concerned with the last two bullets above.

Privatisation

First, businesses such as BP, ICL (Computers) and British Sugar, who were operating in competitive markets, were transferred from public to private ownership. In the mid-1980s, Sealink, Jaguar, British Telecom and British Gas were sold. At the end of the decade and in the early 1990s, more complicated sell-offs such as the water, electricity and rail industries were undertaken. The Labour government in power in 2003 has indicated that it will continue these Conservative policies by privatising National Air Traffic Services (NATS) (air traffic control). However, it has undone some of changes made by the Conservatives by winding up Railtrack and replacing it with the not-for-profit Strategic Rail Authority.

In addition to fitting in with the overall policy of promoting the private sector, privatisation created additional government revenue estimated to have exceeded £60 billion.

The privatisation process

Transferring ownership from the public to the private sector usually takes place in the following way.

- Assets to be sold off are valued.
- A prospectus is published detailing the form and nature of the share offer, including the determination of a number of shares to be issued.
- Individual share prices are set.
- The sell-off is publicised.
- The shares are floated – that is, made available for sale.

From the government's point of view, the third stage is crucial. If the business is undervalued, the government loses potential revenue; if it is overvalued, the actual flotation could fail.

The Conservative governments in the 1980s recognised that the transfer of ownership from the public to the private sectors would not be sufficient to

National Air Traffic Services (NATS) was partly privatised in 2001

protect the public from the abuse of monopoly power. In order to safeguard the public interest, legislation to permit privatisation also contained provision for the creation of regulators. These are independent bodies such as Oftel (communication), Ofwat (water) and Ofgen (gas and electricity) with powers to regulate the actual behaviour of these industries by imposing pricing formulas, insisting on customer service targets and levels of investment.

The most important sanction available to most regulators is over-pricing. In many cases, the freedom of newly privatised firms to raise prices is limited by formulae. Although its application varies between industries, the regulator's formula can be represented as $RPI - X + Y + K$, in which:

- RPI stands for the retail price index
- X is a percentage representing costs saving that the regulator expects to be reflected in lower customer prices
- Y stands for unavoidable cost increases
- K applies to companies as an allowance to cover the costs of environmental improvements.

These regulatory powers are in addition to the legal constraints outlined earlier, and are particularly relevant in the case of natural monopolies.

Natural monopolies

Industries such as water, electricity supply and the railways can be described as natural monopolies, and it has been more difficult to sell them off in such a way as to promote competition and the other benefits that private ownership is meant to bring.

Privatising British Rail

This was one of the Conservatives' last privatisations, and turned out to be especially problematical. On the advice of economists, the Conservative government created an imaginative plan to try to introduce competition into this natural monopoly. It split the industry into three:

- the railway and station network
- rolling stock provision
- rail operating companies.

Privatised rail companiers – better or worse?

Each section was privatised differently.

- Railtrack: the government accepted that this was a natural monopoly that could not be broken up. In 1996, it was sold into private ownership for slightly less than £2 billion. Its market value in January 2000 was £3.25 billion. In the event, Railtrack ran into financial difficulties and after a period in which government subsidised their activities they were wound up and replaced by the Strategic Rail Authority.
- Rolling stock: three rolling stock companies were created whose job was to compete in order to supply engines and carriages to the train operating companies.

■ Train operating companies: investors were encouraged to bid for franchises to run trains over regional and inter-city routes. Successful companies would then pay Railtrack to use 'their' stations and track, and lease rolling stock as required. At the end of 7 to 14 years, new bids would be invited to run services in the future.

Regulation

A powerful independent regulatory regime was introduced to ensure that minimum service levels were met, that profits were not excessive and that government guidelines were followed.

Assessing performance of the privatised rail network

The general perception of the public as revealed in surveys is that the privatisation of the railways has yet to be successful.
■ Train operating companies have used their market power to introduce complicated discriminatory pricing policies.
■ Prices on some services have been dramatically increased.
■ Punctuality and customer service are thought to have deteriorated.
■ Safety may have been given less priority.

The long-term test of the success of this particular privatisation will be the degree to which a natural monopoly re-establishes itself through merger and takeover within the industry. This has already started to occur in the electricity generation and supply industry.

Competition within the public sector

In the 1980s, the Conservative government realised that the total privatisation of the public sector would be both politically unacceptable and very difficult to implement. It chose instead a variety of strategies designed to introduce or mimic market forces within industries and organisations. These included:
■ the creation of internal markets in the British Broadcasting Corporation (BBC) and the National Health Service (NHS)
■ compulsory competitive tendering for a range of central and local government functions
■ greater freedom for educational institutions to control their own budgets.

Internal markets

The creation of internal markets involves the creation of individual cost centres and greater independence in financial decision-making. Thus, in the NHS, budget-holding doctors were given the freedom to purchase medical care from those hospitals providing the most attractive service.

Hospitals were expected to compete for business from General Practitioners (GPs). This represented a radical change in established procedures, which could have had devastating political effects had the government been prepared to allow failing hospitals to go 'bust' and close. The incoming Labour government abandoned these policies in 1997.

A version of an internal market still exists within the BBC in which independent programme makers have the freedom to employ camera operators, directors, costume designers and so on from within the BBC or from outside contractors.

Compulsory competitive tendering

Local and central government departments were compelled by legal changes to put the provision of services out to tender. This means that, rather than a council employing refuse collectors, they were required to invite private companies to bid for contracts to collect domestic and commercial refuse. The rules relating to tendering have now been relaxed to permit councils to tender for the provision of their own services.

Education

The Conservative governments in the 1980s also tried to apply market disciplines to education. Universities were further encouraged to compete with each other. Schools were encouraged to become independent of local authority control, and it was believed that educational standards would benefit if schools competed with each other for students.

Summary

In recent years, UK governments have attempted to encourage the development of more competitive markets through privatisation and the introduction of internal markets and other structures within the public sector. Some of these policies appear to have been more successful than others but it is too early to assess the long-term impact of these changes on society as a whole.

Hot potato

Will competition increase health care and educational standards?

Quickie

Which innovation is most likely to promote competition?

Puzzler

Is the creation of the Strategic Rail Authority back-door nationalisation?

Research task

Select an industry that has been privatised or an area of the public sector that has been opened up to competitive forces and evaluate the effectiveness of these changes.

Activities

Activity 1

Price (AR £)	Quantity demanded	Total revenue	Marginal revenue
10	0	0	–
9	1	9	9
8	2	16	7
7	3		
6	4		
5	5		
4	6		

Table 1 Revenue

a) Complete the rest of Table 1.
b) At what level of output will the marginal revenue equal zero? What is true about the total revenue at this level of output?
c) Work out the price elasticity of demand when the price is cut from £5 to £4. How does this relate to your answer to question b?

Quantity	Total costs	Marginal cost	Average cost
0	9	–	–
1	12	3	12
2	14		
3	15		
4	18		
5	25		
6	36		

Table 2 Costs (short run)

d) Complete the rest of Table 2.
e) Using the information in Tables 1 and 2, work out the profit maximising level of output for the firm. Prove this using analysis of marginal revenue and marginal costs.
f) At what level of output will the firm make normal profit?
g) Which level of output is closest to the productively efficient point?

Pitfalls to avoid

Graphically, MR would be plotted at the halfway point between the two levels of output, for example, MR of 9 would be plotted at an output of 0.5 and MR of 7 at an output of 1.5. We can see that MR is a straight line that would have a value of 8 at an output of 1.

Activity 2

The data below refers to the United Kingdom grocery retailing market in July 2003.

	UK market share by retailer (% sales value, 2003)
Tesco	27%
Asda	17%
Sainsburys	16.2%
Safeway	9.2%
Morrisons	6%

(Source: TNS Superpanel)

Table 3 Market share

From the data in Table 3 it can be deduced that:

A   The industry is monopolistically competitive.
B   A takeover of Safeway by Morrisons would increase the three-firm concentration ratio.
C   The firms in this market are likely to be price takers.
D   The industry most closely resembles an oligopolistic market.
E   The firms are unlikely to compete actively with each other.

Boost your grade

It is important to explain how you get your answer in the supported choice section. You can get some credit by proving the other answers to be incorrect, if you are finding it difficult to write a lot about why your answer is the correct option.

Activity 3

a) Explain five different methods of non-price competition that firms might use.
b) Evaluate the case for spending a large proportion of a firm's revenue on advertising its product.

Activity 4

Using figure 1, identify the output levels that correspond to the following conditions for the firm.
a) Allocative efficiency.
b) Profit maximisation.
c) Sales maximisation.
d) Revenue maximisation.
e) Productive efficiency.

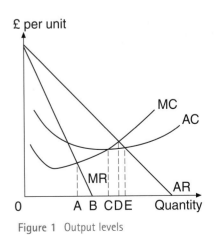

Figure 1 Output levels

Activity 5

Name five different real-world examples of firms practising different forms of price discrimination.

Answers

4.16

Activity 1

a)

Price (AR £)	Quantity demanded	Total revenue	Marginal revenue
10	0	0	–
9	1	9	9
8	2	16	7
7	3	21	5
6	4	24	3
5	5	25	1
4	6	24	-1

b) Marginal revenue is a straight line that will start at the top of the **AR** curve and will cut the *x* axis exactly halfway between the origin and the point that the **AR** crosses it. The data above shows that MR will equal zero at an output of exactly 5. (note: pitfalls to avoid in section 4.14). This is the condition for total revenue maximisation, as any further sales will have negative marginal revenue and the **TR** would fall. We can see that **TR** was maximised at £25 at an output of 5.

c) PED= % change in quantity demanded

—————————————

% change in price.

From £5 to £4:   +20% / –20% = – 1

The demand curve is unit elastic at the point where **MR** is 0 and **TR** is maximised. At prices higher than £5, this demand curve is elastic as a decrease in price will increase total revenue.

d)

Quantity	Total costs	Marginal cost	Average cost
0	9	–	–
1	12	3	12
2	14	2	7
3	15	1	5
4	18	3	4.5
5	25	7	5
6	36	11	6

e) The highest profit level is £6, occuring at an output of 3 and 4. (TR – TC). Between the output levels 3 and 4 the marginal cost equals the marginal revenue (£3). Prior to this level of output the **MR** was greater than the **MC**, thus additional output would have increased profits. After an output of 4 the **MR** is less than the **MC**, thus the profits will decline.

f) **Normal profit** is the break even level from an economist's way of thinking about costs. Supernormal profit is zero at an output of 5 units.

g) Productive efficiency occurs when the resources are being used to produce as much output per input as possible and this will minimise the average cost. The output level closest to this is 4.

Exam hint

Profit maximisation is the most crucial condition to memorise, as it is relevant for all the market structures. Strictly, it occurs where MC cuts MR from below as, in perfect competition particularly, the MC could equal the MR at two levels of output.

Definition

Normal profit includes (as a cost) the profit necessary to reward the entrepreneur with enough return to keep his capital/labour invested in the firm. This will be the opportunity cost, what that money/his time could have earned elsewhere.

Activity 2

D The market is dominated by a few large producers with a three- firm concentration ratio of 27 + 17 + 16.2 = 60.2%. This is clearly an oligopoly, although Tesco has the dominant position and with over 25% market share would be defined as having monopoly power under the 1973 Fair Trading Act. Each of these producers has a degree of brand loyalty, induced by advertising and other non-price methods.

Activity 3

a) Advertising; quality improvements; free gifts/add-on extras; competitions; product placement/sponsorship; credit schemes; restrictive trade practices; vertical integration to control raw materials or outlets.

b) For: Increases the demand from new customers in the market.
              Increases the demand by switching customers from other brands.
              Increases the demand by encouraging more purchases by existing customers of your product.
              Sets up a barrier to entry, in the sunk cost of having to compete with the strength of the incumbent brand.
              Makes existing customers more price and cross-price inelastic.

    Against: Costs a lot of money.
              Advertising may be unsuccessful, even lose demand.
              May provoke retaliatory campaigns from rival producers so that more has to be spent in the future.

Activity 4

a) D Price = marginal cost
b) A Marginal cost cuts marginal revenue from below
c) E Price (AR) = AC at the highest level of output
d) B MR = 0
e) C The lowest point of the AC curve (AC = MC)

Activity 5

By time: London Underground charges more for Travelcards before 9:30 and British Telecom charges more for weekday calls before 18:00.

By Quantity purchased: Mobile phone call charges per minute get cheaper the longer the phone call under certain tariffs and electricity charges are cheaper per unit for larger users.

By age: Cinemas give OAP and student discounts.

By gender: Some clubs let women in free on certain nights and hairdressers charge an entirely different rate for male and female haircuts.

By income: There are lower council house rents for lower-income households and private schools may give bursaries to families with less means.

Exam guidance and practice

Exam guidance

U nit 4 carries 15% of the marks of the full A-level (30% of the A2 component).

The unit 4 paper is split into two sections. Section A consists of ten compulsory supported choice questions, worth 4 marks each. Section B contains two data response questions from which *ONE* must be chosen. Each section carries equal marks. The paper has a one hour and fifteen minute time limit. It is this aspect of the examination that is most likely to present problems to the well-prepared candidate. The paper is particularly hard on timing and you will have to press on to finish it. There is no reason why you must attempt section A first and you may well prefer to start with the data response section. The later questions of section B are worth the most marks.

Section A: supported choice questions

There is one mark available for identifying the correct answer and up to three marks for the justification of why this is the correct option (as with unit 1). Even if you do not get the correct answer you may score up to 2 out of the 4 marks for a sensible justification of the reasons behind your selection. Be certain to *define* all of the economic terms used in the question and the answer that you have selected. You can obtain some credit by proving the other answers incorrect, although this alone will not gain the full marks.

Do not feel constrained to write only on the lines printed in the examination booklet, you can use the full page. This is particularly useful if you choose to annotate a diagram in the question and label your shading as part of your answer. Since many of the supported choice questions will be concerned with the various market structures, you must ensure that you have thoroughly revised all of their assumptions and the short and long run diagrams that illustrate each theory of the firm. You can gain marks for fully labelling and annotating the appropriate diagram to answer a particular question (see exam practice question 1). Do not wait to be asked to draw them. Be sure to *apply* the concepts you develop in your explanation to the particular context given in the question.

Try not to spend too long working out a question that you find particularly difficult, come back to it at the end, as you may be taking up time that you need to score marks elsewhere on the paper. Do not spend longer than 30–35 minutes on section A. You will need time to read through and choose the best data response for you in section B.

Section B: data response question

It is important that you spend a good five minutes, if not a little more, reading through the two data response passages and selecting the most appropriate one. *Read the questions first.* This way you will be searching for the answers as you read the passage for the first time. The passages are intended to supplement your knowledge and the questions should indicate the sections of your studies that you must apply in this particular case. Often, you may be able to answer some of the later questions of the data response with less direct reference to the passage. Do not be put off if you cannot answer the first questions, as they are often descriptive and worth a small proportion of the total marks. The later questions will normally entail some evaluation and you should be aware of the keywords in the question (see boost your grade in section 4.15). You should spend 35–40 minutes answering the data response, most candidates find that they need a little more time on this section.

Exam practice

1) A monopolistically competitive firm in the long run will produce where:

A   it receives supernormal profits.

B   it is productively inefficient but allocatively efficient.

C   the price it receives is equal to the marginal cost.

D   it is allocatively and productively inefficient.

E   it is productively efficient and maximises profits.

D is the answer as the firm is profit maximising where it is only earning normal profits, AR=AC in the long run since there are no barriers to entry. It is not productively efficient as it is not at the bottom of the AC curve (not at point **a**), nor is it allocatively efficient since AR>MC (not at point **b**).

2) A hot-dog vendor lowers his price from £3 to £2.50 and notices that he sells 11 hotdogs an hour rather than 10. What is the marginal revenue of the 11th hotdog?

A   £2.50

B   £27.50

C   £8

D   –£5

E   –£2.50

E is the answer. Marginal revenue is the change in total revenue from the sale of the extra hot-dog. The total revenue is the price multiplied by the number of hotdogs sold. Initially price (£3) × quantity (10) = £30, after the price reduction it is £2.50 × 11 = £27.50. Thus the vendor has lost £2.50 as he must charge a fixed uniform price per hot-dog. Although he gains an extra £2.50 on the sale of the 11th hot-dog, he will lose 50p on each of the 10 sales that he would have made before. This means that his demand is relatively price inelastic as he only gained 10% extra sales from a 16.6% price reduction.

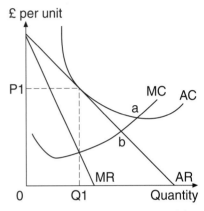

£ per unit

Figure 1 A monopolistically competitive firm's long run equilibrium position

Exam hint

Remember to define all of the terms used in the question and to show full workings for any calculations that you have undertaken. It is a good idea to label the figures in the calculations to show your processes.

Further reading

4.18

4.2
A. Griffiths and S. Ison, *Business Economics*, Heinemann, 2001, Chapter 2.

4.3
A. Griffiths and S. Ison, *Business Economics*, Heinemann, 2001, Chapter 2.
I. Wilson, *The Economics of Leisure*, Heinemann, 2003, Chapter 5.

4.4, 4.5 and 4.6
A. Griffiths and S. Ison, *Business Economics*, Heinemann, 2001, Chapter 1.

4.7
A. Griffiths and S. Ison, *Business Economics*, Heinemann, 2001, Chapter 3.
S. Munday, *Markets and Market Failure*, Heinemann, 2000, Chapters 2 and 4.

4.8
C. Bamford and S. Munday, *Markets*, Heinemann, 2002, Chapter 7.
A. Griffiths and S. Ison, *Business Economics*, Heinemann, 2001, Chapter 4.
I. Wilson, *The Economics of Leisure*, Heinemann, 2003, Chapter 5.

4.9
C. Bamford and S. Munday, *Markets*, Heinemann, 2002, Chapter 7.
A. Griffiths and S. Ison, *Business Economics*, Heinemann, 2001, Chapter 5.
I. Wilson, *The Economics of Leisure*, Heinemann, 2003, Chapter 5.

4.10
C. Bamford and S. Munday, *Markets*, Heinemann, 2002, Chapter 7.
A. Griffiths and S. Ison, *Business Economics*, Heinemann, 2001, Chapter 6.
I. Wilson, *The Economics of Leisure*, Heinemann, 2003, Chapter 5.

4.11
C. Bamford and S. Munday, *Markets*, Heinemann, 2002, Chapters 2, 4 and 7.

4.12
C. Bamford and S. Munday, *Markets*, Heinemann, 2002, Chapter 7.
A. Griffiths and S. Ison, *Business Economics*, Heinemann, 2002, Chapters 6 and 7.
I. Wilson, *The Economics of Leisure*, Heinemann, 2003, Chapter 5.

4.13
A. Griffiths and S. Ison, *Business Economics*, Heinemann, 2001, Chapter 9.

4.14
C. Bamford, *Transport Economics*, 3rd edn., Heinemann, 2001, Chapter 3.
A. Griffiths and S. Ison, *Business Economics*, Heinemann, 2001, Chapter 7.
D. Smith, *UK Current Economic Policy*, 3rd edn., Heinemann, 2003, Chapter 3.

PART 5a
LABOUR MARKETS

5a1 Introduction to labour markets

The study of labour markets is an important and interesting field of study in economics. What type of job people do and how much they earn has a significant impact on the quality of their lives. Some people do interesting, well-paid jobs which provide them with status, stimulation and the finance to enjoy a high material standard of living. Some are in low paid, insecure and unchallenging jobs and others are unemployed.

The nature of the module

You will already have some knowledge and understanding of the workings of labour markets gleaned from part-time jobs, holiday jobs and the experiences of friends and relatives. Module 5a provides you with the opportunity to study labour markets in some depth. You will make use of what you learned at AS level on price determination, the nature, causes and consequences of market failure, unemployment and income distribution. For instance, you will apply the concepts of elasticities of demand and supply and the mobility of labour. You will also learn new concepts and pick up additional information, including marginal productivity theory, the role of trade unions and Lorenz curves, in your studies of this topic.

Among the topics you will study are how wages are determined, why some people earn more than others, the effects of discrimination, the impact of the National Minimum Wage, the significance of our ageing population, why wealth is not evenly distributed and the causes of poverty.

The exam

The module is assessed in a unit paper lasting one hour and fifteen minutes. The examination counts for 15 per cent of your total A-level mark and consists of one data response question from a choice of two.

Maximising your grade

To achieve a high grade, it is particularly important that you develop your analytical and evaluative skills. In assessing labour market issues, you need not only to apply relevant economic concepts but also to explain the points you are making using appropriate economic analysis and, for the higher marked questions, to make judgements supported by economic evidence and theory. The sections in this unit are designed to provide you with the relevant information and to help you to develop the skills you will need

There is also widespread coverage of labour market issues in newspaper articles, magazines and websites. Information and analysis of wage differentials, discrimination, immigration, labour disputes, poverty and other issues are regularly reported. So, keep in touch with developments in labour markets by regularly reading relevant articles and visiting appropriate websites. Also regularly check and analyse labour market data. Such data can be found in ONS (Office for National Statistics) publications and on its websites. The section on labour markets in *Social Trends* is particularly informative.

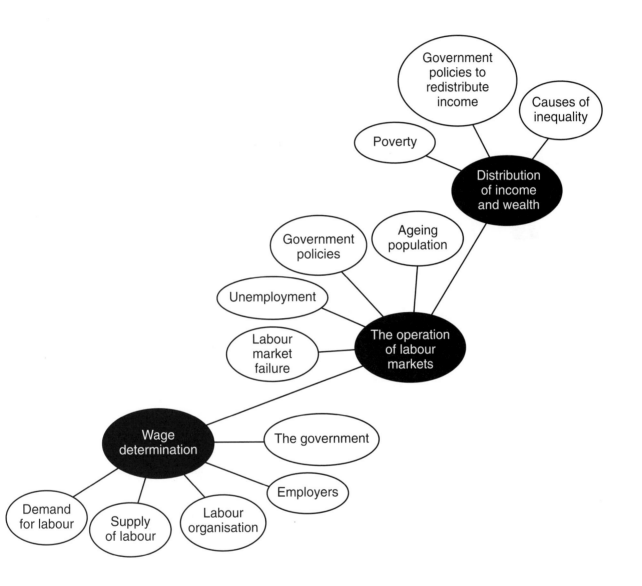

5a.2 The supply of labour

The supply of labour can be examined in a number of ways, from what influences how many hours an individual works to the total supply of labour in an economy. As with the supply of goods and services, there are a number of key influences on the supply of labour. One of the main influences is the price of labour, that is the wage rate. Due to its importance, economists measure the elasticity of supply of labour.

The individual supply of labour

The number of hours a worker decides to work is influenced by the number of hours on offer and the relative importance that the worker attaches to income and leisure.

Many workers are unable to alter the number of hours they work in their main jobs. They are contracted to work, say, 38 hours a week and are not offered the opportunity to vary these hours. However, with increasing flexibility in labour markets, more workers are now able to choose how many hours they work.

It is thought that at low wage levels, a rise in the wage rate will cause an extension in supply, with a worker being prepared to work more hours. However, after a certain wage is reached, the offer of a higher wage rate may cause a worker to choose to work fewer hours. They may decide that a given income level is sufficient to meet their financial requirements and may prefer to have more leisure time in which to enjoy their earnings.

For example, a worker may currently work 40 hours at £15 per hour. This gives a gross income of £600 per week. A rise in the wage rate to £20 would enable the worker to earn the same wage rate by working 30 hours, giving 10 hours more leisure time. This change in response to an increase in the wage rate gives rise to the backward sloping supply curve as illustrated in Figure 1. Up to the wage rate of £15 the supply of labour extends, but any rise above £15 causes supply to contract. The behaviour of the worker can be explained by the income and substitution effects.

Synoptic links

This section draws on AS sections 1.11, 1.12 and 3.8. You will apply your understanding of supply, price elasticity of supply and the causes of changes in productive potential to labour markets.

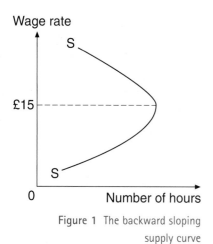

Figure 1 The backward sloping supply curve

The aggregate supply of labour

The total supply of labour is influenced by these three key factors:
- size of the population
- size of the working population
- number of hours worked.

Making connections

Explain the income and substitution effects of a rise in income tax.

Population

The larger the population size, the greater the potential supply of labour. So, for example, the USA, with a population of 280 million, has a greater supply of labour than France, which has a population of 60 million.

As well as the total size of population, the age distribution of the population, school leaving age and retirement age all influence the size of the labour orce. The higher the proportion of the population in the working age range, the greater the supply of labour. In the UK, the population of working age consists of those aged between 16 and 65.

This proportion could rise as a result of a rise in the birth rate that occurred sixteen or more years before, net immigration (since most immigrants are aged between 20 and 40), a lowering of the school leaving age or a raising of the retirement age. In a number of countries, including the UK, USA, Germany, France and Japan, the proportion of people of working age is declining as a result of the population ageing.

The working population

The **working population** or labour force consists of those in employment and those seeking employment. This is not the same as the population of working age. Some of those who are older than the school leaving age and younger than the state retirement age may not be **economically active**. The main groups who are not actively participating in the labour force are those still in full-time education, those who have retired early, those who are long term sick or disabled and those who are homemakers.

There are various factors that influence the **participation rate** of the population of working age in the labour force.

- Wage rates – higher wage rates will tend to encourage more people to seek to enter or stay in the labour force.
- Employment opportunities – the greater the number and quality of jobs on offer, the higher the participation rate is likely to be.
- Social attitudes to women working – countries in which it is acceptable for women and, in particular, married women to work, have a large pool of workers to call on.
- Provision for the care of the very young and the elderly – those countries in which there is state and private provision will tend to have a higher working population rate than those in which the very young and the elderly are looked after solely by relatives at home.

The hours worked

As well as the number of workers, the hours they work influences the supply of labour. The hours worked, in turn, is influenced by the length of the working week, the number of holiday days and the number of days lost through industrial action. The more hours worked, the greater the supply of labour in terms of quantity. However when workers work long hours, with few holidays, the quality of what they produce may decline.

Workers in the UK work longer hours than those in most other EU countries. On 1 October 1998 the Working Time Regulations came into force. This requires employers to 'take all reasonable steps' to ensure that employees do not work, against their will, more than an average of 48 hours a week. Despite this, in 2002 more than a sixth of UK workers worked more than 48 hours a week in their main jobs.

Definitions

Working population means those who are economically active, for example, in employment or unemployed.

Economically inactive means people who are neither in employment nor unemployed, for example, children, the elderly, retired and housewives.

Participation rate means the proportion of those of working age in the working population (labour force).

Making connections

Discuss two policies a government could employ to increase the participation rate of disabled adults.

The supply of labour to a particular occupation

The number of people willing and able to work in a given occupation is influenced by:

- The wage rate – the higher the wage rate, the more people are likely to want to do the job. For example, a relatively high number of people seek to become accountants because of the high wages on offer.
- The convenience and flexibility of hours – long and unsociable working hours are likely to discourage potential workers. For example, nursing homes find it difficult to recruit night-time nursing staff. However, flexibility of hours may attract people to a given occupation. For example, salespeople may, to a certain extent, be able to decide when they work.
- Status – the high status achieved by, for example, pilots makes it an attractive job.
- Promotion opportunities – some people are prepared to work initially for relatively low wages in, for example, the media in the hope than they will progress on to high paid jobs.
- Flexibility of location – it is becoming increasingly possible in certain occupations, such as architects and designers, to work at least some days from home. This increases the attractiveness of the occupations.
- Qualifications and skills – the higher the qualifications and skills required, the fewer the number of people who are able to undertake the occupation. Whilst the supply of sales assistants is relatively high, the supply of brain surgeons is low.
- Job security – the more secure a job is, the more attractive it is likely to be. University lecturers and professors in the UK used to be given tenure for life. This made some people willing to enter an academic life even though pay was not very high. However, security of tenure has now ended and this, combined with the relatively low pay for a job requiring high academic qualifications, has coincided with a decrease in the numbers wanting to become university lecturers.
- Pleasantness of the job – everything else being equal, more workers will be attracted to more pleasant jobs. It might be expected that the supply of sewage workers would be low as it is not a particularly pleasant job. However, the unpleasantness is more than offset by the low level of qualifications required. Some sewage workers may not be particularly keen to work in the occupation but they may not have the qualifications to switch to alternative jobs.
- Holidays – long holidays are likely to attract workers. Some people may be encouraged to become teachers because of the relatively long holidays on offer. However, this benefit is likely to decrease. Already lecturers in further education have experienced reductions in their holiday entitlement.
- Perks and fringe benefits – company cars, paid trips abroad, profit sharing schemes, free private health care and good company pension schemes are likely to make an occupation more attractive. For example, pilots receive benefits including free or very cheap flights for their families, good company pension schemes and an early retirement age.

Thinking like an economist

Why are UK farmers finding it difficult to recruit fruit pickers?

The supply of labour to a particular firm

Most of the factors that influence the supply of labour to a particular occupation also apply to the supply of labour to particular firms. In addition, supply is influenced by:

- The quality and quantity of training on offer – the greater the quality and amount of training that workers can gain from the firm, the greater the number of workers that are likely to be attracted.
- The location of the firm – firms based in major cities have a greater pool of labour from which to select.
- The level of employment – firms often find it difficult to recruit workers when there is a low level of unemployment.
- The reputation of the firm – this is similar to the status of an occupation.
- The recent performance of the firm – potential workers are encouraged to apply to firms which are doing well and expanding. This is linked to the previous influences, as an expanding firm may be expected to offer higher wages, more training, greater promotion opportunities and more job security than static or declining firms.
- The opportunity to work overtime – some people are keen to raise their incomes by working extra hours at higher rates.

The elasticity of supply of labour

The extent to which the supply of labour changes as a result of a change in the wage rate is measured by the **elasticity of supply of labour**. The formula is:

$$\text{Elasticity of supply of labour} = \frac{\text{percentage change in supply of labour}}{\text{percentage change in wage rate}}$$

The factors which influence the elasticity of supply of labour are:

- The qualifications and skills required – the supply of skilled workers is more inelastic than the supply of unskilled workers as there are fewer skilled than unskilled workers.
- The length of training – a long period of training may discourage some people from undertaking the occupation. So a rise in the wage rate will still not attract many new workers.
- The level of employment – if there is high unemployment, supply of labour to many occupations is likely to be elastic. This is because the wage rate will not have to be raised by much to attract a high number of applicants from people seeking employment.
- The mobility of labour – the easier workers find it to switch jobs (occupational mobility) and the easier they find it move from one area to another (geographical mobility), the more elastic supply will be.
- The time period – as with demand, supply will be more elastic the longer the time period involved. A rise in the wage rate of barristers, for example, may not have much effect on the supply of barristers in the short run. However, in the long run it is likely to since more students will be encouraged to undertake the necessary training.

Definition

Elasticity of supply of labour is the responsiveness of the supply of labour to a change in the wage rate.

Making connections

Explain why an increase in the elasticity of supply of labour would be likely to raise efficiency.

A profile of the working population

Women are continuing to form an increasing proportion of the UK's labour force. In 1971, women formed 38.5 per cent of the working population. This had risen to 44.7 per cent by 2002. This rise reflects an increase in the participation rate of women and a decline in the participation rate of men.

In 1986, 88 per cent of males of working age were economically active and 68 per cent of females. By 2001 this had changed to an economic activity rate for males of 83 per cent and 72 per cent of females.

The major rise in the participation rate of women has come in the 25-44 age range. In 1971, just over half were economically active. This had risen to over three quarters by 2002. Amongst others, the reasons women are participating more include increased job opportunities, increased pay, changing social attitudes and increased expectations of living standards. Women are also tending to have children later and are returning to work more quickly.

The working population is also ageing. In 2002, there were 3.5 workers supporting each person over 65 but in 2036 this will have dropped to 2.4 putting ever-greater strain on health services and pension provision.

There have been a number of other changes in the UK's working population in recent years. These include rises in part-time employment, self-employment and in the number of people with second jobs.

While most people still work on a full-time basis, the number of people working part-time increased by more than 30 per cent between 1986 and 2002. More women than men work part-time.

The proportion of the labour force that is self-employed continues to rise. The three main industrial categories in which people are self-employed are: construction; distribution, hotels and restaurants; banking, finance and insurance. In 2002, the number of workers with second jobs increased to more than 1 million. This represents a 68 per cent increase since 1985.

Quickies

1   Distinguish between the income and substitution effects of a fall in the wage rate offered to a worker.
2   What effect does a fall in unemployment have on the elasticity of supply of labour?

Puzzler

Should the UK raise the retirement age?

The demand for labour is influenced by its function as a factor of production. Firms will demand more labour if demand for the products they produce rises. **Marginal productivity theory** seeks to explain what determines the number of workers a firm employs. A change in the wage rate obviously has an impact on the demand for labour. Elasticity of demand measures the extent to which demand responds to a change in the wage rate.

Derived demand

As with demand for factors of production, demand for labour is a **derived demand**. Factors of production are not wanted for their own sake but for what they can produce. So the number of workers that firms wish to employ depends principally on the demand for the products produced. If demand rises, firms will usually seek to employ more workers.

The aggregate demand for labour

The aggregate (total) demand for labour depends mainly on the level of economic activity. If the economy is growing and firms are optimistic that it will continue to grow in the future, employment is likely to rise. However if output is declining or even growing at a slower rate than the trend growth rate and firms are pessimistic about future levels of aggregate demand, employment is likely to fall.

A firm's demand for labour

How many workers, or working hours, a firm seeks to employ is influenced by a number of factors. These include:

- Demand and expected future demand for the product produced – this is the key influence.
- Productivity – the higher the output per worker hour, the more attractive labour is.
- Complementary labour costs – as well as wages, firms incur other costs when they employ labour. So, for example, if National Insurance contributions rise, demand for labour is likely to fall.
- The price of labour – a rise in wage rates above any rise in labour productivity will raise unit labour costs and is likely to result in a contraction in demand for labour.
- The price of other factors of production which can be substituted for labour – if capital becomes cheaper, firms may seek to replace some of their workers with machines.

Marginal productivity theory

Marginal productivity theory suggests that demand for any factor of production depends on its marginal revenue product (MRP) and that the

Synoptic links

Before starting this section, reread AS sections 1.5, 1.7 and 1.12.

Definitions

Derived demand is the demand for one item depending on the demand for another item.

Marginal productivity theory is the view that demand for a factor of production depends on its marginal revenue product.

Thinking like an economist

Why is the demand for vets increasing?

Making connections

Why may economic growth be below the trend rate?

Definitions

Marginal revenue is the change in revenue brought about by changing production by one unit.

Marginal revenue product of labour is the change in a firm's revenue resulting from employing one more worker.

quantity of any factor employed will be determined by where the marginal cost of employing one more unit of the factor equals the marginal revenue product of that factor.

The marginal product of labour is the change in total output which results from employing one more worker. As more workers are employed, output may initially rise rapidly as increasing returns are experienced so marginal product may increase. However, once a certain level of employment is reached, marginal product may fall as diminishing returns set in.

No. of workers	Total output	Marginal product		Marginal revenue (Price £)		Marginal revenue product (MRP)	Total revenue (£)
1	20	20	×	10	=	200	200
2	80	60	×	10	=	600	800
3	160	80	×	10	=	800	1600
4	220	60	×	10	=	600	2200
5	260	40	×	10	=	400	2600
6	280	20	×	10	=	200	2800

Table 1 Marginal revenue product of labour

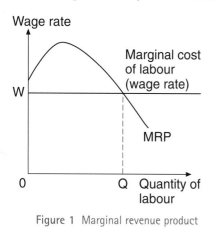

Figure 1 Marginal revenue product

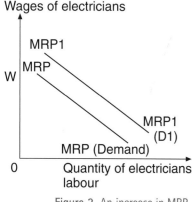

Figure 2 An increase in MRP

Marginal revenue product of labour is found by multiplying marginal product by **marginal revenue** as shown in Table 1. In a perfectly competitive market marginal revenue will be equal to price.

If the wage rate is constant at £400, the firm will employ five workers, since this is where the marginal cost of labour equals MRP. At this level of employment the total cost of workers will be 5 × £400 = £2000. This level of employment is the one where the gap between total revenue and total cost of labour is greatest, that is £2600 – £2000 = £600.

The marginal revenue product of labour curve shows the quantity of labour demanded at each wage rate, as shown in Figure 1. So the marginal revenue product curve of labour is the demand curve for labour.

The MRP, and hence the demand curve for labour, will shift out to the right if the marginal product of labour and/or marginal revenue increase. For example, the demand for electricians will increase if the productivity of electricians rises, perhaps due to increased training, and/or if the price of their services rises, for example, due to a switch from gas to electrical appliances. This increase in MRP is illustrated in Figure 2.

In practice, it can be difficult to measure MRP. This is because workers often work in teams so it can be difficult to isolate the contribution one worker makes to changes in output. In addition, it is difficult to measure the marginal product of a number of people who work in the tertiary sector. For example, is a doctor who treats twenty people in a day for varicose veins more productive than one who carries out one multiple-organ transplant?

The elasticity of demand for labour

Whilst a change in marginal productivity or marginal revenue will shift the demand curve for labour, a change in the wage rate will cause a movement along the demand curve for labour. The extent to which demand will contract or extend as a result of a change in the wage rate is measured by the **elasticity of demand for labour**. The formula is:

$$\text{Elasticity of demand for labour} = \frac{\text{percentage change in demand for labour}}{\text{percentage change in wage rate}}$$

A number of factors influence the elasticity of demand for labour.

- The price elasticity of demand for the product produced – if demand for the product is inelastic, demand for the labour that produces it is also likely to be inelastic. This is because the rise in the price of the product that will result from a rise in the wage rate will cause a smaller percentage fall in demand for the product. So, as output will not change by much, employment will not fall significantly.
- The proportion of wage costs in total costs – if wages account for a significant proportion of total costs, demand will be elastic. This is because a change in the wage rate will have a large impact on total costs. If the wage rate falls, total costs will fall by a noticeable amount and demand for labour will rise by a greater percentage.
- The substitution of labour by other factors – if it is easy to substitute capital for labour, demand for labour will be elastic. A rise in the wage rate will cause workers to be substituted by machines. Demand for labour will fall by a greater percentage than the rise in the wage rate.
- The elasticity of supply of complementary factors – if wages fall and it is easy to obtain more of the factors that are used alongside labour, demand for labour will be elastic.
- The time period – demand for labour is more elastic in the long run when there is more time for firms to reorganise their production methods.

Definition

Elasticity of demand for labour is the responsiveness of demand for labour to a change in the wage rate.

Quickies

1 What effect will a rise in vegetarianism have on demand for butchers?
2 Explain two possible causes of an increase in the MRP of hairdressers.
3 Why is it difficult to measure MRP?
4 Why is the demand for pilots more elastic than demand for air stewards?

Puzzler

Would a trade union want demand for the labour of the workers it represents to be elastic or inelastic?

Wage determination and wage differentials

Price determination and changes in price were covered in AS sections 1.13–1.15. In this section you will examine how the price of labour is determined in different labour markets.

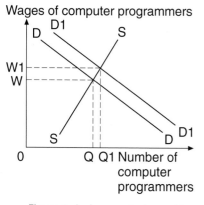

Wages of computer programmers

Figure 1 An increase in demand for computer programmers

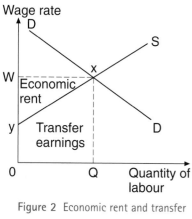

Wage rate

Figure 2 Economic rent and transfer earnings

hy did the pay of barristers increase in 2002? Why are financial advisers paid more than checkout assistants? In examining how wages are determined and why they differ between groups of workers, it is important to consider the demand for and supply of labour.

Wage determination

The market forces of demand and supply play a key role in determining relative wages. The wage rate of a group of workers will rise if either the demand for their services increases or their supply decreases. For example, the wages of computer programmers have risen as the spread of information technology has increased demand for their services. This effect is shown in Figure 1. In contrast, the wage of clerical workers has fallen relative to other groups as their supply has increased and demand for their services has fallen.

Economic rent and transfer earnings

The level of demand and supply and their elasticities determine not only the level of wage rates but also the proportion of wages which consist of economic rent and the proportion which consist of transfer earnings.

Transfer earnings are what a worker can earn in their next best paid job – the opportunity cost of performing the current job. Transfer earnings are the equivalent to the minimum which has to be paid to keep the worker in their current job.

Economic rent is the surplus over transfer earnings and is total earnings minus transfer earnings. For example, a woman may earn £580 a week as an optician. If the next best paid job she is willing and able to do is as an advertising executive earning £494 a week, her economic rent is £86 and her transfer earnings are £494.

Figure 2 shows that the total earnings received by the workers is $0WxQ$. Of this yWx is economic rent and $0YxQ$ is transfer earnings. This figure shows that economic rent is the area above the supply curve and below the wage rate. The amount of economic rent earned by the workers will vary.

The first worker employed would have been prepared to work for considerably less than the wage rate actually paid. So, a relatively high proportion of their earnings will be economic rent. Whereas the last worker employed would have be prepared to work only for the going wage rate and so earns no economic rent.

The proportion of earnings which constitute economic rent depends on the elasticity of supply. Economic rent will form a large proportion when supply is inelastic. For example, many footballers playing in the premier leagues of England and Scotland are thought to earn a large amount of economic rent. Supply is inelastic since most footballers enjoy playing football and would continue to play, even if their wage rate was cut, as most would earn considerably less in their next best paid jobs.

These footballers are also highly paid. Demand for their skills is high since they attract not only large attendances at matches but also promote high merchandise sales, whereas the supply of skilled players is limited. Figure 3 shows the market for premier league players.

Wage differentials

Wage differentials are differences in wages. Wage differentials occur between occupations, industries, firms and regions and within these categories. Table 1 shows the differences in pay earned by workers in a number of occupations.

Wages are likely to be high when demand is high and inelastic and supply is low and inelastic. In contrast, wages are likely to be low where supply is high relative to demand and both demand and supply are elastic.

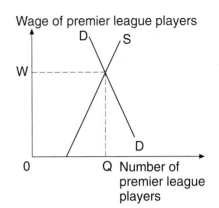

Figure 3 The market for premier league football players

Great Britain	Average gross weekly pay (£)
Highest paid	
Treasurers and company financial managers	1059
Medical practitioners	964
Organisation and methods and work study managers	813
Management consultants, business analysts	812
Underwriters, claims assessors, brokers, investment analysts	775
Police officers (inspector or above)	766
Computer systems and data processing managers	757
Solicitors	748
Marketing and sales managers	719
Advertising and public relations managers	690
Lowest paid	
Educational assistants	212
Other childcare and related occupations	205
Counterhands, catering assistants	196
Launderers, dry cleaners, pressers	196
Hairdressers, barbers	190
Waiters, waitresses	189
Petrol pump, forecourt attendants	189
Retail cash desk and check-out operators	185
Bar staff	184
Kitchen porters, hands	184

Source: Table 5.8 (page 93), Social Trends 2002, ONS.

Table 1 Highest and lowest paid occupations, April 2000

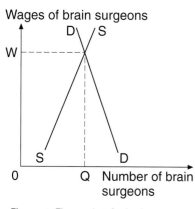

Wages of brain surgeons

Figure 4 The market for brain surgeons

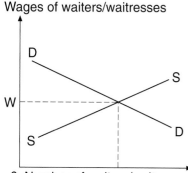

Wages of waiters/waitresses

Figure 5 The market for waiters and waitresses

Thinking like an economist

Why are solicitors paid more than bar staff?

A good example would be brain surgeons, who are paid considerably more than waiters and waitresses. The supply of brain surgeons is low relative to demand. It is limited by the long period of training involved and the high qualifications required to undertake that training. These features also make supply inelastic. A rise in the wage rate will not attract many new brain surgeons in the short run. Demand is also inelastic as brain surgeons are a vital part of an operating team and there is no viable substitute. Figure 4 shows the market for brain surgeons.

In contrast, the supply of waiters and waitresses is high and elastic. The job requires no qualifications and the minimum of training. So there is a large number of people capable of doing the job and a rise in the wage rate will attract a greater percentage in supply. The marginal revenue productivity of waiters and waitresses is also low and so demand is low. Figure 5 shows the market for waiters and waitresses.

Wage differentials between particular groups

Skilled and unskilled workers

Skilled workers are paid more than unskilled workers, principally because the demand for skilled workers is higher and supply is less. The marginal revenue productivity of skilled labour is high because their skills will lead to high output per worker. The supply of skilled labour in many countries is below that of unskilled workers. It is also more difficult to substitute skilled labour with machines or unemployed workers than is the case with unskilled labour. Figure 6 shows the markets for skilled and unskilled workers.

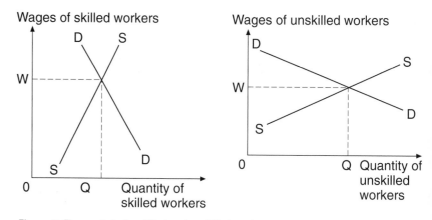

Figure 6 The markets for skilled and unskilled workers

Male and female workers

Despite equal pay legislation, men are still paid more than women. When comparing weekly pay, part of the explanation lies in the fact that more women work part-time than men. However, even when hourly rates are compared, men still earn more than women.

There are a number of reasons why women still earn less than men. One is that on average, the marginal revenue productivity of women is lower than that of men. In the past, a significant reason was that the qualifications of men were greater than that of women. More males went to university than females. Nowadays, the gap in the qualifications, and hence the marginal productivity, between men and women is narrowing.

However, the marginal revenue productivity of women remains below that of men because women are disproportionately concentrated in low paid occupations which generate low marginal revenue. In addition, a smaller percentage of women belong to trade unions and professional organisations and so have lower bargaining power.

Some women also lose out on promotion opportunities because of leaving the labour markets at crucial times in their career in order to have and raise children. Another factor which still exists is sexual discrimination, with some employers undervaluing the services of female workers.

Part-time and full-time workers

Part-time workers, on average, receive less pay per hour than full-time workers. Again there are a number of reasons to explain this. One is that the supply of people wanting to work part-time is quite high relative to the demand. Part-time work is convenient for a number of people bringing up children, pursuing university studies, other interests or careers. Part-time workers are also less likely to receive training, both on and off the job, than full-time workers so their productivity tends to be lower. In addition, a smaller proportion of part-time workers belong to trade unions and professional organisations. Finally, with the wage gap between men and women as discussed above, a higher proportion of part-time workers are women.

Ethnic groups

Those from ethnic minorities tend to be lower paid than white workers. One particular group which receives low pay is workers of a Bangladeshi origin. There are again a number of reasons for this. One is that a high proportion of Bangladeshis work in the catering industry which is low paid. Another is that the qualifications of Bangladeshis, particularly Bangladeshi women, are currently, on average, below those of the rest of the population. Another factor is discrimination.

Making connections

Explain how discrimination creates inefficiency.

Quickies

1   Distinguish between economic rent and transfer earnings.
2   What is the significance of elasticities of demand for, and supply of, labour in wage determination?
3   Why are skilled workers paid more than unskilled workers?
4   Why is the gap between male and female wage rates narrowing?

Puzzler

Should economic rent be taxed?

5a.5 The role of labour organisations

In practice, many wages are not determined in competitive labour markets. In these markets, factors, in addition to the free market forces of demand and supply, play a role in determining wages and the level of employment. One such factor is labour organisations. Workers may join together to sell their labour through one body. This may be a **trade union** or professional body.

The role of labour organisations

Labour organisations seek to promote the interests of their members. Probably their best-known function is to negotiate pay and conditions of employment with employers.

Negotiations can take place at both a national and local level. For example, the AUT (Association of University Teachers) negotiate lecturers' pay at a national level with the Higher Education Funding Council and will negotiate with individual universities over possible redundancies. Unions lobby the government through the TUC (Trades Union Congress), the national body of the trade union movement.

In addition to their negotiating role, labour organisations also carry out a number of other functions. A number provide benefits and services for their members including financial services and legal advice. Some are also involved in lobbying national government on behalf of their members and setting minimum qualification standards.

The effect of labour organisations on wages and employment

If all the workers in a labour market are members of a trade union or a professional organisation, the body will act as a monopoly seller. This will alter the supply curve of labour.

Figure 1 shows the effect of a trade union forcing the wage rate up from W to W1. The supply curve now becomes W1×S. All workers would now be prepared to work for W1 or above.

The diagram also shows employment falling from **Q** to **Q2**. This might occur if trade unions force up the wage rate paid by firms producing under conditions of perfect competition or monopolistic competition in the product market. In these two market structures, firms earn only normal profit in the long run. So, a rise in their costs will cause marginal firms to leave the industry, thus causing output and employment to fall.

The trade union may seek to avoid loss of jobs by supporting measures to increase labour productivity (for example, participating in training initiatives) or measures to increase demand for the product (for example, participating in an advertising campaign). In both cases, if the measures are successful, the marginal revenue productivity, and hence the demand curve, will shift to the right.

Synoptic link

In many labour markets, wage rates and employment levels are influenced by labour organisations. The effect of trade unions was touched upon in AS section 3.19.

Definition

A **trade union** is an association of workers.

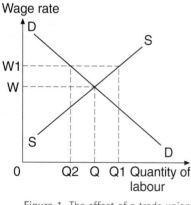

Figure 1 The effect of a trade union on the labour market

A union may be in a stronger position to raise the wage rate of its members if the employer operates under conditions of monopoly or oligopoly in the product market. This is because the firms may be earning supernormal profits in the long run.

Factors influencing a labour organisation's bargaining strength

A labour organisation will be stronger, the:

- greater the financial reserves of the organisation
- higher the proportion of workers in the organisation
- more inelastic the demand for the firm's product
- lower the degree of substitution between capital and labour
- lower the proportion of labour costs in total costs
- lower the rate of unemployment
- greater the support the workers have from the general public
- more legislation favours the rights of workers
- more disruption any industrial action would cause.

For example, most brain surgeons are members of the British Medical Association (BMA), a strong professional organisation. The Association has large funds and has built up a close relationship with Ministers of Health. Any industrial action it may take would have significant consequences and brain surgeons cannot be replaced by **capital equipment** or other types of doctors.

In contrast, waiters and waitresses have low bargaining power. Very few belong to a trade union and they can usually be replaced by unemployed workers.

Trends in trade union membership

The trend in trade union membership is downwards. Table 1 shows that membership has fallen by more than 1.1 million between 1990 and 2000. One reason for the decline was the rise in unemployment in the early years of the 1990s – there were fewer people in jobs to join trade unions. An increase in employment, in part, explains the short-term rise in membership between 1997 and 2000.

The reasons why trade union membership has been declining are thought to include a change in the composition of the working population and a decline in union power. There has been a fall in the number of workers employed in areas which are heavily unionised and a rise in the number of workers employed in areas with low union density. For example, the number of workers in the public sector, engineering and large companies has declined while the number of workers in the private sector, small companies, self-employment and part-time work has increased.

Thinking like an economist

What factors will limit how high a labour organisation seeks to push up the wage rate of its members?

Making connections

Why are labour organisations stronger during an economic boom than a recession?

Definition

Capital equipment is man-made goods used to produce goods and services.

Year	No. of members (millions)
1990	9.96
1991	9.56
1992	9.17
1993	8.85
1994	8.30
1995	8.11
1996	7.98
1997	7.84
1998	7.89
1999	7.94
2000	7.82

Source: Table 7.26 (page 115), Annual Abstract of Statistics, 2003, ONS.

Table 1 Trade union membership 1990–2000

Unions have become less powerful because of legislation, introduced in the 1980s and 1990s, which restricted their rights and by the rise in the number of companies deciding not to recognise unions. When a company does not recognise a union it means that the union does not have the right to negotiate on behalf of its members. This would make it difficult for the union to recruit members.

Labour disputes

In the last two decades there has been a noticeable decline in labour disputes. This is reflected in the three measures of labour disputes. These are:

- the number of stoppages arising from labour disputes
- the number of workers involved in the stoppages
- the number of working days lost through stoppages (probably the main measure).

In 1980, for example, there were 1330 stoppages and 11.97 million working days as a result. This is in contrast to 212 stoppages and 499,000 working days lost in 2000.

In comparison with other EU countries, the UK has recently had a good record in labour relations. In 2000, for instance, the UK lost 11 days per 1000 employees to labour disputes, compared with the EU average of 50.

Quickies

1 What are the key functions of a labour organisation?
2 In what sense may a labour organisation be a monopoly?
3 Explain three factors that influence the bargaining power of a labour organisation.
4 Why is trade union membership declining?

Puzzler

Does a reduction in labour disputes necessarily imply an improvement in labour relations?

G overnment intervention affects wages and employment in a number of ways. These include the government's employment of public sector workers, its general macroeconomic and microeconomic policies and the legislation it passes which affects labour markets.

Government intervention

Government policy influences wages and employment in a variety of ways. Despite the major privatisation programmes of the 1980s and 1990s, the government remains a major employer. The pay and number of people working in the public sector, for example nurses, civil servants and teachers, is affected by the level of government expenditure.

Government measures which increase aggregate demand will tend to stimulate employment and raise wages. Conversely, measures which reduce aggregate demand will tend to constrain wage rises.

Changes in tax rates and welfare benefits can affect wage rates. New classical economists believe that cuts in tax rates and benefits will stimulate a rise in the supply of labour and reduce upward pressure on gross wages. In contrast, Keynesians believe the effects of tax cuts are more uncertain and that reductions in benefits may reduce employment by lowering aggregate demand.

Government policies on particular markets can affect wage rates and employment in those markets. For example, raising tax rates on cigarettes is likely to result in a fall in demand for cigarettes and thereby put downward pressure on wages. The government also passes legislation, including anti-discrimination acts, which affects labour markets.

The government operates the Advisory, Conciliation and Arbitration Service (ACAS), which conciliates in disputes between employers and employees. In addition, it has in the past acted directly as an arbitrator in wage disputes between employers and trade unions.

Discrimination

Discrimination occurs when a group is treated less favourably than other workers. Groups that experience discrimination include ethnic minority workers, women, the disabled, the old and the young. If an employer believes, because of prejudice, that the marginal revenue of ethnic minority workers is lower than it actually is, the wage rate paid to these workers (W) and their employment (Q) will be below the allocatively efficient levels (WX and QX), as Figure 1 shows.

This discrimination is likely to have a knock-on effect throughout the labour market. Those who cannot gain employment with the discriminating employer will seek employment with those employers who do not discriminate. This will increase the supply of labour to the non-discriminating employers and lower the wage rate, as shown in Figure 2.

Synoptic links

This section builds on the knowledge and understanding of market failure and minimum wage you gained in AS sections 2.1–2.3. It also expands on the Working Time Directive discussed in A2 section 5a.2.

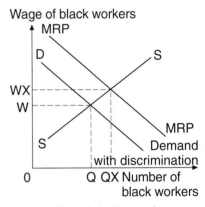

Figure 1 A discriminating employer labour market

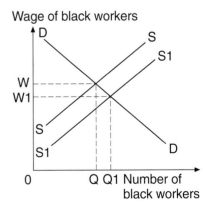

Figure 2 The effect on a non-discriminating employer labour market

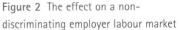

Discrimination legislation

A government can pass legislation making discrimination illegal. In the UK the Equal Pay Act of 1970, which was implemented in 1975, sought to end the differences in pay between men and women undertaking the same or broadly similar work or for work rated as equivalent under a job evaluation study. The Sex Discrimination Act made unequal treatment on the grounds of gender or marital status in aspects of employment other than pay, which was already covered, illegal. In 1983, both Acts were consolidated and broadened under the Equal Pay (Amendment) Regulation.

The Race Relations Act of 1976 makes it illegal to discriminate the grounds of colour or race. In 1995 the Disability Discrimination Act came into force which made discrimination on the grounds of disability illegal. The government is planning to introduce anti-ageism legislation in October 2006. This will make it unlawful to advertise for young workers and to discriminate on the grounds of age in promotion, training and the provision of health and pension benefits.

Making connections

Why is discriminating against a particular group of workers likely to raise a firm's costs?

Such discrimination legislation may change attitudes over time. Employers may find that a group, which they had previously discriminated against, is more productive than they first thought. However, at least in the short run, employers may seek to get round any such legislation by, for example, claiming that workers from a certain group are less well-suited than others for the jobs on offer and redefining jobs undertaken by workers from different groups. In practice, it can often be difficult to prove that discrimination has occurred.

Thinking like an economist

How might the ending of age discrimination benefit society?

Minimum wage legislation

Minimum wage legislation is introduced to help raise the pay of low-paid workers. To have any effect, the minimum wage has to be set above the market equilibrium wage rate.

New classical economists argue that such government intervention in the operation of free market forces raises firms' costs of production. Figure 3 shows that the setting of a minimum wage of W1, above the equilibrium wage rate of W, causes an extension in the supply of labour but also a contraction in the demand for labour. This, in turn, causes a shortfall of employment of Q2-Q1. Compared to the situation before the intervention of the government, employment falls from Q to Q2.

However, some Keynesian economists argue that the introduction of a national minimum wage may not result in higher unemployment. Low-paid workers often have low bargaining power relative to their employers. In these cases, the introduction of a minimum wage could raise both the wage rate and employment.

There are also other reasons why a minimum wage may not cause unemployment. One is that the first effect of its introduction is to raise

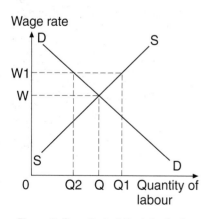

Figure 3 The effect of the introduction of a minimum wage

wages. This in turn raises demand for goods and services, which in turn may increase demand for labour. The higher wages may also raise the morale and productivity of those affected.

Productivity will also increase if employers seek to gain higher returns from the now higher-paid workers by providing more training. Rises in demand for products and increases in productivity will shift the marginal revenue productivity (demand for labour) to the right and increase employment, as illustrated in Figure 4.

Despite paying higher wages, firms' labour costs may be reduced if the introduction of a minimum wage reduces labour turnover. It is expensive to advertise for new staff, interview them and train them.

A national minimum wage (NMW), affecting the pay of 1.8 million workers, was introduced in the UK in April 1999. The minimum pay for adults was initially set at £3.60 per hour, with £3.00 for 18-21 year olds and workers aged 16 and 17 made exempt. From October 2003 it was £4.50 for workers over 21 and £3.80 for 18-21 year olds.

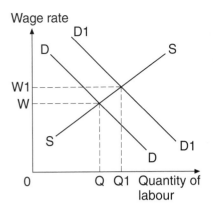

Figure 4 An increase in demand resulting from the introduction of a minimum wage

The Working Time Directive

When the UK government was considering implementing the Working Time Directive, employers expressed concern that the directive might raise their labour costs and reduce the flexibility of their labour force. The UK government negotiated an opt-out from the full implementation of the 48 hour week, subject to later review. This allows employers to ignore the limit if staff agree. UK trade unions oppose the opt-out. Other EU countries also want the opt-out ended as they claim it gives the UK an unfair economic advantage.

Quickies ✓

1   How does discrimination affect the wages and employment of those discriminated against?
2   Why is anti-discrimination legislation not always successful?
3   Which groups do not benefit from the NMW?
4   What effect may a NMW have on unemployment?

Puzzler

Should the national minimum wage be raised?

Low paid workers

Monopsonistic employers

I n some labour markets, employers exercise considerable market power. In such markets the wage rate and employment level may be driven below the efficient levels.

Synoptic link

AS section 2.5 discussed how market power can influence markets. This section focuses on the effect of market power in labour markets.

Definitions

A **monopsonist** is a single buyer.

An **oligopsonist** is one of a few dominant buyers.

Employers with labour market power

Those employers who employ a high percentage of workers in a particular labour market can influence the wage rate. In a labour market, a **monopsonist** is a firm which is the only buyer (that is, the employer) and an **oligopsonist** is one of a few dominant firms buying a certain type of labour. An example of a monopsonistic employer is the Ordnance Survey, which is the main employer of mapmakers in the UK. In some areas where there are only a few veterinary practices, vets and veterinary nurses sell their labour in an oligopsonistic market.

Determination of wages and employment

Monopsonists and oligoposonists are price makers. They influence the wage rate. To employ more workers, they have to raise the wage rate. So the marginal cost of labour (MCL) will exceed the average cost of labour (ACL), which is equivalent to the wage rate.

No. of workers	Average cost of labour (wage rate) per hour	Total cost of labour per hour	Marginal cost of labour per hour
1	10	10	10
2	11	22	12
3	13	39	17
4	16	64	25
5	20	100	36
6	25	150	50

Table 1 Labour costs

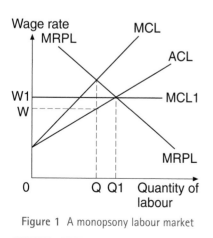

Figure 1 A monopsony labour market

Table 1 shows how the average cost of labour exceeds the marginal cost of labour. For example, attracting a fourth worker costs the employer an extra £25 since they not only pay that worker £16 but also pay an extra £3 to each of the first three workers employed.

In this circumstance, a union can raise the wage rate without causing unemployment. Figure 1 shows that in the absence of union action the number of workers employed will be **Q** (where MRPL equals MCL) and the wage rate will be W (found from the ACL curve).

The union may then raise the wage rate to W1. This then becomes the new marginal cost of labour (MCL1) as there will be one wage rate for all union members. Employment now rises to **Q1**.

It also means, however, that once the wage rate has been settled by negotiation, the monoposonist will not have to increase the wage rate to attract labour.

Bilateral monopoly

When a monopoly trade union negotiates with a monopsonist employer, the situation is referred to as a **bilateral monopoly**. In this case, the wage rate will be determined by the relative bargaining strengths of the two sides. If the monopsonist is powerful, the outcome will be a wage rate close to that which they would have chosen to pay without trade union intervention.

The upper limit will be the maximum the monopsonist can pay without threatening the existence of the firm. The stronger the trade union is, the closer the wage rate will be to this limit. Figure 2 shows the lower limit and a possible upper limit.

Employer's bargaining strength

An employer will be stronger the:
- greater the financial reserves it has with which it can last out any dispute
- lower the proportion of its workers that are in the union
- greater the degree of substitution between capital and labour
- higher the rate of unemployment, since this will mean it can substitute existing workers with unemployed workers
- lower the support workers have from the general public
- lower the disruption any industrial action would cause to production
- the more branches the firm has which employ either non-union labour or labour in different unions, so that production can be moved in the case of a dispute
- the more legislation favours employers.

Definition

A **bilateral monopoly** is a market with a single buyer and seller.

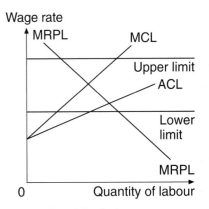

Figure 2 Bargaining limits

Making connections

What effect is globalisation having on employers' bargaining strength?

Quickies

1   In the case of a monopsonistic labour market, why does the marginal cost of labour exceed the average cost of labour?
2   Why might employment rise if a union negotiates a pay rise for its members from a monopsonist employer?
3   Identify three factors that could increase the strength of an employer's bargaining power.

Puzzler

Will the working conditions of people working for a monopsonist employer be better or worse than those of people working for employers in a competitive labour market?

Unemployment and labour market failure

Synoptic links

A2 section 5a.7 discussed one possible cause of labour market failure. This section examines a number of other causes as did AS section 2.9.

Making connections

What policies might a government employ to reduce unemployment?

Labour market failure occurs when the market forces of demand and supply do not result in an efficient allocation of resources. Evidence of labour market failure occurs in a number of forms. The most obvious is unemployment. Other examples include shortages of skilled labour, workers being in jobs that they are not best suited for, a lack of training and wage rates being above or below their equilibrium rate.

Unemployment

Unemployment means that labour markets are not clearing. Some of those willing and able to work cannot obtain a job. The existence of unemployment means that a country will not be producing on its production possibility curve and so will not be achieving productive efficiency.

The extent to which unemployment causes labour market failure is obviously influenced by the number of people who are out of work. It is also influenced by how long people are out of work. The longer someone is unemployed, the more they get out of touch with the skills required and the greater the risk that they may give up hope of gaining a job.

Dominant buyers and sellers

Trade unions may push the wage rate above the equilibrium and thereby cause unemployment. A trade union would not push up the wage rate indefinitely, since such a policy would result in one paid member. Trade unions may also engage in restrictive practices such as job demarcation in which workers will only undertake tasks outlined in their job descriptions. This will influence the flexibility of the labour force.

In labour markets with monopsonist and oligopsonist employers who have the power to determine the wage rate and employment, both are likely to be lower than in a perfectly competitive labour market.

Lack of information

Workers may be in jobs which are less well paid and which they enjoy less than other jobs they are capable of doing because they are unaware of suitable vacancies. Similarly, employers may not appoint the most productive workers because they are not in touch with all the potential workers.

Obtaining information on job vacancies and potential workers, applying for jobs and interviewing workers involves a variety of costs. For workers it takes time, effort and money to look for a new job, fill out application forms and attend interviews. Employers incur costs in advertising jobs, assessing applications, interviewing people and inducting new staff. So both groups have to weigh the benefits of searching for a better situation against the costs of searching.

Other causes of labour market failure

Any or all of the following can cause labour market failure.

- Attachment between workers and employers – some workers may stay in less well-paid jobs because they like working for their employers; they have a good working relationship. Employers may also feel a sense of loyalty to their existing workforce. This attachment reduces the mobility of labour and makes supply more inelastic.
- Inertia – workers may not move to higher paid jobs and employers may not seek to replace less productive workers out of laziness.
- Externalities – training is a merit good. It has positive externalities but, if left to market forces, too few resources would be devoted to it. This is because some workers and some firms take a short-term view and underestimate the benefits of training. In addition, some firms are afraid that other firms may reap the benefits of their expenditure by poaching their staff.

Discrimination

Negative discrimination results in an inefficient allocation of resources and inequitable wage differentials. Its costs include the following.

- The group discriminated against clearly suffers. The people within it are likely to be paid less than other workers doing the same job. They are also likely to find it harder to gain employment. In addition, some may have to settle for less demanding jobs than they are capable of undertaking. They may also be overlooked for promotion and may not be selected to go on training courses. The existence of discrimination may discourage members from the discriminated group from applying for well-paid jobs and from seeking to gain higher qualifications.
- Producers who discriminate have a smaller pool of labour to select from. They may also not make the best use of any ethnic minority or female workers they employ. This will raise their costs of production and make them less competitive against rival firms at home and abroad.
- Consumers will experience higher prices if producers discriminate.
- The government may have to pay out more welfare benefits to groups that are discriminated against, and may have to spend time and money introducing and monitoring legislation to end discrimination and tackle social tension.
- The economy will lose out as a result of the misallocation of resources. Output will be below the potential output, which could be achieved if the group were not discriminated against in terms of employment, pay, promotion and training.

Theories of negative discrimination

Various theories have been put forward to explain negative discrimination, including:

- Becker's theory
- statistical discrimination.

Becker's theory

Gary Becker, Professor of Economics at Chicago University (USA), argues that some people may be prepared to experience higher costs rather than come into contact with members of a particular group. In effect, the individuals pay in the form of lower profits to avoid employing, for example, women workers and in the form of higher prices to avoid buying from firms employing female workers.

Statistical discrimination

This arises because of imperfect information. Some economists argue that employers discriminate as a result of seeking to reduce their costs. They do not know in advance the productivity of job applicants and may find it difficult to measure the productivity of existing workers. So when deciding who to employ, how much to pay and who to promote and train, they make decisions based on generalisations about groups of workers.

For example, an employer may assume that workers aged 50 years and over are less productive and will have a shorter time with the firm than younger workers. As a result, the employer may use age as a screening device when deciding on job applicants, may not promote older workers or send them on training courses, and, if deciding on redundancies, may select older workers first.

Quickies

1   In what sense is unemployment an example of labour market failure?
2   Why, if left to the private sector, would training be under-provided?
3   Why might a worker not leave her current job for a better job for which she is qualified?
4   Explain three costs to the economy arising from discrimination.

Puzzler

Who should bear the costs of training workers – firms or the government?

Section 5a.8 discussed some of the causes of labour market failure. Another major cause of labour market failure is a lack of geographical and occupational mobility. Such a lack of mobility reduces the flexibility of labour markets. The government seeks to tackle the problem of immobility in a variety of ways.

Labour immobility

Labour immobility comes in two main forms:
- geographical
- occupational.

Geographical immobility

This is caused by the obstacles workers experience in moving from jobs in one area to jobs in another area. When there is geographical immobility, shortages of workers in one area and surpluses in other areas are not corrected and regional unemployment continues to exist.

Geographical immobility arises for a number of reasons. These include differences in the availability and price of housing in different areas, family and social ties and a lack of information.

Occupational immobility

This arises due to the obstacles which workers experience in changing occupations including differences in qualifications, skills, social barriers and again lack of information. Occupational immobility contributes to structural unemployment.

Flexibility of the labour force

Immobility of labour reduces the ease with which the labour force adjusts, in terms of the number of hours worked and the amount of pay received, to changes in market conditions.

The flexibility of labour is influenced by how easy it is for firms to 'hire and fire' labour and how easy workers find it to adapt to new tasks and technology. It can be interpreted in terms of temporal flexibility (ability to change the hours people work), locational flexibility (ability to change where people work – at home or their place of employment) and functional flexibility (ability to change the tasks workers perform).

Flexibility allows firms to respond to increased demand without encountering capacity constraints and without putting upward pressure on wages and allows them to adjust smoothly and quickly to falls in demand. However, it can create greater insecurity for workers. For example, if they are working on a casual contract, they may find it difficult to obtain a mortgage.

Policies to influence the mobility of labour

Synoptic links

AS section 2.9 discussed factor immobility. This section builds on that section and is also linked to A2 section 5a.8.

Thinking like an economist

Why do some workers not seek to improve their skills and qualifications? How does this affect their mobility in the labour market?

Making connections

What effect is locational flexibility likely to have on pollution and congestion?

Tackling immobility

Governments try to tackle immobility in a number of ways, including:

- providing labour market information
- regional policy
- training
- education
- cutting marginal tax rates
- reducing unemployment benefit.

Labour market information

To offset the lack of labour market information, which reduces mobility of labour, the government provides information in a variety of forms. There is a state-funded careers service which provides details about requirements, working conditions and pay of a variety of occupations. Careers education is also part of the curriculum of state schools and most private sector (public) schools. Government job centres provide information about job vacancies and welfare benefit officials discuss with the unemployed what jobs are on offer and how to apply for them.

Regional policy

Regional policy seeks to influence the distribution of firms and people. To reduce the problem of geographical immobility of labour and regional unemployment, governments employ a variety of measures. Financial assistance may be given to workers to relocate to areas where there are vacancies requiring their particular skills. More commonly, however 'work is taken to the workers' by providing financial assistance for firms to locate and relocate in areas of high unemployment. Firms can also experience geographical and occupational immobility, but it is thought it easier for firms to move from one location to another than for workers to move.

Training

A better-trained labour force will be more occupationally mobile. A government can seek to raise the level of training to the allocatively efficient level in a variety of ways. It can provide training itself directly to its own employees and to the unemployed and those changing jobs, it can subsidise individuals to engage in training and/or firms to provide training and it can pass legislation requiring firms to engage in a certain level of training.

Making connections

What effect may increased government spending on education and training have on long run aggregate supply?

Education

Increases and improvements in state educational provision should raise the qualifications and skills levels of workers. This should increase the occupational mobility of the labour force, reduce the shortage of skilled labour and raise the productivity of labour.

Measures to raise the qualifications and skills of workers are referred to as investment in human capital. If there is investment in developing the abilities of a wide range of people, the problem of social exclusion (people not feeling a part of society) should also be reduced.

Cutting marginal tax rates

Firms will find it easier to adjust to changes in demand if the supply of labour is responsive to changes in wage rates.

New classical economists believe that reducing marginal direct tax rates will raise the incentive for existing workers to increase the number of hours they work, for the unemployed to seek work more actively and for those considering retiring early to stay in the labour force for longer. They think that the substitution effect of any rise in net pay resulting from a tax cut will exceed the income effect. However, studies have shown that a large proportion of workers are not free to alter the hours that they can work and of those who can, as many choose to work fewer hours as work more hours. However, cuts in marginal tax rates do seem to have some influence on people's decision as to when they will retire if they have some choice in the matter.

The effect on unemployment is a controversial matter. Keynesians believe that the main cause of unemployment is a lack of aggregate demand and hence job vacancies. They do not think that people remain unemployed because they are not prepared to work for the going wage rate.

Reducing unemployment benefit

Some new classical economists have suggested that in addition to cutting marginal tax rates, the gap between paid employment and benefits (for example, Jobseekers' Allowance) should be increased by reducing benefits. They believe that this makes unemployment a less attractive prospect and so reduces the time that the unemployed spend searching for a job.

Again Keynesians argue that the unemployed are not voluntarily unemployed. They also believe that cutting Jobseekers' Allowance will actually increase unemployment by reducing aggregate demand. The unemployed spend a high proportion of their income. A cut in their benefits will reduce their spending which will have a knock-on effect on the spending of the people they buy goods and services from and so on.

The New Deal

Quickies

1   What are the main causes of geographical and occupational immobility of labour?
2   Why may locational flexibility reduce firms' costs?
3   How does the government provide labour market information?
4   How should improved education and training increase the mobility of labour?

Changing structures of UK and EU labour markets

In recent years, there have been some noticeable changes in the labour market in the UK and other EU countries. These include changes in migration, changes in participation rates, an increase in temporary employment and employment in the tertiary sector and a rise in the average age of the working population.

Synoptic link

This section draws on the knowledge and understanding you gained in A2 section 5a.2.

Participation rates

Women are continuing to form an increasing proportion of the UK labour force. This reflects both an increase in the participation rate of women and a decline in the participation rate of men. The participation rate of women increased from 56 per cent in 1971 to 72 per cent in 2001. The most significant rise has been in the 25–44 age bracket. In contrast, there has been a decline in the participation rate of men from 91 per cent in 1971 to 83 per cent in 2001.

UK participation rate figures indicate that the gap between male and female economic activity rates is narrowing. They also show that the UK's economic activity rates are above those of the EU's average. Within the EU there is a wide variation, as shown in Table 1, with participation rates for women in southern EU countries being low while those of Scandinavian countries are high.

	Males %	Females %	All %		Males %	Females %	All %
Denmark	84.0	75.9	80.0	France	75.3	62.5	68.8
Finland	79.4	74.1	76.8	Irish Republic	79.1	55.7	67.5
Sweden	77.2	73.4	75.3	Belgium	73.8	56.6	65.2
UK	83.0	67.8	75.5	Luxembourg	76.4	51.7	64.2
Netherlands	83.9	65.7	74.9	Spain	77.1	50.7	63.7
Austria	83.9	65.7	74.9	Greece	77.1	49.7	63.0
Germany	78.8	63.0	71.0	Italy	73.8	44.2	59.9
Portugal	78.8	63.6	71.0	EU average	78.1	59.8	68.9

Source: Table 4.7 (page 73), Social Trends 32, 2002, ONS.

Table 1 Economic activity rates by gender, EU comparison, 2000

Making connections

What is the connection between a country's labour market participation rate and its productive potential?

The main change in the participation rate of men has come in the age range 60–64 because of the rise in early retirement.

Temporary employment

Although the proportion of workers in temporary employment in the UK is increasing, it is still below that of most of the other EU countries. In 2000, 13 per cent of all EU employees were in temporary work. The percentage was very high in Spain at 32 per cent. In the UK it was 7 per cent, and only the Irish Republic and Luxembourg had smaller percentages. In every EU country the percentage of female employees in temporary employment was higher than males.

The rise in temporary employment is a reflection of increased flexibility in the labour market. Employers wishing to increase their responsiveness to changes in demand are offering more jobs on temporary contracts.

Sectors and occupations

The proportion of workers employed in manufacturing and construction continues to decline while the proportion in the tertiary sector increases. In 1981, one out of every three male employees worked in manufacturing. By 2001 this proportion had fallen to one out of five. The fastest growth in the tertiary sector is occurring in distribution, hotels and catering, and financial and business services. This picture is reflected throughout the EU, although some EU countries, for example Greece, have much larger agricultural sectors.

Second jobs

More women than men have second jobs, and most of those with a second job work part-time in their main job. The growth in the number of second jobs rose in the first half of the 1990s but has fallen slightly since. In 2000, approximately 500,000 male workers had a second job and 700,000 female workers.

Workers' rights

In 1997, the newly elected Labour government reversed the UK's opt-out from the Social Chapter of the Maastricht Treaty. It has adopted various EU directives on employment legislation, which include the right to paternity leave and paid holidays, maximum working hours and emergency unpaid time off to care for dependants.

Ageing population

In many industrialised countries, including those of the EU, falls in the birth rate and increases in life expectancy are causing the average age of the population, including the working population, to rise. This trend has a number of implications for the labour market and for the government.

Older workers used to be regarded as less adaptable to change and more geographically and occupationally immobile. While they are probably more geographically immobile than young workers, there is increasing evidence that they are just as occupationally mobile and adaptive to change.

Use aggregate demand and
aggregate supply analysis to compare
the effects of increasing income tax
and raising the retirement age.

As the number of young people entering the labour force continues to decline, firms will increasingly have to draw on the services of older workers. To attract people to stay in the labour force for longer and to encourage some of those who have retired early to re-enter the labour force, firms will have to offer flexible work patterns. They will also have to engage in regular retraining of their labour force.

The ageing population also has implications for governments. As the number of retired people dependent on the working population increases (the so-called demographic time bomb), governments have to consider how the increasing burden can be reduced or financed. One possible solution, being considered by a number of governments, is to raise the retirement age in line with rising life expectancy. This would simultaneously reduce the number of dependants and raise the size of the working population. EU governments are also operating more lenient immigration and work permit policies in a bid to raise the size of their working populations and reduce labour shortages.

Ways of coping with the burden are to encourage the development of private pension schemes and/or to raise the rates or coverage of taxation.

Quickies

1   What is happening to participation rates in the EU?
2   What are the advantages and disadvantages of taking up temporary employment?
3   Identify a UK sector which is experiencing a decline in employment and one which is experiencing a rise in employment.
4   How are governments seeking to defuse the demographic time bomb?

Puzzler

Which occupations are likely to expand in the next ten years and which are likely to contract?

T hroughout most of the twentieth century, income and wealth became more evenly distributed. However, the last two decades of the twentieth century saw a reversal of this trend and, now, at the start of the twenty-first century a quarter of the UK population live in households with incomes below half the national average.

The distribution of income and wealth

Wealth

Wealth is a stock of assets that have a financial value. Economists distinguish between marketable and non-marketable wealth. Marketable wealth is wealth that can be transferred to another person, for example houses and shares. In contrast, non-marketable wealth is wealth which is specific to a person and cannot be transferred, for example pension rights.

The distribution of wealth can be considered in terms of how it is distributed between the population (size distribution), the forms in which it is held and according to the characteristics of those holding wealth.

Synoptic links

This section builds on the knowledge and understanding you gained in AS sections 1.15, 2.9, 3.4 and particularly 3.16.

The size distribution of wealth

Wealth is very unequally distributed among the UK population. Table 1 compares the size distribution of marketable wealth in the UK in 1986 and 1999.

	Percentages	
	1986	1999
Marketable wealth		
Percentage of wealth owned by:		
Most wealthy 1%	18	23
Most wealthy 5%	36	43
Most wealthy 10%	50	54
Most wealthy 25%	73	74
Most wealthy 50%	90	94
Total marketable wealth (£ billion)	955	2752

Source: Table 5.25, Social Trends 30 and 32, ONS, 2000 and 2002.

Table 1 Distribution of wealth in the UK

The table shows that wealth has become more unequally distributed between 1986 and 1999. It also shows the extent of inequality. In both years the wealthiest 10 per cent of the population owned half or more than half of the country's wealth.

Wealth distribution between assets

Wealth can be held in a variety of forms, including life assurance and pension funds, property, securities and shares, banking and building society deposits and cash.

Life assurance and pension fund holdings have, in the past, accounted for the largest percentage of wealth held, forming more than a third of all household wealth in 1997. This form of wealth is more evenly distributed than property, securities and shares.

The proportion of a particular asset in the wealth of the household sector is influenced not only by the amount accumulated but also by changes in its value. For example, in the late 1980s, the share accounted for by property in the form of residential houses rose as a result of increases in owner-occupation and rises in the price of houses. In contrast, the fall in property prices in the early 1990s was reflected in a decline in property as a percentage of the wealth of the household sector.

Wealth distribution between different groups

As would be expected, wealth is unevenly distributed between age categories. For example, people in their 40s and 50s have had more time to accumulate savings than people in their 20s and 30s and do indeed have greater wealth.

However, the amount of wealth held also varies between ethnic groups and genders. White adults have more wealth than adults from ethnic minorities. The group which currently has the lowest holding of wealth per head is people of a Bangladeshi background. Women also have less wealth than men.

Source of wealth

A person can become wealthy in four main ways:
- Inheritance – this is the main way people become wealthy.
- Saving – a person could accumulate wealth by saving. However, to achieve significant wealth, saving has to be on a large scale. This is easier to achieve by people with high incomes, which may themselves be generated by significant holdings of wealth. Indeed, wealth creates wealth.
- The use of entrepreneurial skills – some people are self-made millionaires as a result of building up a business. For example, Bill Gates of Microsoft has built up a fortune in excess of £36.25 billion.
- Chance – lottery winners receive a considerable amount of publicity and a number of people are made 'instant millionaires'. However even a £2 million lottery win pales into insignificance when compared with the approximately £1750 million that the family of the Duke of Westminster stand to inherit.

Causes of the inequality of wealth

The causes of the inequality of wealth are obviously linked to the sources of wealth and include the following.

- The pattern of inheritance – in the UK, significant holdings of wealth have traditionally been passed on to the next generation on the basis of primogeniture (the right of the eldest son to inherit to the exclusion of others). Major estates and the connected titles are still passed on to the eldest son, making wealth progressively less evenly distributed, whereas in countries where property and other assets are distributed amongst the children on the death of the parents, wealth becomes more evenly distributed over time.
- Marriage patterns of the wealthy – the wealthy tend to marry other wealthy people. This further concentrates wealth in the hands of the few.
- Inequality of income – as already noted, people with high incomes are more able to save and earn interest.
- Different tendencies to save – those who save a higher proportion of their income will accumulate more wealth than those who save a smaller proportion.
- Luck – this plays a part in terms of the success of businesses that people start and in terms of who wins money.

Making connections

Explain the effect a rise in wealth is likely to have on consumption.

Wealth and income distribution

Wealth is more unevenly distributed than income. While a person can survive without owning any assets by, for example, renting a house, it is not possible to survive without any income. In addition, due to inheritance, the highest amount of wealth a person can hold at any one time exceeds the highest amount a person can earn.

Distribution of income

The distribution of income within a country can be considered in terms of how income is shared out between the factors of production (functional distribution of income), between households (size distribution) and between geographical areas (geographical distribution of income).

The functional distribution of income

Income is a flow of money over a period of time. Income can be earned by labour in the form of wages, by capital in the form of interest, by land in the form of rent and by entrepreneurs in the form of profits. In the UK, wages still account for the largest percentage but that percentage is falling. In 1987, 61 per cent of household income came from wages but by 2000 it was down to 57 per cent. In contrast, income from dividends, interest and rent (collectively known as investment income) has been rising.

In addition to earned income and investment income, households can receive income in the form of social security benefit. The relative shares of earned income, investment income and transfer payments depend on a variety of factors but principally on the level of employment and the relative power of labour and capital.

Measuring the size distribution of income

A common method of measuring the degree of inequality of income and wealth distribution between households is the Lorenz curve. This is named after the American statistician, Max Otto Lorenz.

As well as measuring the extent of industrial concentration, Lorenz curves can be used to compare the distribution of income and wealth over time and between countries. The horizontal axis measures the percentage of the population, starting with the poorest. In the case of income distribution, the vertical axis measures the percentage of income earned.

A 45° line drawn between the axes is called the line of income equality, as it shows a situation in which, for example, 40 per cent of the population earned 40 per cent of the income and 80 per cent of the population earned 80 per cent of the income.

The actual cumulative percentage income shares are then included on the diagram. In practice this will form a curve which starts at the origin and ends with 100 per cent of the population earning 100 per cent of income, but which lies below the 45° line. The greater the degree of inequality, the greater the extent to which the curve will be below the 45° line. Figure 1 shows that income is more unevenly distributed in Country A than in Country B.

In Country A, the poorest 20 per cent of the population earn only 5 per cent of the income, whereas in Country B they earn 12 per cent. The distribution can be measured in terms of, for example, quintiles of the population (fifths) or deciles (tenths).

The Gini coefficient is an international measure of inequality. It measures precisely the degree of inequality shown on a Lorenz curve. It is the ratio of the area between the Lorenz curve and the line of inequality in relation to the area below the line of income inequality.

In Figure 1 Country A, this is the ratio of $a \div a + b$. Complete equality would give a ratio of 0 and complete inequality would give a ratio of 1 (100 per cent). So in practice, the ratio will lie between 0 and 1 and the nearer it is to 1, the more unequal the distribution of income.

The size distribution of income in the UK

In recent years, the distribution of income has become more unequal. The widening of the gap between those with high incomes and those with low incomes was particularly noticeable between 1980 and 1990. In the first half

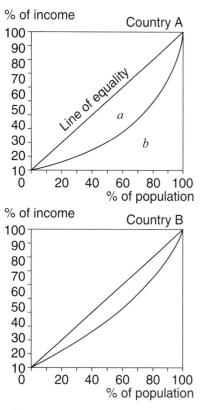

Figure 1   Lorenz curves – a comparison of inequality

Thinking like an economist

The Gini coefficient for the UK increased from 29 per cent in 1985 to 35 per cent in 2002. Explain what this means.

of the 1990s, income distribution appeared to stabilise but since then there appears to have been a further small increase in inequality.

There are a number of reasons for this rise in income equality. One was the cut in the top tax rates in the 1980s and 1990s. Another is the rise in top executive pay, which was sparked initially by privatisation but which has continued in the 2000s. At the other end of the income range, there has been a decrease in the real value of benefits, particularly Jobseekers' Allowance, and a toughening up of the eligibility rules. There has also been a rise in the number of lone parents. The percentage of families with dependent children headed by lone parents more than doubled between 1971 and 2002. The lack of support in bringing up the children means lone parents are often not in work or only in part-time jobs.

The causes of income inequality between households

These include the following.

- Unequal holdings of wealth – as wealth generates income in the form of profit, interest and dividends, differentials in wealth cause differences in income.
- Differences in the composition of households – some households may have three adults working, whereas other households may have no one in employment. Indeed, low income is closely associated with a dependency on benefits.
- Differences in skills and qualifications – those with high skills and qualifications are likely to be in high demand and hence be likely to be able to earn high incomes.
- Differences in educational opportunities – those who have the opportunity to stay in education for longer are likely to gain more qualifications and develop more skills and so, as indicated above, are likely to increase their earning potential. Lifetime earnings of graduates are noticeably higher than those of non-graduates.
- Discrimination – the income of some groups is adversely affected by discrimination in terms of employment opportunities, pay and promotion chances.
- Differences in hours worked – most full-time workers earn more than part-time workers and those who work overtime earn more than those who work the standard hours.

Thinking like an economist

Is the current distribution of income equitable?

The geographical distribution of income in the UK

Income is unevenly distributed between the regions of the UK. For example, in 1999, the gross domestic product (GDP) per head in London was 130 per cent of the UK's average, whilst it was 77 per cent in the north-east of England and in Northern Ireland.

Regional income differences are even greater in Germany and Italy. Germany has a very wide gap between former East Germany and former West Germany. There is a north–south divide in Italy, where the southern Mezzogiomo region is much poorer than the north.

There are a number of causes of differences in the geographical distribution of income, including differences in:
- unemployment rates
- the proportion of the population claiming benefits
- the qualifications and the skills of the labour force
- industrial structure
- occupational structure
- living costs, such as London allowances.

Of course, there are also variations within regions. Even though London as a whole has a high income per head, it has some of the most deprived districts in the UK.

Government policies

The extent to which a government intervenes to affect the distribution of income and wealth depends on the extent to which it believes that the free market distribution would be inequitable, the effects such inequality will have on society and the effects it believes any intervention will have on incentives and efficiency.

New classical economists do not favour significant intervention. This is because they believe that differences in income act as signals encouraging workers to move jobs and differences in wealth promote saving and investment. They also think that the provision of benefits above a minimum level for those who cannot work, such as the disabled and sick, can encourage voluntary unemployment.

In contrast, Keynesians believe that intervention is justified, as market forces will not ensure an efficient allocation of income and wealth and that low levels of income and wealth can cause considerable problems for the households involved, including having a detrimental effect on the educational performance of the children. They also think that significant differences in income and wealth can cause social division, with the poor feeling socially excluded.

Ways in which governments affect the distribution of income and wealth

Governments influence the distribution in a number of ways including:
- taxation
- cash benefits
- benefits in kind
- labour market policy
- macroeconomic policy.

Taxation

To assess the effects of taxation on the distribution of income and wealth, pre- and post-tax distribution can be compared. In the UK, the overall effect of the tax system is to reduce inequality. However, while progressive taxes, such as income tax, which take a higher percentage of the income or wealth of the rich make the distribution more equal, regressive taxes, such as VAT, which take a higher percentage of the income of the poor make the distribution more unequal.

The provision of cash benefits.

There are two types of cash benefits – means-tested and universal. Means-tested benefits such as family credit are available to those who claim them and who can prove their income is below a certain level, whereas universal benefits are available to everyone in a particular group irrespective of income.

For example, all families with young children receive child benefit. Means-tested benefits reduce inequality and universal benefits form a larger percentage of the income of the poor.

The provision of benefits in kind.

These include the provision of health care, education and school meals. The take up of these benefits depends on the age composition of the household (for example, the elderly make the most use of the NHS) and attitudes and opportunities to access the provision (for example, more middle class children stay on in education after 16 than working class children).

Labour market policy

The Minimum Wage Act of 1999, the anti-discrimination acts and government subsidising of training reduce income inequality.

Macroeconomic policy

This influences the distribution of income and wealth in a number of ways. For example, measures to reduce unemployment may benefit low-income households and regional policy reduces geographical inequalities of income and wealth.

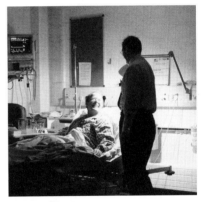

State provision of health care

Research task

Using the most recent 'Social Trends', assess the effects of state benefits and taxes on the distribution of income.

Quickies ✓

1 What are the main ways people can become wealthy?
2 What are the main causes of wealth inequality?
3 How are wealth and income inequality related?
4 Identify three ways in which the government influences the distribution of income and wealth.

Poverty

t is estimated that a third of children (4.5 million) in the UK live in poverty. In understanding the problem of poverty it is important to consider the meaning, measurement and consequences of poverty, plus the policy measures that a government can take to reduce poverty.

Absolute poverty

Economists distinguish between **absolute poverty** and **relative poverty**. People are said to be in absolute poverty when their income is insufficient for them to be able to afford basic shelter, food and clothing. Even in rich countries, there are some people who still do not have any housing. It has been estimated that in England in 2000 there were 1600 people sleeping rough. Of course, the problem of absolute poverty is more extensive in poor countries.

If a country experiences a rise in income, absolute poverty may fall. However, if those on high incomes benefit more than those on low incomes, relative poverty may rise.

Relative poverty

Relative poverty varies between countries and over time. Fifteen years ago in the UK, a personal computer might have been regarded as something of a luxury for a household. However, these days it might be viewed as necessary to participate in the activities of society.

While people in the UK may consider themselves poor if they are living in poor accommodation, have a television but no video recorder and can only afford to go out once a week, people in, say, Mali might regard themselves as well off if they had the same standard of living. This reflects the difference between absolute and relative poverty.

People are relatively poor when they are poor in comparison to other people in their country. They are those who are unable to afford a certain standard of living at a particular time. As a result, they are unable to participate in the usual activities of the society in which they live.

The concept of human poverty, introduced in the Human Development Report 1997, sees poverty as a situation where people not only lack material goods but also lack access to those items needed to enjoy a long, healthy and creative life, including self-esteem and the respect of others.

Measuring poverty

To assess the extent to which poverty is a problem, it has to be measured. Economists often define as poor those whose income is less than 60 per cent the average income (adjusted to take account of family size).

Synoptic link

In AS section 3.16, the consequences of poverty were touched on. This section examines the topic of poverty in more depth.

Definitions

Absolute poverty is the inability to purchase the basic necessities of life.

Relative poverty is a situation of being poor relative to others.

The Labour government elected in 1997 set itself the task of eradicating child poverty by 2020, and now publishes a poverty audit. This includes poverty statistics and assesses the government's performance against a set of indicators. Among the indicators included are:

- an increase in the proportion of working-age people with a qualification
- improving literacy and numeracy at age 11
- reducing the proportion of older people unable to afford to heat their homes properly
- reducing the number of households with low incomes
- reducing homelessness
- reducing the number of children in workless households.

The poor

Particular groups are more prone to poverty than others. These include the old, the disabled, the sick, lone parents with children, the unemployed and those from ethnic minorities. For example in 1999–2000, 35 per cent of lone parent families were in households earning below 60 per cent median income.

Causes of poverty

Essentially, the amount of poverty experienced depends on the level of income achieved and how it is distributed. The reasons why particular people are poor include the following.

- Unemployment – this is a major cause of poverty, with some households having no one in employment.
- Low wages – some workers in unskilled, casual employment earn very low wages. For example, a significant proportion of workers in Northern Ireland and the north-east of England are on low wages. However, just because someone earns low wages does not necessarily mean they are poor. It is possible that this person could live in a household with a high-income earning partner or parents.
- Sickness and disability – most of the long-term sick and disabled are dependent on benefits and this takes them into the low-income category.
- Old age – for pensioners, state benefits are the largest source of income. However, occupational pensions and investment income are forming an increasing proportion of the income of some of the old.
- The poverty trap – this arises when the poor find it difficult to raise their disposable income because any rise in gross income results in them having to pay more in taxes and receiving less in benefits.
- Being a lone parent – not having a partner to cope with the raising of a child may make it difficult for someone to obtain full-time employment.
- Reluctance to claim benefits – a number of people do not claim benefits that could help to supplement their incomes. This is because either they are unaware of their entitlements or they fear social stigma.

Making connections

Explain how studying might enable someone to escape poverty.

The effects of poverty

Poverty, especially absolute poverty, has a number of serious harmful effects on those who experience it. The poor tend to suffer worse physical and mental health and indeed have a lower life expectancy.

The children of the poor suffer in terms of education. They are less likely to stay in full-time education post-16, have few books at home and attend low-performing schools. They are also less likely to have a personal computer in the home and to travel abroad. All these factors tend to result in them gaining fewer qualifications and skills. This reduces their employment and wage prospects.

Government policy measures to reduce poverty

Governments may seek to reduce absolute poverty by introducing measures to raise the income of the poorest groups. They may also try to reduce relative poverty by introducing measures which reduce the gap between the rich and the poor. Among the various measures which they might use are:

- operating a national minimum wage
- cutting the bottom rates of income tax
- increasing employment opportunities
- improving the quantity and quality of training and education
- making use of the trickle down effect
- increasing benefits
- increasing the provision of affordable child-care.

Operating a national minimum wage

If set above the equilibrium rate, this will help the low paid who stay in employment. However, there are disputes about the effect that such a measure may have on the employment of unskilled workers. Also, not all the low paid are poor and of course not all the poor are in low paid jobs, for example the old and the disabled. In addition, if over time the minimum wage is not raised in line with earnings, it will cease to have any effect.

Cutting the bottom rates of income tax

This is something the current Labour government has done in order to reduce the extent of the poverty trap and provide a greater incentive for people to work. In order to have an effect though, in addition to the incentive there also have to be jobs available.

Increasing employment opportunities

This is thought to be significant as a major cause of poverty is unemployment. However economists disagree about the best methods of increasing the number of jobs on offer.

Improving training and education

This is a long-term measure but again is an important one as it will increase the productivity and potential productivity of those affected and thereby improve their job prospects and earning potential.

Making use of the trickle down effect

This is a more controversial measure favoured by some supply-side economists. The idea is to cut the rate of corporation tax and the high rates of income tax with the intention of encouraging entrepreneurs to expand and thereby create employment for the poor. It is also thought that the higher spending which the rich may undertake may also stimulate the economy. However, it can be debated how the rich will react and whether the poor will benefit from any expansion that does occur. For example, will they have the skills for any new jobs created and what about the poor who are unable to work?

Increasing benefits

Economists differ on their views about the effects of raising benefits for the unemployed. Keynesians think that it can raise aggregate demand and thereby create jobs, while new classical economists believe it will increase voluntary unemployment. However, there is more agreement on increasing benefits for those unable to work or who are retired. Those dependent solely on state sickness, disability benefit or the state pension fall into the lowest quintile of income and many of these would be unable to take out private insurance or invest to raise their income.

Increasing the provision of affordable child-care

This would enable more lone parents to undertake full-time employment and raise themselves out of poverty.

Thinking like an economist

Assess the arguments for and against raising benefits to reduce poverty.

Quickies

1 Why might absolute poverty fall whilst relative poverty increases?
2 What are the main causes of poverty?
3 What are the main costs of poverty?
4 Explain three measures a government could employ to reduce poverty.

Puzzler

Should an income tax rate of 50 per cent on those with incomes over £100,000 be introduced to combat poverty?

Activities

Activity 1

a) Using demand and supply analysis explain why a professional footballer earns more than a nursery school teacher.

b) Why might the economic rent earned by the footballer be much greater than that of the nursery school teacher?

Activity 2

Wage rate (ACL) per hour	Number of workers	Total costs	Marginal cost of labour (MCL)
£2	11	£22	–
£3	12	£36	£14
£4	13		
£5	14		
£6	15		
£7	16		
£8	17		

Table 1 The monopsonist's supply of labour

a) Complete Table 1.

b) Explain why this upward sloping supply of labour would give the employer the incentive to restrict employment levels.

c) What effect would the introduction of a professional qualification to become a member of this occupation have on the above figures?

Number of workers	Marginal revenue product of labour
11	£34
12	£24
13	£16
14	£11
15	£6
16	£3
17	£1

Table 2 The monopsonist's demand for labour

d) Using the information in Tables 1 and 2, what would be the profit maximising level of employment? What wage would the firm pay per hour?

e) Assume that the government now enforces a national minimum wage of £6 per hour. Show the impact of this on the average, total and marginal cost curves.

f) What would be the effect of the national minimum wage on the profit maximising level of employment in this marketplace?

Activity 3

Explain how the following government policies might affect the distribution of income and the incentives to work in the UK:

a) The cutting of the basic rate of income tax.

b) The introduction of the lower rate of income tax on earnings just over the **personal allowance**.

c) The introduction of the Working (Families) Tax Credit and Child Tax Credit. (In April 2003 the UK government reformed these benefits. The Working Tax Credit aims to tackle persistent poverty among, working people over 25 without children working 30 hours or more a week, or working people with children if they work 16 hours or more a week, effectively guaranteeing a minimum income for those in work. The Child Tax Credit extends the system of universal child benefit with further means-tested allowances in an attempt to meet the governments stated commitment to halve child poverty by 2010).

d) The raising of the national minimum wage from £4.20 to £4.50 per hour for workers aged 22 or over from October 2003.

e) An increase in employees National Insurance Contributions of one percentage point.

Activity 4

a) How might the rising **female participation rates** in the UK be explained?

b) Why are salaries much higher in some regions of the country?

Pitfalls to avoid

Be sure to separate the concepts of poverty and inequality. Economists distinguish absolute poverty from relative poverty for this reason. Although absolute poverty may have declined in recent years through government action, inequality may have widened as the incomes of richer groups have grown faster than poorer ones through economic growth.

Definition

Personal allowance is the amount of income that can be earned before paying income tax (£4615 for a single person under 65 in 2003-4).

Boost your grade

The lower rate of income tax is 10% on the first £1920 a year earned above the personal allowance in 2003-4.

Definition

Female participation rate is the % of women that are either employed or unemployed using the International Labour Organisation's definition of unemployment calculated in the Labour Force Survey. They are said to be economically active.

Answers

5a.14

Activity 1

a) *Demand side:*

- A premiership footballer generates a large amount of marginal revenue for his club, particularly a premiership side, which can win lucrative television deals and merchandising rights. The nursery school teacher has a lower marginal revenue since the price of the nursery place is quite small and the teacher can only cope with a small number of children at once. The footballer may be bringing thousands of paying customers to the ground each week.
- The players may have greater bargaining powers with their clubs than individual nursery teachers have with their employers.

Supply side:

- The footballer possesses unique skills that may be the product of years of training. The nursery school teacher's skills/qualifications may be more abundant.
- Education may be seen as a vocation by the teachers. They may be willing to accept a lower wage because of job satisfaction.
- Convenient working hours for teachers may provide flexibility, resulting in them being willing to accept a lower hourly wage.
- The footballer bargains for his wage individually, whereas an increase in the state salary for a nursery teacher might have to be paid to thousands of workers.

b) The elasticity of labour supply for the footballer is much more inelastic than that for the teacher (skills/training). This means that it is more difficult to attract another similar footballer with a higher wage than it is to hire another teacher. The footballer is in a powerful bargaining position to command a wage in excess of his transfer earnings.

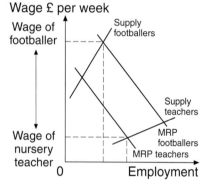

Figure 1 A comparison of the markets for premiership footballers and nursery school teachers

Activity 2

a)

Wage rate (ACL) per hour	Number of workers	Total costs	Marginal cost of labour (MCL)
£2	11	£22	–
£3	12	£36	£14
£4	13	£52	£16
£5	14	£70	£18
£6	15	£90	£20
£7	16	£112	£22
£8	17	£136	£24

b) The firm would want to restrict employment because it must pay a uniform wage. The effect of this is clear from the MC column. The twelfth worker may be willing to work for £3 an hour but his employment will raise the salary bill by £14 an hour as each of the previous eleven workers also receives another £1 per hour. The larger the workforce, the more expensive additional employment becomes.

c) The supply of labour would get more inelastic. This would make the supply (AC) curve steeper and would increase the marginal cost.

d) The **profit maximising level of employment** would be 13 workers and a wage level of £4 per hour.

e)

Wage rate (ACL) per hour	Number of workers	Total costs	Marginal cost of labour (MCL)
£6	11	£66	–
£6	12	£72	£6
£6	13	£78	£6
£6	14	£84	£6
£6	15	£90	£6
£7	16	£112	£22
£8	17	£136	£24

f) The minimum wage may raise the total cost of employment for the firm, but the MC has fallen so there is now less incentive to restrict employment levels. MRP = MC (£6) with 15 workers now.

Activity 3

a) This would not help those without an income. The biggest gains would go to those who earn the most. It would therefore increase inequality. If the substitution effect outweighs the income effect, the incentives to work increase as the worker keeps more of any additional income earned.

b) Those in work with income gain, higher earners gain more, making the distribution less equal, but it is likely to increase incentives to work.

c) The link of WTC to the number of hours worked obviously raises incentives to work. It is also means-tested and helps lower income workers more, lowering inequality. CTC is not related to work, but is means-tested and will lower inequality.

d) This is likely to lessen inequality and raise the incentives to look for low paid work.

e) This is a progressive tax that would decrease inequality and be likely to reduce the incentives to work.

Activity 4

a) ▪ the growth of the UK tertiary sector.
   ▪ delaying of marriage and child-bearing.
   ▪ increased availability of part-time employment.
   ▪ equal pay and anti-discrimination legislation.
   ▪ more firms offering flexi-hours and job sharing facilities.
   ▪ subsidies for child-care/nursery vouchers/crèches at work.

b) ▪ Deindustrialisation in areas of the north-east Scotland and Wales compared to the rapid growth of tertiary sector employment in the south-east has changed the demand for labour. This is then compounded by multiplier effects on other industries in these areas causing desertification and migration.
   ▪ Low occupational mobility of the structurally unemployed.
   ▪ Low geographical mobility of the regionally unemployed.

Exam guidance

Unit 5a is worth 15% of the overall A-level grade (30% of the A2 marks).

You must attempt *ONE* of two data response questions with a time constraint of one and a half hours. Most candidates find this a little less of a problem than in Unit 4. Question selection is clearly vital here and it is certainly advisable to spend *up to the first 15 minutes* reading the passages to make the appropriate choice. There will probably be four questions totalling 60 marks on each data response. Try and ensure that you allocate your time according to the marks for each question, for example, a 20 mark question should take about a third of your writing time, or about 25 minutes, if you spend the full 15 minutes reading the passages.

Exam hint

Read the questions before each passage to make better use of your time. You could use different coloured pens to annotate the passages as you read them, to highlight sections that are relevant for particular questions.

Exam hint

Remember that the data and prose has been deliberately selected for the questions set. It is unlikely that there would be irrelevant material. It is often a useful exercise to consider whether each table or excerpt provides any suitable source material for each question. This will maximise your 'application' marks.

Exam practice

Sales assistant and checkout operators	10.2
Other sales and services	7.5
Numerical clerks	6.8
Secretaries/personal assistants/typists	6.3
Health related occupations	6.0
Teaching	5.8
Health associated professionals	5.4
Clerks	4.7
Childcare and related	4.2
Catering	3.6

Source: The Kingsmill Review of Women's Pay and Employment, February 2003. (More than 77 professions were surveyed).

Table 1 % of total UK female employment in the 10 most popular professions for women

	Male			Female		
	Manual	Non-manual	All	Manual	Non-manual	All
Public sector	326.70	561.50	492.20	258.80	414.30	398.80
Private sector	323.80	509.10	393.60	219.20	308.20	285.70

Source: The New Earnings Survey April 2002.

Table 2 A comparison of public and private sector full-time earnings (£ per week), April 2002

	Male			Female		
	Manual	Non-manual	All	Manual	Non-manual	All
Full-time	7.50	13.70	10.30	5.90	9.90	9.20
Part-time	5.70	9.40	7.00	5.60	7.90	7.00

Source: The New Earnings Survey April 2002 (includes overtime hours)

Table 3 A comparison of full-time and part-time earnings (£ per hour), April 2002

In 2000, women comprised 47% of total UK employment, 11.5 million of the 24.4 million. 69% of women of working age were in employment. By February 2003, women working full-time earned on average 82% of the male full-time mean gross hourly earnings. Women working part-time earned only 61% of male full-time earnings. This divide is compounded by the fact that full-time women work on average 37.2 hours a week (male – 41.2), and average 0.6 hours of overtime a week (male – 2.9). Since the Equal Pay Act 1975 the full-time pay gap has narrowed from 31% points to 18 and since the introduction of the national minimum wage in April 1999 the gender gap has narrowed by 2% points. 70% of the 1.2 million people who have benefited have been women. With the continuing expansion of public sector employment beyond a quarter of the workforce, women seem likely to make further gains towards statistical equality.

Source: adapted from the Kingsmill Review and the Low Pay Unit reports.

a) Explain the factors that might account for the gender pay divide in 2003.
b) Assess the arguments in the passage for why the pay divide has been narrowing in recent years.

a) ■ the clustering of women into low-paying occupations.
    ■ You should use Table 1 to illustrate this, for example, more than 60% of total female employment occurs in these 10 professions alone. You could expand using MRP theory on why some of these professions are comparatively poorly paid.
    ■ the higher proportion of women in part-time work.
    ■ This should be supported by using the figures from table 3 and the 61% pay divide statistic. This flexibility of hours provides a negative compensating differential explaining the willingness to work for less.
    ■ Smaller numbers of hours worked and overtime received.
    ■ Lower human capital.
      Although educational qualifications are similar in the under 35s, older age groups may be affected by this. Certainly part-time staff tend to receive less on the job training.
    ■ Lower promotion prospects? Due to the prospect of maternity leave?
    ■ Discrimination in hiring or promotion?
b) You must explain the effects of and weigh up the importance of the Equal Pay Act, the minimum wage and the growing public sector points from the passage. Table 2 is useful to show the lower pay divide in the public sector than the private sector.
    Counter-arguments should also also be made:
    ■ Might the Equal Pay Act result in discriminatory hiring?
    ■ Will the minimum wage result in more equal pay but less female employment?
    ■ Are the women receiving the minimum wage the ones in need or second-income earners?
    ■ What about the gender differentials for part-time pay in the public sector? (The male/female pay divide is actually wider here, 25% points, than in the private sector).
    ■ The 61% part-time figure has not improved markedly in recent years and part-time employment continues to accelerate fast.

Boost your grade

Remember that many of these arguments could be supplemented by using a labour demand and supply diagram. Do not wait for the question to ask for 'illustration'. You can raise your 'analysis' marks by using properly labelled and fully integrated diagrams.

Boost your grade

Another evaluative approach could be to suggest that the passage's arguments are less relevant than other broader reasons for growing equality such as; the growth of tertiary sector employment that is less gender biased, the equalisation of educational skills in younger age groups.

Further reading

5a.2 and 5a.3
C. Bamford and S. Munday, *Markets*, Heinemann, 2002, Chapter 6.
G. Hale, *Labour Markets*, Heinemann, 2001, Chapter 1.

5a.4
C. Bamford and S. Munday, *Markets*, Heinemann, 2002, Chapter 6.
G. Hale, *Labour Markets*, Heinemann, 2001, Chapter 2.

5a.5
G. Hale, *Labour Markets*, Heinemann, 2001, Chapter 3.

5a.6
G. Hale, *Labour Markets*, Heinemann, 2001, Chapters 4 and 5.

5a.7
G. Hale, *Labour Markets*, Heinemann, 2001, Chapter 4.

5a.8
G. Hale, *Labour Markets*, Heinemann, 2001, Chapter 3.

5a.9
G. Hale, *Labour Markets*, Heinemann, 2001, Chapter 4.

5a.10
G. Hale, *Labour Markets*, Heinemann, 2001, Chapters 8 and 9.

5a.11
G. Hale, *Labour Markets*, Heinemann, 2001, Chapter 6.
D. Smith, *UK Current Economic Policy*, 3rd edn., Heinemann, 2003, Chapter 2.

5a.12
G. Hale, *Labour Markets*, Heinemann, 2001, Chapter 7.

PART 5b

ECONOMIC DEVELOPMENT

5b.1 Introduction to economic development

conomic development is one of the most controversial areas of economic study as different schools of economic thought clash over the most effective ways of promoting economic development. Choose this option if you want to really sharpen up your skills as an economist and get involved in heated debate.

At its crudest, those who believe in the application of free market principles believe that the best way of achieving economic development is for governments, both nationally and internationally, not to intervene in the free working of global markets. In the opposite corner are those that believe that economic development can only occur if revolution occurs and resources are equally distributed.

Between these extremes of right and left wing approaches there are many different approaches to how governments should best encourage economic development. As in many areas of this subject, there are no right and wrong answers and it is incumbent upon you as a young economist to always question the evidence that is used to support particular analyses or policy suggestions to tackle problems of economic development.

The challenge of this topic is not just that economists can differ radically in their views but that it addresses issues vital to most of those living on the planet. In 2003, it is estimated that:

- 840 million people in the world are malnourished
- hunger kills 6 million children a year
- 20 per cent of the world's population live on less than $1 (60p) a day
- 36 million people in sub-Saharan Africa are living with AIDS
- The USA contains 4 per cent of the world's population but consumes 25 per cent of the world's energy resources.

These inequalities are not confined to developing countries. In the USA, 31 million people are judged to be living in poverty and in the UK, one out of every four children are considered to be living in poverty. It is easy to let data such as this wash over us but problems of inequality and poverty are closely tied to social instability, which can pose a threat to us all.

We would all be better off if fewer people lived in poverty. It is a matter of simple economics, more income means more consumption which means more demand which means more production which means more jobs and higher incomes ... Enough preaching – let's get down to business which, in this case, means helping you get a top grade on this module.

What you have to learn

To quote directly from the Edexcel specification:

This unit explores issues associated with the economic development of those countries mainly in the southern hemisphere seeking to achieve faster economic growth and an enhanced quality of life for rapidly growing populations. At the end of this unit, students should be able to understand the causes, costs and benefits of economic growth in developing countries. They should also be able to appraise the benefits and disadvantages to those countries of alternative sources of finance from developed countries.

In order to do this the specification is divided up into four overlapping areas:

- development indicators
- theories about economic development
- differences in economic development
- strategies to promote economic development.

These are illustrated in more detail in the diagram below, and this structure is very logical. Firstly, we have to agree how best to measure economic development. This is followed by developing an understanding of different theories about economic growth, but to get a good grasp of the complexities of the topic, you also need to know why and how different countries have developed. Finally, you are expected to be able to critically evaluate the possible effectiveness of different policies to promote economic growth.

The exam

You can only take this in June so your chances of a retake are limited. By then your understanding of global economic issues will help you with development. You have to answer one data response question from a choice of two, and in section 5b.14 there is advice from a leading Edexcel examiner on the type of questions you are likely to get and the best ways of getting a top grade.

Web link

For links to some useful development websites visit www.heinemann.co.uk/hotlinks and click on this section.

Thinking like an economist

Doing development can depress you because you have to deal with human misery. Remember, that even though they might make mistakes, economists can help by developing strategies which can help many people improve their lives.

Learning tip

Read Joseph Stiglitz's *Globalisation and its discontents.*

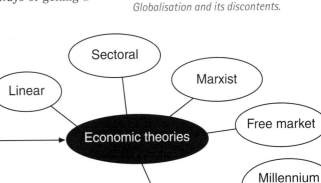

Development indicators

This section is directly linked to work that you have done for AS on using Gross Domestic Product (GDP) as a macroeconomic measure. This is a good topic to help you see the various connections between different aspects of economics. Edexcel expect you to understand different indicators, especially in relation to sub-Saharan Africa, Asia and Latin America. In this section, data of countries from these areas have been included along with comparative data from two of the most well-off countries, Switzerland and the UK.

Synoptic links

If you cannot remember the arguments about the value and limitations of the GDP measure, look back at section 3.3 of the AS book. You will also use what you have learned about economic growth and government polices for AS and for A2.

Definition

Trickle down is the argument that if the incomes of the better-off improve, the poor will also benefit.

Development Indicators

Historically there have been three different ways in which economic development has been defined. In the 1960s and 1970s, the United Nations (UN) focused upon positive changes in real GDP or GNP and set developing nations the target of hitting a 6 per cent percent growth rate per annum. It was assumed that the benefits of such growth would **trickle down** to benefit the mass of population of any given country. Most economists now realise that it was a mistake to equate economic development with economic growth. While it is true to argue that people will not become better off without economic growth, this is not a sufficient condition to ensure that the welfare of most people is improved. For example, a country may produce more goods and services but if these are very unevenly distributed and if they are produced at the cost of damage to the environment, it can be questionable whether economic development has occurred.

An alternative view of development became more widely accepted in the 1980s. It acknowledged the importance of economic growth but also included reference to the reduction of poverty, inequality and unemployment. Although the 'trickle down' approach was still considered valid by such organisations as the World Bank and the IMF, by the end of the 1990s there was broad acceptance of the wider definition of development.

Some economists use an even wider definition of development to focus on human rather than economic values such as empowerment, self-esteem and freedom. Meeting targets, such as these often requires institutional and attitudinal change as well as a faster rate of economic growth. It is important for you to understand the strengths and weaknesses of using different measures in relationship to the needs of developing countries. These include:
- GDP
- infant mortality and life expectancy
- literacy rates
- proportion of the population employed in agriculture
- compound measures – the two best-known ones are the UN's Human Development Index (HDI) and the Human Poverty Index (HPI).

GDP

You should already be familiar with the problems of using GDP as a macroeconomic measure in a developed economy such as the UK. Even if real GDP per capita is used, this measure may fail to account for:

- the mix of goods produced
- inequalities in income
- the production of externalities
- the output of the **social economy**.

It can also be distorted by recording and accounting problems.

These factors also apply to countries with developing economies and some are even more important. In a worst case scenario, it is possible to consider economic growth occurring in the context of gross inequalities of income, resulting in the production of luxury goods rather than basics for survival. This growth could be unsustainable, involving the once and for all consumption of non-renewable resources, whereas the mutual support offered by poorer groups and extended families would not be recognised. Finally, if government and civil services are weak it is likely that official statistics would be incomplete. This extreme scenario illustrates the shortcoming of relying on GDP as a measure of development.

GNI stands for gross national income per capita and the measures that are used in this section are those used by the World Bank. Although it is not possible to make judgements about development using this data alone, the underlying significance of GNI must never be underestimated. If per capita income figures are low, as is the case with Angola as shown in Table 1, it follows that poverty, suffering and starvation will be major problems and that such countries are always going to be faced with massive problems in terms of financing development programmes.

Moreover, it is important to consider the nature of the economic growth being experienced. For economic growth to take place, the economic growth must be sustainable, that is achieved in a way which does not reduce future populations' ability to produce more. Some developing nations, particularly in Africa, have achieved relatively high levels of growth in the past but at the opportunity cost of using up non-renewable resources.

Infant mortality and life expectancy

These two measures are commonly used to give a quick notion of the quality of life in different countries. This is illustrated in Table 2 overleaf.

Infant mortality is regarded as a very useful measure as it acts as a proxy variable for many other factors – quality of health care, clean water, the diet of mothers and so on. The data for Angola confirms the serious difficulties faced by its people, whereas those for Cuba indicate the priority given to healthcare in an otherwise poor country.

Definition

Social economy refers to the value of outputs not captured by GDP, such as childcare by other members of the family.

Country	GNI per capita (atlas method) 2001
Angola	$500
Argentina	$6940
Belarus	$1290
Cuba	unknown
Switzerland	$38,330
Syria	$1040
Thailand	$1940
UK	$25,120

Source: World Development Indicators Data Base, April 2003, World Bank

Table 1 GNI per capita

Country	Infant mortality 2001	Life expectancy 2001
Angola	154	46.6
Argentina	16	74.1
Belarus	17	68.1
Cuba	7	76.6
Switzerland	5	79.8
Syria	23	70.0
Thailand	24	69.0
UK	6	77.4

Source: World Development Indicators Data Base, April 2003, World Bank

Table 2 Infant mortality and life expectancy

Literacy rates

There are different ways in which this indicator can be measured. The World Bank currently includes measures of both males and female aged 15 and above who are illiterate. The data for the countries identified above is shown in Table 3.

Country	Illiteracy total (% aged 15 and above) 2001	Illiteracy female (% aged 15 and above 2001
Angola	unknown	unknown
Argentina	3.1	3.1
Belarus	0.3	0.4
Cuba	3.2	3.3
Switzerland	unknown	unknown
Syria	24.7	38.4
Thailand	4.3	5.9
UK	unknown	unknown

Source: World Development Indicators Data Base, April 2003, World Bank

Table 3 Literacy rates

Sectorial analysis

Another measure that is used is to consider the importance of the agricultural sector in a given economy. The World Bank compares the proportion of GDP added by the agricultural, industrial and service sectors.

The usefulness of this measure is based on the proposition that as countries develop, the agricultrual sector becomes less important, relative to the contributions of the industrial and service sectors. The data for the eight countries chosen is shown in Table 4.

Human Development Index (HDI)

An alternative and more comprehensive set of measures of economic development are those developed by the United Nations Development Programme (UNDP) which focus on the human impact of various economic factors. It is assumed that development should focus on three aspects of human development:

- how long people might expect to live
- access to knowledge and learning
- standard of living.

The HDI (first published in 1990) gives equal weighting to these three. In the words of the authors of the most recent UNDP report:

> 'The concept of Human Development looks beyond per capita income, human resource development, and basic needs as a measure of human progress and also assesses such factors as human freedom, dignity and human agency, that is, the role of people in development. The HDR argues that development is ultimately a process of enlarging people's choices, not just raising national incomes.'
>
> Source: UNDP July 2002

This most recent UNDP report also highlights that over 50 countries have been faced with declines in their development. Two, Jamaica and Madagascar, are worse off than they were over 25 years ago, and many countries who were part of the old communist block, as well as most African countries, are becoming worse off.

Human Poverty Index (HPI)

The HPI measures how progress is distributed in a country and takes into account the proportion of people who are left behind – the extent of deprivation.

HPI-1

This measures poverty in developing countries. It takes into account:

- the percentage of people expected to die before the age of 40
- the percentage of adults who are illiterate
- the percentage of people without access to health services and safe water
- the percentage of underweight children under 5.

Country	Value added in agriculture (% of GDP) 2001
Angola	8.0%
Argentina	4.8%
Belarus	10.9%
Cuba	6.7%*
Switzerland	1.7%
Syria	22.5%
Thailand	10.2%
UK	1.0%

* 2000 data
Source: World Development Indicators Data Base, April 2003, World Bank

Table 4 Proportion of GDP added by agriculture

Web link

The best portal for data on development can be accessed by visiting www.heinemann.co.uk/hotlinks and clicking on this section.

HPI-2

This measures poverty in rich, industrialised countries and accepts that human deprivation varies with the social and economic conditions of the country. It takes into account:

- the percentage of people likely to die before the age of 60
- the percentage of people whose ability to read and write is far from adequate
- the percentage of people with disposable income of less than 50 per cent of the median
- the percentage of long-term unemployed (12 months or more).

Summary

There are a range of indicators which can be used to judge development in different countries. The World Bank uses measures which focus on more economic dimensions to development, whereas the UN focuses more on social factors. Both organisations generate amazing amounts of easily accessible data. Whatever measures are used, this data shows that the least developed countries are to be found primarily in sub-Saharan Africa. These indicators also show that over 50 countries in the world are becoming worse off than they were in the past.

The following sections will try to help you understand which factors are likely to aid economic development and those which act as barriers. With growing instability in the world it could be argued that having a better understanding of global inequalities is one of the most important challenges for all of us.

Quickie

What global patterns can you find in the data about development contained in this section?

Exam hint

Examiners often ask students to evaluate the usefulness of national income statistics in helping measure economic development in different countries.

Puzzler

The Gini Co-efficient for Zambia is 49.8% compared to 36.1% for the UK. What are the implications for the effects of positive economic growth in Zambia?

This section has been written to remind you of concepts which can be applied to economic development and are useful in understanding the effectiveness of different development strategies and the particular constraints which they have to overcome. It can even be argued that the costs associated with negative externalities can make some forms of growth undesirable.

Back to basics

Although there may be arguments as to what constitutes economic development and how this can best be measured, there is little dispute that if countries are to tackle the poverty and hunger associated with a lack of development, they have two options. Firstly, they can redistribute wealth from the wealthy minority to the mass of people. This could be described as a revolutionary approach to development and has occurred in the past in Russia, China and those countries which have had communist governments.

Redistribution of wealth is not a painless or peaceful process but it can produce dramatic effects. According to the UN, Cuba is one of the quickest rising countries with a medium stage of human development. The average monthly income is around US$20, but education, healthcare, and basic foodstuffs are available to everyone. This has been achieved by the redistribution of wealth but has not been without serious social problems. Most better-off Cubans have left the country over the last 40 years, many settling in Florida.

Although income inequalities are great in many developing countries, even if available wealth and income were shared equally, countries such as Angola, Sierra Leone and Niger all have per capita incomes of less than US$500 a year. This is not enough to ensure that hunger, disease and early death are not commonplace. Logically, developing countries need to create more wealth in order to develop.

Five simple tools of analysis are useful in understanding the prerequisites for economic growth: simple input/output analysis, production possibilities frontiers, circular flow, AD/AS analysis and market failure.

Input/output analysis

This should take you back to one of your first classes in economics. In order to produce wealth four factors of production are required: land, labour, capital and enterprise.

Lack of any of the above is likely to limit economic growth and the production of wealth. Most developing countries have access to different natural resources and almost all are characterised by large supplies of labour. However, if educational investment is low, labour is not likely to be productive.

Almost without exception, developing countries lack capital. Levels of investment in infrastructure, health care, plant and machinery are all constrained by lack of finance.

Synoptic links

Your AS course should have helped you understand the economic processes which are needed in order for economic growth to occur (see AS section 3.4). Economists use different tools to analyse growth (see AS section 3.2 and A2 section 5b.2) and this can all be applied to the problems facing developing countries. Moreover, you will also be aware from your AS course of the significance of different forms of market failure (see AS section 2.2) and the benefits or otherwise of government intervention (see AS sections 2.3 and 2.12).

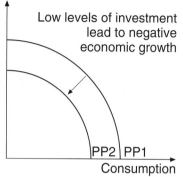

Figure 1 Negative economic growth

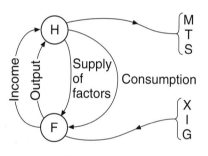

Figure 2 Circular flow model

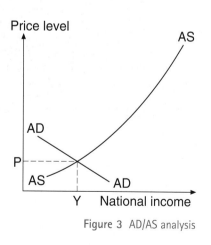

Figure 3 AD/AS analysis

The availability of enterprise is more debatable. Survival in extreme and life threatening conditions requires great enterprise. However, not all cultures attach the same significance to personal material possessions and individual profit, which, in turn, is associated with the notion of entrepreneurship.

Production possibilities

This is another concept from the very beginning of your course which is really useful in understanding how hard it is for poor countries to develop. If a country is really poor, almost all its resources will be devoted to consumption. The opportunity cost of this is that less is available for investment. In many cases, this is not likely to be sufficient to maintain the value of existing capital, in which case economic welfare as indicated by the production possibility frontier is likely to decline. This is illustrated in Figure 1.

Circular flow

Introductory macroeconomics introduced you to the classic Keynesian circular flow model that can be used to identify the conditions in which economic growth and the expansion of incomes are to occur. To recap, if there are unused resources within an economy and if inflows of investment, export earnings and government spending exceed outflows of savings, spending on imports and taxation economic growth will occur, and the multiplier effect will increase the eventual impact of any stimulus. This model is illustrated in Figure 2.

Many developing countries are faced with low export earnings, high imports, low levels of government spending, investment, and in some cases high levels of taxation, all of which are unlikely to compensate for low levels of saving. This simple analysis points to the likely situation of negative economic growth and falling levels of income.

AD/AS analysis

This is another way of looking at low levels of economic growth. Both aggregate demand and aggregate supply in poor countries are likely to be relatively low. Inability to invest is likely to push AS to the right and reduce productive capacity. AD is also likely to be low but even modest levels can lead to potential inflation. This is illustrated in figure 3 where the price level is P and the level of National income is Y.

Market failure

Market failure can occur when markets produce socially unacceptable outcomes. If incomes are very unequally distributed, it is possible for a country to produce and import luxury goods to meet the demands of a wealthy elite, while at the same time failing to produce enough food or medical supplies to meet the needs of those without income to translate their needs into effective demand.

They can also be said to fail if externalities exist. Externalities, both positive and negative, probably have a bigger impact on the working of markets in developing countries than they do in countries considered more developed.

Some transnational corporations have regarded the natural resources of some countries almost as free goods to be exploited and exported to developed countries with no consideration of the short and long-term impact on local economies. So, workers can be expected to work in conditions which would not be accepted in the developed countries, for example tin miners in Bolivia, child labour in Laos and asbestos workers in South America. Low levels of pay and poor health or even death are a constant threat to families and wider communities.

Countries such as Brazil and Indonesia are also responsible for massive deforestation. This results in the local and international negative externalities of soil infertility, erosion and global warming.

The most obvious positive externalities which a free market system is unlikely to provide are those which derive from improved access to education and health care. Healthier, better-educated workers are likely to be more productive, to the benefit of the whole society.

Markets also fail if monopoly power exists. Industries in some small economies are easily dominated by firms with monopoly power, either publicly or privately owned. Although it is possible for dominant firms to produce at lower cost and in greater volume than would be the case if there were more competition, there is also the likelihood of higher prices, less choice and lower outputs.

Finally, market failure occurs if markets are imperfect. In addition to monopoly power, market imperfections are likely to be significant in developing countries. This is especially the case where asymmetric information or imperfect knowledge exists; this is especially likely to occur in major trading transactions.

An asbestos worker in South America

Research task

Pick a developing country and see how far the analytical tools revisited in this section might explain low levels of economic growth.

Summary

None of the theory in this section should be new to you, but using what you have done for AS to understand some of the broad issues faced by developing countries may come as a surprise. This section has dealt in very general terms with the theoretical basis upon which policies are promoted.

Returning to the concept of market failure should help underline that strategies that rely on market solutions, and which could work in the developed world, may fail in developing countries.

Puzzler

Is market failure a bigger problem in developing countries?

5b.4 Development theories

Theories about economic development can be broken down into four groups:
- linear stages
- structural change
- dependence
- new classical.

Synoptic links

There are direct links between the macroeconomics that you did for AS and for A2. Keynes' 'circular flow' model in AS section 3.9 and A2 section 5b.3, the treatments of aggregate demand and aggregate supply in AS sections 3.5–3.8, and the study of economic growth are all relevant.

Linear stages

These approaches tended to dominate thinking in the 1950s and 1960s. In the developed world, these decades were a period of fairly continuous economic growth, helped in Europe by the USA who provided significant inputs of aid in the form of the 'Marshall Plan'.

Economists tended to think that development was a structured process, which could be applied to all countries with a kick-start of high savings, investment or foreign aid.

Harrod and Domar

Firstly, two economists, Harrod and Domar, working independently from each other, were credited with developing a simple model focusing on the savings ratio. They argued that economic development would follow once the savings ratio was high. This, they argued, would lead to high levels of investment, which in turn would promote the growth in employment and income, leading to a virtuous cycle of development.

Harrod and Domar were important as their model highlighted one of the key constraints limiting development. Poor countries, it was argued, were likely to have high average propensities to consume and it followed that their savings ratios would tend to be low. Such economies would be forced into a 'hand-to-mouth' economic system, which could only be broken if radical steps were made to increase savings. This could be forced on people as in Stalin's Soviet Union or could be provided by foreign direct investment.

Rostow's model

A similar approach was taken in 1960 by an American economist W.W. Rostow in his book *The Stages of Economic Growth: A Non-Communist Manifesto* (Cambridge University Press). He argued that all economies passed through five different stages on their road to full economic development:
- traditional
- transitional
- take off
- drive to maturity
- high mass consumption.

Traditional economies were largely dependent upon subsistence, which was followed by a period of change, usually in agriculture, such that more would be produced. Rostow argued that growing surpluses at this stage would lead to rapid expansion in investment. Higher investment would in turn promote greater growth while rising incomes would feed into increases in aggregate demand. Expanding investment, aggregate demand, employment opportunities and growing incomes would lead to the development of the infrastructure and the human and physical capital associated with a mature economy. This would culminate in the final stage in which high levels of mass consumption would provide sustained demand for the outputs of a developed economy.

The crucial part of this model is 'take off'. The implication is that additional savings and/or investment could set off a chain reaction of development, culminating in sustained economic development.

Structural change

This suggests that development can be increased by transferring workers from low productivity agriculture into the higher productivity manufacturing and service sectors.

Sir Arthur Lewis argued that in some developing countries that had a large number of underemployed people working in agriculture, some of the workers have zero marginal productivity. For instance, a small farm with three family members working on it might not experience an increase in output if an additional family member started work on the farm. If there are workers who do not contribute anything to agricultural output that could be moved into other sectors, then national output could be increased by a reallocation of resources.

It follows that development would be prompted by additional investment in the urban manufacturing sector and facilitating the movement of workers from the rural to urban sectors. However, this presupposes there are job vacancies in the other sectors. In practice, in a number of developing countries the migration from rural to urban areas can cause problems. These include pollution, congestion and underused social capital in rural areas and a shortage of social capital in urban areas.

Dependence

In the 1970s, there was a backlash in response to the application of the linear and structuralist models that suggested that the causes of underdevelopment were to be found within developing countries. Various Marxists and neo-Marxists argued that underdevelopment was the result of external factors. Development did not take place because it was not in the interests of the leading economic powers. Indeed, the comparative wealth and high levels of development of these leading powers were said to be partly the outcome of their exploitation of developing countries.

It was further argued that elite groups within developing countries often formed an alliance with interests from developed countries to ensure that inequalities and exploitation continued.

Thinking like an economist

It is now clear that simple models of development such as the linear stages model do provide insights into the process of development but they do fail to capture the very complex process of social change which has to occcur if development is going to to take place.

The most extreme policy implications of this approach to development are those that have been argued by various revolutionary groups. These include the arguments that foreign influences have to be removed, local ruling elites need to be replaced and land and wealth needs to be redistributed from the rich to the poor.

New classical

In almost complete contrast to Marxist and neo-Marxist perspectives were those approaches to economics of the 1980s and 1990s and the governments of President Reagan in the USA and UK Prime Minister, Margaret Thatcher. New classical economists used the arguments that you should be familiar with from other parts of your course. They believed that freely operating markets would ensure that development took place. They argued against any forms of government intervention in the form of subsidies to help the poor or import controls to protect domestic employers.

Such policies were energetically pursued in the 1990s by the World Bank, the IMF and the US government. In many cases, aid was only given to countries on condition that market reforms, such as privatisation, freeing-up capital markets and removing trade barriers, were introduced. When these policies appeared to fail, the developing countries were often blamed for not making changes quickly enough or for allowing corruption to go unchecked. New classical economists appeared to fail to recognise that it has taken countries such as the UK hundreds of years to develop the legal checks and balances needed if markets are going to operate fairly and effectively.

Usefulness of theories of development

It is very hard to evaluate the usefulness of these different theoretical approaches to development. Some elements have been successful. High savings ratios in many east Asian countries have contributed to relatively long periods of economic growth. The creation of more competitive markets in Poland has resulted in improvements in living standards for some elements of the population, and the redistribution of wealth from the rich to the poor in Cuba has led to very high educational and health standards for the all.

Web link

For access to thousands of indexed items on development issues, visit www.heinemann.co.uk/hotlinks and click on this section.

However, as the data in the previous section indicated, many countries have been going backwards. There is little doubt that both the investments in heavy industry undertaken during communist rule in Russia and eastern Europe did not lead to a sustained transformation of their economies, and the free market changes introduced during the 1990s have actually led to a fall in living standards in these countries.

Development issues might be so complex that applying economic models is too limiting. Some developmental theorists adopt a more multidisciplinary approach while others advocate small incremental changes that cumulatively result in sustainable change.

Other factors

As this section has shown, there are many links between economic and political change. Economic development is much harder to achieve in times of political instability. For about 40 years from 1945 onwards, the Cold War between the USA and the Soviet Union provided a form of global stability. Conflicts occurred, but much of the world was effectively divided between Soviet and American spheres of influence.

During this period, development appeared to have been relatively more successful. The end of the Cold War appears to have created much greater instability. Many of the poorer African countries have been affected by civil war, and conflict has also been evident in the middle and near east. Perhaps the poor development record results from political instability rather than the failings of particular economic policies.

Research task

Who is Paulo Freire and why is his work important to understanding development?

Quickie

Which countries in the world have the highest savings ratios? Have they experienced high levels of economic growth?

Puzzler

How would you sort out the relative merits of the different development theories outlined in this section?

Latin America

5b.5

Synoptic links

This and the following two sections are each devoted to looking at development issues in three parts of the world. They all follow directly from the preceding sections on indicators of development and theories of development.

Web link

For more international statistics visit www.heinemann.co.uk/hotlinks and click on this section.

For A2, you need to know about development issues in three regions:
- Latin America
- Asia
- sub-Saharan Africa.

The development of each region is illustrated by maps and statistics, and each of these three sections includes consideration of the factors which will have influenced development within the region. This involves considering the broad inter-relationship between historic, political and economic factors.

Latin America

This section focuses on Latin America. Latin America includes countries at different stages of development but in terms of the UNDP most Latin American countries fall into the middle group of countries. Most have significant raw materials and levels of education for most people are not exceptionally low. However, there tend to be huge inequalities in the distribution of income and wealth, which have been a source of political instability for over 100 years. This instability has had a very negative effect on development.

Historical factors

Prior to colonisation by the Spanish and Portuguese from 1492 onwards, Latin America was a comparatively under-populated continent. It supported extensive and complex civilisations such as the Mayans and Aztecs, as well as tribal societies living in what some would call subsistence economies but others would describe as self-sustaining and stable. Considerable advances had been made in agriculture, development of cures for disease and in understanding ecological systems. It would be a mistake to describe these various cultures as undeveloped.

European invasion

The European invasions, which followed early voyages of discovery by Columbus, Vespucci and others, brought massive change and most of the indigenous people of the West Indies, and the more accessible coastal fringes of Latin America were exterminated. Those surviving fled to less accessible regions. The Spanish and Portuguese were primarily looking for wealth to take back to Europe. The Spanish were especially successful in expropriating rich reserves of gold and silver which was shipped back to Europe to provide the financial basis for the expanding political and social power of the Spanish during the sixteenth century. The riches of countries like Peru and Columbia financed the growing power of the Spanish.

Colonisation

These early stages of colonisation involved the use of considerable military resources to establish new colonies under the direct control of Spain and Portugal. The British, French, Dutch and Swedish also established small colonies, especially in the Caribbean, and tended to be in conflict both with each other and with the Spanish.

Sixteenth and seventeenth centuries

In the late sixteenth and early seventeenth centuries, more direct colonisation took place. The richer and more productive lands were incorporated into large estates and ownership was taken up by Spanish families who were already wealthy. The tobacco and sugar industries flourished, creating more income for their owners, which tended to flow back to Europe.

Profits were boosted by the importation of slaves from West Africa, especially to the West Indies and Brazil. In short, most of South America consisted of feudal economies supporting a small number of very wealthy Europeans and a large mass of slaves and peasants living in conditions of exploitation and extreme suffering.

Nineteenth century

In the latter part of the nineteenth century, there were relatively large migrations of Europeans, especially from Spain and Italy but also from Germany and other European countries, who helped form a small but growing middle-class.

Spain's economic and political power was by then declining and from the 1820s onwards the inequalities arising from these still feudal societies led to a series of independence movements. This coincided with conflict between the USA and Spain, which led to the independence of Cuba and an increasing US commercial and political interest in the continent. By the beginning of the twentieth century, most countries had achieved independence from Spain but were increasingly regarded by the US as part of its growing empire.

In the 1880s countries like Chile, Uruguay and Argentina had made reasonable progress in terms of early economic development. Chile was the world's largest producer of guano – bird droppings – which was used as a fertiliser, while other countries in the south of the continent produced wheat and beef for international markets.

Some studies show that Argentina was roughly equal with the US in terms of its economic development. It shared vast reserves of natural resources, enjoyed high levels of investment from Europe, and had a growing agricultural sector and similar political and commercial institutions. Although less developed, other countries like Uruguay, Chile and Brazil had extensive natural resources and relatively small populations, seemingly set for 'take off' according to Rostow's model. This, however, has never really happened and Argentina, along with most other countries in South America, has achieved slow and erratic economic development.

Twentieth century

In the twentieth century, further investment led to greater industrialisation but most countries were largely dependent on exports of primary products to the USA and Europe. The economies of Latin American countries tended to follow economic cycles in the countries to which they exported. Wars in Europe tended to promote greater development of import substituting industries, leading to an increase in living standards but no significant changes in the distribution of wealth and income.

There have been periods of economic growth, reaching 10 per cent per annum in the 1960s in Brazil, some improvements in infrastructure but most Latin American economies have also experienced hyper-inflation, social unrest, and many continue to be dependent upon the export of primary products. In the 1970s and 1980s there were large movements of foreign capital into Latin America and many international financiers believed that the long awaited take off of these economies was about to occur. This did not happen and many countries in Latin America have been left with very high levels of international debt which can only be repaid at the expense of domestic investment. Over the last decade many countries in Latin America have experienced falling growth rates, increased social unrest, and some have been ruled by brutal right wing dictatorships.

Although there are differing views as to why a well-resourced continent should grow so erratically, the following factors are significant.

A Favella in Rio

Inequalities in wealth and income

Inequality means great wealth for the few and relative poverty for the many. This is readily apparent in most cities in Latin America where the rich live side by side with the poor and, as noted earlier, provides a breeding ground for both criminal and revolutionary activity. Rio is currently terrorised by rival drug gangs whose violence is such that normal daily activities are limited. These inequalities are greater in Latin America than in most other parts of the world, as shown in Table 1.

Gini Coefficients

This is a measure of equality in the distribution of incomes. It contrasts the incomes of the richest 10 per cent of a population with that of the poorest 10

Country	Gini index score	World ranking
Slovakia	18.2	Most equal distribution of income in the world
UK	36.1	
Costa Rica	47.0	
Chile	56.5	
Paraguay	59.1	
Brazil	60.0	
Sierra Leone	62.9	Least equal distribution of income in the world

Table 1 Gini coefficients for Latin America

per cent. Zero would represent perfect equality and 100 per cent perfect inequality.

These inequalities are partly attributable to great disparities in the distribution of wealth. Resources tend to be owned by a small minority of the population. This has meant that the benefits of periods of economic growth tend to be enjoyed by small elites. It also means that their great wealth has reduced the incentive to invest in technologies which would increase productivity, both in industry and agriculture.

Undemocratic institutions

Inequalities in wealth and income create the conditions for civil unrest, which has in turn been used by the armed forces to justify military coup, resulting in the suspension of democratic processes and ruthless suppression of dissent. In the last 50 years, every country in Latin America has experienced a period of military rule, while at other times totalitarian governments have been kept in power by the support of the military. It is now realised that persistent inequalities and lack of democratic institutions are major barriers to economic development.

Lawlessness and civil conflict have been exacerbated by the enormous potential profits to be made from the international trade in illegal drugs. In countries such as Columbia, these profits have been used to finance the arming of private armies, largely beyond the control of governments. Other governments, in countries such as Bolivia, Panama and in the West Indies, have used drug money to stay in power.

One of the further outcomes of the persistence of conflict is that resources are diverted into military expenditure at the expense of investments that might lead to economic development.

Lack of competitiveness

In the 1950s and 1960s, a number of South American countries applied the two-sector development model and invested heavily in the development of manufacturing, protecting their infant industries with tariffs and import controls. This created excessive short term profits but little incentive to invest further.

It has proved hard for these industries to compete in international markets, while at the same time investment in agricultural improvements is limited. For many Latin American countries this has resulted in repeated balance of payment crises, to which the response of governments has often been to cut domestic demand, leading to acute social problems because so many people were living at or below the poverty line.

Another economic problem with similar causes and consequences has been periods of rapid inflation caused by falling exchange rates, excessive growth

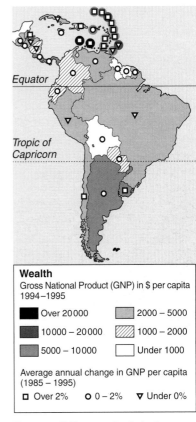

Wealth
Gross National Product (GNP) in $ per capita
1994–1995

■ Over 20 000		▨ 2000 – 5000
■ 10 000 – 20 000		▨ 1000 – 2000
■ 5000 – 10 000		□ Under 1000

Average annual change in GNP per capita
(1985 – 1995)
□ Over 2%　　○ 0 – 2%　　▽ Under 0%

Figure 1 GNP per capita in Latin America

Hot potato

How far do you agree that the experience of South America shows that economic theories are little use in understanding development issues?

in the money supply and limited productivity gains. Deflationary policies have often caused further suffering and social unrest.

Foreign interference

As examined on pages 134–6, Latin American countries have been dominated firstly by Spain and, more latterly, by the USA. Some economists have argued that it was in the interest of these countries not to promote and support economic growth and to regard these countries as important sources of raw materials.

The USA instituted and has maintained a trade blockade on Cuba since the establishment of a left wing government in 1959. This has had direct repercussions on the ability of the Cuban government to trade with other countries. Similarly, right wing military governments have tended to be supported by successive US governments, especially where their activity has threatened to disrupt the activities of western multinationals producing oil. This US interference has probably helped in the overthrow of a democratically elected government in Chile and aided fighting revolutionary forces in Columbia, Venezuela and Ecuador.

More recently, the USA has had a strong influence on the policies of the World Bank and the IMF. In the 1990s, Argentina had been forced to open up its financial sector to foreign banks and when in 2001 and 2002, the country was faced with a severe financial crisis, foreign owned banks responded by cutting their lending to local businesses. This drove many to bankruptcy. This led to the collapse of some banks and the savings of many of the middle-classes were lost.

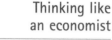

Thinking like an economist

It must be stressed that looking at development on a continental wide basis, as Edexcel requires you to do, helps us make some useful generalisations about development in different regions but also tends to hide significant differences in development between neighbouring countries, for example Uruguay and Paraguay. Find out more about development in Latin American countries.

Quickie

What contribution do each of the theories outlined in section 5b.4 make to understanding the pace of economic development in Latin America?

Asia 5b.6

conomic development in many Asian countries is very different to that of those in Latin America. Their experience of colonisation has been more varied and some Asian economies have maintained high rates of economic growth over the last 30 years.

A significant number of Asian countries were part of the former Soviet Union and they have shared many problems in moving from command to market based economies. In terms of HDI rankings, there are proportionally as many Asian countries in the high category as there are in the low. As with Latin America, the majority of Asian countries fall into the middle category. Although there are exceptions, countries in Asia have generally made better development progress than those of sub-Saharan Africa or Latin America.

This section follows section 5b.5 by focusing on the interplay between historical, political and economic factors, which go some way towards helping understand economic development in the world's largest continent.

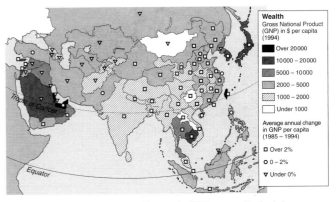

Figure 1 GNP per capita in Asia

Historical Factors

Asia supported a number of civilisations predating capitalist developments in Europe. Indeed, contact between Arab and other eastern cultures are seen to be one of the driving forces for economic growth and development in medieval Europe. Venice's growth and expansion from around 1250 onwards was directly related to growing trade with countries in eastern Europe. Prior to this, Arab cultures were far more advanced in terms of mathematics and the sciences and these, in turn, were interlinked via trade with cultures further east.

There was a similar historical relationship between the Scandinavian countries and central Asia and these trading links lasted for many years until challenged by more aggressive policies of colonisation which started in the 1700s when Britain tried to develop closer ties with countries such as India.

By this time, Asia was dominated by four countries: China, Japan, India and Russia. Russia was a feudal monarchy with relatively low levels of development but the other countries were highly developed in terms of technologies, urbanisation, state organisation, bureaucracy and internal trade. In this respect, Asia was different to Latin America and sub-Saharan Africa – both had previously supported advanced civilisations but these had had relatively less impact on what, to European eyes, were undeveloped, primitive societies.

At the same time, European navigators were exploring and charting Latin America. Voyages of discovery first revealed to Europeans the full extent of Africa and then opened up new sea trading routes to southern Asia, firstly by travelling around Africa and then, in the middle part of the seventeenth century, by sailing westwards to central and south America. Although the Portuguese established early settlements in India, the British pursued more aggressive trade and colonial policies by supporting a state-run monopoly, the British East India Company.

The British were able to exploit differences between local rulers to establish increasing political influence. India became an important source of raw materials, especially cotton, which was imported into Britain to be turned into clothing and other cotton goods, some of which were then exported back to India. In some ways, southern Asia provided the impetus for the industrial revolution which occurred between 1750 and 1850 in Britain. Evidence of the power which Britain exercised is provided in her ability to forbid the manufacture of cotton goods in India in order to prevent competition for the newly established cotton industry in Lancashire.

In the latter part of the nineteenth century, there was much stronger competition between European countries and Russia to establish empires. The Russians pushed eastwards and southwards, Britain expanded from its bases in India, and also tended to dominate the Middle East. The French established colonies in Indo China (what is now Vietnam, Laos and Cambodia). The Dutch took over most of what we now call Indonesia but both China and Japan were much stronger in resisting these colonial powers.

Britain and America forced China into the growing pattern of world trade by establishing their right to trade in opium within China and they were able to extend their power at the expense of a relatively weak Chinese political system. Japan remained largely closed to foreigners.

These emerging empires were challenged in the twentieth century. This century was one of conflict in different parts of Asia including the following.

- Late 1880s and early 1900s – Japan wanted to extend its influence and attacked Chinese and Russian controlled areas of north-west Asia.
- 1919 – The Communists took over what became the Soviet Union and the country went through a period of civil war.
- 1942 – World War II was escalated by the Japanese attack on Pearl Harbour, followed by the rapid military occupation of the bulk of south-east Asia.
- 1949 – Communist revolution in China lead to their takeover of political power and the founding of the People's Republic of China.
- 1954 – Defeat of the French in Indo China.
- 1975 – The Americans were defeated in their attempt to prevent independence and communist control in Vietnam.
- 1979 – The Soviet Union occupies Afghanistan, to be finally defeated in 1989.
- 1992 – The first Gulf War.
- 2003 – The second Gulf War.

Although this list is not comprehensive, it does indicate a very different recent history which has centred on conflicts between the USA and Japan, the USA and the Soviet Union, and now the USA and UK conflicts with Iraq. The former colonial powers have been resisted strongly and had less impact on economic and social development than has been the case in other parts of the world.

The rest of this section concentrates on those counties of south and east Asia which, in spite of war and conflict, have tended to be the most successful in terms of their development – China, South Korea, Taiwan, Thailand, Singapore and Malaysia. In many ways, the centre of world economic power has now shifted to south-east Asia. The following factors have contributed to this relatively good economic record.

Greater equality in wealth and income distribution

Although there are significant inequalities in income, these are less extreme than in other parts of the world (see Table 1). In their short period of occupation the Japanese redistributed land and broke up the power of large landowners. The countries which have developed most rapidly have used their growing wealth to ensure that most people have access to good quality education and that attention is also focused on meeting the needs of the less well-off. Although these countries have faced periods of social unrest, these have not been on the scale or intensity of revolutionary and criminal activity in Latin America.

Country	Gini index score	World ranking
Slovakia	18.2	Most equal distribution of income in the world
Vietnam	36.0	
UK	36.1	
India	37.8	
China	40.3	
Thailand	41.4	
Sierra Leone	62.9	Least equal distribution of income in the world

Table 1 Gini coefficients for Asia

Government intervention

Although there are variations, the governments of each of the south-east Asian countries have taken a leading role developing policies and structures which will lead to long-term economic growth. This is reflected in the importance that has been attached to investment in human capital through education, investment in high technology and information systems and careful control of imports and exports.

There has been little hesitation about using the power of the state to ensure that there are few challenges to government, and most of the growing countries in south-east Asia have poor human rights records. The Chinese government appears to have controlled the transition to a highly competitive, fast-growing economy, in which western influences have been accommodated without seriously weakening the control of the Communist government.

Research task

Pick a country in Asia and present a paper to the rest of your class assessing the likely prospects for economic development.

Competitiveness

The economies of these countries are also characterised by a very high savings ratio, which lends support to the linear stages theorists. This has provided a high proportion of investment funds without controls and influence from foreign investors.

Hot potato

How far do you agree that the history of colonisation in Asia is all about access to raw materials and the monopoly power of developed countries?

Productivity has also been relatively high, giving these countries a clear competitive advantage in the production of a wide range of manufactured goods and an increasing share of the financial services market. It has been very difficult for the USA and European countries to compete with these growing economies.

Foreign interference

Although countries in south-east Asia have generally been able to have much more power in determining appropriate economic policies, their progress has been threatened by foreign interference. There have been long and acrimonious arguments between the USA and China on the admission of the latter to the World Trade Organisation (WTO).

Although local savings ratios have been high, there have been also been high levels of foreign lending and pressure from the IMF and the World Bank that the economies of the south-east Asian countries should be liberalised. This has included pressures to open up capital markets.

One of the results of this was the collapse in the exchange rates of countries like Thailand, South Korea and Indonesia in the late 1990s. Speculation forced exchange rates down leading to severe economic problems. The IMF urged further liberalisation and free market reforms, which led to civil unrest in Indonesia and a collapse of the Thai economy. Some countries such as Malaysia and South Korea resisted the imposition of free market solutions and they appear to be recovering more quickly from the crisis than those less powerful economies who had severe deflationary policies forced upon them.

Research task

Investigate the collapse of the Asian Tiger economies in the late 1990s.

Quickie

Why has China been the fastest growing economy over the last two decades?

Puzzler

Is there a relationship between development and democracy in Asian countries?

I n the final of these three sections on different world regions and their
development the focus is on sub-Saharan Africa. Most countries in this
region have suffered negative economic growth over the last two decades,
and in terms of the UNs HDI, the bottom 27 countries on their list of worst
off countries all come from this region. The highest ranking country in
South Africa is ranked 107th in the world.

These low or negative rates of development can be partly explained by looking
at the interrelationships between historical, political and economic factors.

History, politics and economics

Prior to exploration and settlement by Europeans, sub-Saharan Africa was
settled by tribal and pastoral groups, who had some contact with Arab traders
from the north. Although there is evidence of past civilisations in countries
like Zimbabwe, comparatively little is known of their culture and impact.

Fifteenth century

From the mid-1400s, Portuguese sailors gradually sailed and mapped their
way round Africa reaching the Cape of Good Hope in 1497. This exploration
continued gradually northwards, with Vasco de Gama eventually reaching
India in 1498. Small trading centres were established around the coast but
the central part of the continent was largely unexplored by Europeans.

Eighteenth and nineteenth centuries

The pattern of exploration described above continued and expanded greatly
in the eighteenth century as the demand for slaves to work in the Caribbean
and southern states of the USA grew. Trade in slaves had long been a feature
of complex relationships between Europeans and people from north and west
Africa. A mixture of force and financial incentives was used to lure Africans
into captivity to be transhipped westwards. It is estimated that between 10
and 28 million Africans were forcibly moved from their homelands. Those
that survived the sea crossing were often brutally treated, families were
broken up, and local customs and cultures were ignored. A similar trade but
on a much smaller scale existed between Arab countries and east Africa.

From the middle of the eighteenth century, relatively small numbers of
Dutch and Flemish settlers established farming communities in what we now
know as South Africa. However, colonisation of sub-Saharan African
happened only towards the end of the nineteenth century, when what has
been variously described as the scramble or race for Africa began.

This was an outcome of intense rivalry between the newly industrialised
countries of Europe – Britain, Germany, France, Italy, Belgium and Portugal
– who rushed to conquer new territories. Each had different policies but each
of the countries in sub-Saharan Africa was clearly ruled by a foreign power,
supported by occupying armies of various sizes.

Sub-Saharan Africa

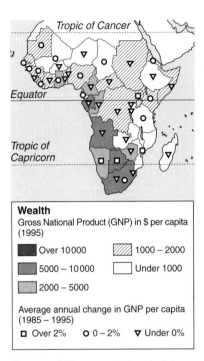

Wealth
Gross National Product (GNP) in $ per capita
(1995)

Over 10000   1000 – 2000

5000 – 10000   Under 1000

2000 – 5000

Average annual change in GNP per capita
(1985 – 1995)

☐ Over 2%   ○ 0 – 2%   ▽ Under 0%

Figure 1 GNP per capita in sub-Saharan
Africa

Part of the motivation for this rush to Africa was to 'civilise the dark continent', to bring Christianity to the black masses, but also to acquire rights to increasingly important supplies of natural resources. Diamonds from South Africa, rubber from the Congo, gold from Sierra Leone, copper from northern Rhodesia.

The colonising countries sought ways of making their colonies pay, meaning the introduction of taxation which forced local Africans into work and membership of a cash-based economy that was previously less extensive. Some of the new rulers were particularly barbaric. Belgium rubber merchants forced local people in the Congo to go out into the jungle to collect rubber. The punishment for failing to harvest sufficient quantities was the removal of one arm. The response to further failures was equally barbaric, and many perished.

Twentieth century

One of the outcomes of World War I was the loss of the German colonies in south-west Africa and Tanganyika (Tanzania). In the 1930s, Mussolini tried to capture Ethiopia and in the late 1940s, the UK granted self-government to South Africa, which became increasingly dominated by white racists of the Nationalist Party. In other parts of Africa there was a growth in independence movements, which in some countries such as Kenya, resorted to armed struggle.

In the 1960s, there was a rush by the largest colonial power, the UK, to give independence to its former colonies and this followed by the French. The colonial powers moved out more quickly than they had moved in, leaving behind poorly educated populations, ill trained civil servants and tribal rivalries which had been kept in check under colonial rule.

Conflict in central Africa

In southern Africa, white dominance was more deeply entrenched. South Africa embarked on policies euphemistically called 'separate development', which in reality condemned the bulk of the black population to low skill, low pay jobs and limited access to education. Black opposition was ruthlessly suppressed, and the South African government funded white settlers in Rhodesia (Zimbabwe) to remain in power and also supported anti-government movements in the newly independent countries of Angola and Mozambique. International pressure and armed resistance from the ANC led by Nelson Mandela eventually brought about the overthrow of the white regime in 1992.

Over the last 20 years, sub-Saharan countries have suffered disproportionately from starvation, especially in 1985 in Ethiopia and Somalia, and civil war. Living standards have fallen and genocide in Rwanda, Burundi, Congo and Sierra Leone have all contributed to misery and suffering that cannot be described.

Causes of negative economic growth

Why has this happened in Africa? The continent, although not all the countries, is resource rich and some countries such as Uganda and Cape Verde have made progress. The power and influence of South Africa is growing but this is not the norm. Economists and political scientists disagree as to the causes of the decline in living standards for most in sub-Saharan Africa but there is general agreement that the following factors have been important:

- poverty
- one crop dependence
- bad governance.

Country	Gini index score	World ranking
Slovakia	18.2	Most equal distribution of income in the world
Ghana	32.7	
UK	36.1	
Uganda	39.2	
Zimbabwe	56.8	
South Africa	59.3	
Sierra Leone	62.9	Least equal distribution of income in the world

Table 1 Gini coefficients for sub-Saharan Africa

Poverty

Most sub-Saharan countries are too poor to invest in human and physical capital. They inherited colonial infrastructures that were designed to facilitate the export of raw materials but not much more. Continuous under-investment has led to a decline in productive capacity and an inability in some cases to deal with natural disaster, for example changing climatic conditions that reduce rainfall and make it less predictable

One crop dependence

Many sub-Saharan countries have historically been dependent upon exports of a single crop or raw material. Falling world prices for copper, coffee, and sisal have meant that countries such as Zambia, Ethiopia and Tanzania have been faced with dramatic cuts in their foreign earnings, forcing further cuts in investment and/or increasing reliance on foreign borrowing.

Bad governance

Governance is a term used to cover the effectiveness of all aspects of government and legal systems. Newly independent sub-Saharan countries have inherited European models of governance, which have not been robust enough to survive without military intervention. Democratic institutions are not well established and a number of countries have been ruled by totalitarian despots with little regard for development.

It is estimated that the late President Mobuto of Zaire (the Congo) removed over US$4 billion to foreign bank accounts in the 18 years he was in power. Moreover, dictators have spent a disproportionate amount on weapons and the break down of law and order in some countries such as Sierra Leone, Liberia and the Congo is fuelled by the easy availability of guns and other weaponry.

Web link

You might have looked at this before but access Bized's virtual economy of Zambia by visiting www.heinemann.co.uk/hotlinks and clicking on this section.

As noted in section 5b.5, poverty provides a breeding ground for instability and unlawful activity, and this, coupled with weak governance, can lead to the break down of civil society as has happened in Somalia, the Congo and Liberia.

Foreign indifference and interference

Some of the worst episodes in recent African history, such as the genocide in Rwanda and the current wave of killings in the Congo, could probably have been prevented by more vigorous intervention from the UN and former colonial powers. Like other developing nations, some in sub-Saharan Africa have been subjected to inappropriate advice from the IMF and the World Bank. Their reliance on free market solutions has not been appropriate where markets do not necessarily exist and where the legal and financial structures and safeguards are lacking. The only way that really poor countries can repay foreign debt or invest in human and social capital is by further decreasing living standards. Such strategies depress rather than encourage economic development.

Summary

Clearly, history has left very different marks on the three regions investigated in this and the two preceding sections. Both Latin America and sub-Saharan Africa have colonial pasts in which they were exploited for their raw materials, and in Africa's case, their labour. Many African countries lack basic facilities to prevent starvation, still less democratic and legal frameworks to support the effective working of markets.

Both central planning in the ex-communist countries and the application of free market ideology in Latin America and Africa appear to have failed. Interestingly, those countries in south-east Asia which have developed the most have followed strategies in which there has been close collaboration between the private and public sectors, and have ignored conventional economic wisdom.

Research task

Pick a country in sub-Saharan Africa and present a paper to the rest of your class on why economic development has been so slow.

Quickie ✓

Give the strongest three economic arguments as to why development has been so slow in sub-Saharan Africa.

Puzzler

Can economics aid development?

This section builds on the previous sections about development, and leads onto examination of development in the different subcontinents and involves consideration of those economic factors which are considered to be obstacles to economic growth. These include:

- population
- dependence on primary products
- debt
- missing markets.

Synoptic links

This section links to earlier theoretical and descriptive accounts of development issues in A2 sections 5b.4–5b.7.

Population

Demographic changes can provide a constraint to development. Historically, there has always been the fear that population growth might outstrip the ability to increase supplies of food, water and energy to prevent starvation and even death. Rapid population increases, especially in developing countries, has been seen to cause particular problems. In the last 20 years, however, the spread of AIDS is presenting a very different population problem – rising death rates amongst the potentially most productive people in poor countries.

Population growth

During the twentieth century, the world's population increased from 1.6 million in 1900 to over 6 million in 2000. The bulk of this growth has been in developing countries and although rates of growth are slowing from a high of 2.5 per cent 30 years ago, growing populations present an obvious constraint on developing countries and their attempts to improve living standards and reduce poverty. Current rates of growth in a sample of countries are shown in Table 1.

Generally speaking, most less-developed countries have rates of increase above 2 per cent. The relationship between population growth and development is complex. Populations grow because birth rates exceed death rates. Any changes which improve the chances of children surviving their early years or improvements which results in people living longer will decrease death rates. Thus population increases can indicate positive changes and improving living standards.

However, increasing population growth means that many developing countries have very young populations, with some African countries having 50 per cent or more of their population under 15 years. This can provide a potential constraint upon economic growth because it cause the following problems.

- It places greater demands for food and healthcare on those countries with least capacity to respond. Such problems often become evident when crop failures lead to mass starvation, as is currently being experienced in Zimbabwe, Malawi, Ethiopia and Somalia.
- It leads to higher dependency ratios, which mean that a relatively small working population has to support a large number of dependents.
- It increases pressure on urbanisation, especially if conditions in cities are perceived to better by those growing up in rural areas.

Country	Current annual rate of increase in population (%)
Chad	3.3
China	0.7
Ecuador	2.2
Hungary	– 0.4
South Africa	1.1
UK	0.1

Table 1 Current population growth rates in selected countries

- It will lead to growing labour forces requiring employment. If a developing country already has problems in ensuring that there are job opportunities, this problem will become more acute.

It is now widely recognised that people living in poverty with little welfare provision will have large families as an insurance against old age. Looked at in this way, population growth is partly a function of poverty. Those countries such as China and India that have developed policies to limit population growth are also those who have tended to sustain higher rates of economic growth. Conversely, those in which population control has been less effective tend to be the least well-off.

HIV AIDS

HIV AIDS is causing a fall in life expectancy in a number of African and Asian countries. Currently, it is estimated that 10 per cent of females aged between 15 and 24 are infected with HIV in sub-Saharan Africa. The spread of AIDS is particularly associated with poverty. This reduces access to contraception, makes potentially life-saving drugs too expensive, and reduces the impact of education and preventative programs. Some African countries have been slow to take action and transnational drug companies have tried to prevent the use of cheaper generic drugs. Apart from the human tragedy, HIV AIDS is now, along with indebtedness, the major constraint limiting economic growth in sub-Saharan Africa, and parts of south-east Asia.

Primary product dependency

Many developing countries are reliant on sales of one or two primary products for export earnings. Over 50 per cent of Zambia's foreign trade earnings come from copper sales. Half of Jamaica's exports are accounted for by bauxite and alumina, and a number of tropical islands, including Cuba, Mauritius and St Kitts, have traditionally relied on exports of sugar.

This dependence has been very harmful to many developing countries because fluctuating community prices directly impact on export earnings. In turn, this has a direct effect on the standard of living of those working in that sector and, more generally, makes long-term investment and planning difficult. As commodities are traded globally, many factors, far beyond the influence of individual countries, can have an effect on their world price.

In addition, long-term trends in most commodity prices are downwards with the **terms of trade** of primary commodity exporters deteriorating. There are a variety of reasons for this, including technological improvements in developed countries, which mean that smaller volumes of commodities are required. Increased world production, including subsidised outputs in developed countries, will also push commodity prices downwards. The USA, for example, gives its cotton farmers bigger subsidies than African producers receive as income from their production.

Hot potato

Prosperity is the best method of birth control. Do you agree?

Thinking like an economist

Use AD/AS analysis to assess the impact of HIV AIDS on Malawi.

Making connections

Use demand and supply analysis to show the problems of primary product dependency. Is that the end of the problem?

Definition

Terms of trade is the ratio of export prices to import prices.

Debt

Many economists would agree that the debt burden faced by developing countries is the biggest single barrier to development. The scale of the problem is illustrated by the following:

- estimates show that developing nations pay the developed world nine times more in debt repayments than they receive in aid
- Africa alone spends four times more on repaying its debts than it spends on health care
- 32 of the most debt-distressed countries in the world are in Africa.

The origins of the debt crisis go back to the 1970s and were one of the consequences of OPEC's intervention in the oil market, which saw a quadrupling of the price of oil, leading to massive inflows of dollars to OPEC countries. This was reinvested in western banks, who in turn lent heavily to countries in the developing world, including communist-ruled states in eastern Europe.

Initially, most lending went to Mexico, Brazil, Argentina and Venezuela. These loans were from private sector banks, as distinct from earlier lending from governments. Paying interest and repaying these loans is called 'debt service' and this had to be paid in foreign exchange, which meant that debt servicing had to be met directly out of export earnings. When the loans were originally made, the four Latin American economies were growing relatively rapidly, with average growth rates of 7 per cent and more. During the 1970s, these countries continued to borrow but growth in their economies was maintained which meant that debt service payments continued to be paid.

> **Definition**
>
> **Debt service** is the proportion of a country's foreign earnings required to pay interest and repay foreign loans.

The recession in Europe and the USA in the early 1980s led to a slowing in international trade and a fall in commodity prices but with further increases in the price of crude oil. All resulted in falling export growth, which meant that debts could not be repaid. The situation was made dramatically worse as better-off people in the Latin American countries preferred to invest in developed countries, leading to massive outflows of capital. The initial response to this was for the debtor nations to further increase their borrowing.

The net effect of this whole process was that in 1988, $35.2 billion was being transferred to the developed world from the developing world. Another statistic which shows the scale of the problem is that between 1970 and 1992, the debt of developing countries had increased by more than 2000 per cent.

In 1982, the debt crisis was finally recognised as Mexico threatened not to repay outstanding debts, and for the last 21 years various attempts have been made to solve the debt crisis. Unfortunately, many of the strategies that have been used have been designed to protect the investments made by western banks rather than to address the problems of developing countries.

The overall effect has been to inflict lasting damage on the economies of the developing countries but this is explored more fully in section 5b.11, which deals with the role of the IMF and World Bank. Eventually, these institutions adopted HIPC (Highly Indebted Poor Country) by which it was to be agreed that the debts of the worst off countries would actually be written off. However, they had to agree a range of policies to liberalise their economies. By 2003, only eight of the 26 HIPCs have had their debts written off and more, previously unidentified countries are faced with problems of debt repayment.

It should be clear from the above that until the problem of debt is tackled effectively, many developing countries are going to be faced with falling levels of growth and even declining living standards. It is this that explains:

- the growing reluctance in developing countries to accept strategies advocated by west countries
- the growth in anti-**globalisation** movements across the world
- grudging acceptance that IMF/World Bank policies, far from reducing world poverty, have actually resulted in its increase.

Missing markets

Section 5b.7 contained a reminder that market failure is an especial issue in developing countries. Not only are markets more likely to fail, but they might not even exist.

The concept of missing markets has been highlighted by development economists. In very simple terms, shortages and the inability to pay for imports of foodstuffs or inward investment means that markets that we take for granted in the developed world simply do not exist. There are no market mechanisms by which the buyers and sellers of particular goods might be brought together.

This can happen for a great variety of reasons but the outcomes present a significant constraint upon development. In many cases, governments try to intervene and deal with missing markets by controlling access to foreign currency and granting import licences and so on. However, this can cause more problems since in developing countries this creates further market imperfections, which result in the development of unofficial markets and provide an incentive for bribery and corruption. This is a complex issue but in some countries like Nigeria, Benin and Congo, corruption is endemic.

Although corruption is less of an issue in other developing countries, all have ill-developed capital markets. Investors are not necessarily protected by law. They may lack the support of legal and financial controls and frameworks, and large sections of trade may be controlled by criminal elements. This is particularly the case in Russia, where a local commentator recently remarked, 'You only pay your creditors if they can kill you' – hardly the conditions for freely operating markets to work.

Definition

Globalisation is the development of the world into one marketplace.

Thinking like an economist

Analyse the economic effects of not having a financial market from which small businesses can obtain overdraft facilities.

Hot potato

The developed countries have a lot to answer for when it comes to understanding development issues. Do you agree?

Quickie

Prioritise the five factors constraining economic development covered in this section. Justify your decisions.

Trade and development

All countries in the world operate within a global economy and those in the developing world are particularly dependent on the import and export of key commodities and products. This section explores the implications of the theory of international trade and highlights its importance as a means of both aiding and constraining development. The issues are highly topical as poorer countries are often in conflict with those from the developed world and the growing anti-globalisation movement shows that many in the world are concerned about the effects of globalisation.

Absolute and comparative advantage

The key theory in understanding why countries trade is that relating to absolute and comparative advantage.

Absolute advantage

A country is said to have an absolute advantage in producing a product when it is better at producing it than other countries. More technically, it means that it can produce more of the product from each unit of resource than other countries – that is, it has a greater productivity.

Table 1 is based on the assumption that there are ten workers in the USA and ten in Malaysia. Initially, each country divides its workers equally between car and rubber production. It is further assumed that each worker in the USA can make either 6 cars or 10 units of rubber, and each worker in Malaysia can make either 2 cars or 60 units of rubber.

The table shows that the USA has the absolute advantage in the production of cars, as it can make three times as many cars per worker as Malaysia. Alternatively, Malaysia has the absolute advantage in rubber production, as it can make six times as much rubber per worker as the USA.

The implication of this simple analysis is that both countries would become better off if specialisation took place. The total production of both cars and rubber would be increased if the USA specialised in the production of cars and Malaysia in the production of rubber.

This analysis provides a good argument for the use of specialisation and trade to promote economic growth in both countries but, as will be indicated later, it contains a number of in-built assumptions which might reduce the usefulness of the application of this theory.

Comparative advantage

A more compelling argument in favour of trade to aid development is derived from the principal of comparative advantage, which can be applied to the production of similar products. A country is said to have a comparative advantage if it can produce a particular product at a lower opportunity cost than another country.

Synoptic links

Check back on the work that you did for AS in section 1.4. This A2 section takes the theory introduced in AS and applies it to issues relating to development strategies which are explored more fully in A2 section 5b.10.

	Output	
	Cars	Rubber
USA	30	50
Malaysia	10	300
Total	40	350

Table 1 Absolute advantage

Rubber tapping in Malaysia – Malaysia has an absolute advantage in rubber production

	Output	
	Cars	Toys
USA	30	600
Malaysia	10	400
Total	40	1000

Table 2 Comparative advantage

	Output	
	Cars	Toys
USA	48	240
Malaysia	–	800
Total	48	1040

Table 3 Position after specialisation

	Output	
	Cars	Toys
USA	35	630
Malaysia	13	410
Total	48	1040

Table 4 Position after specialisation

Exam hint

Including a simple numerical example like the one discussed here helps to explain comparative advantage.

The application of the theory of comparative advantage indicates that both countries will benefit from specialisation and trade, even if one country is more efficient at making both products, as long as there is a difference in its relative efficiencies.

Table 2 assumes there are ten workers in the USA and ten in Malaysia and that the workers are divided equally between the two products. In the USA each worker can make either 6 cars or 120 toys. In Malaysia each worker can make either 2 cars or 80 toys.

In Table 2, the USA has the absolute advantage in the production of both of the goods. Its comparative advantage, however, lies in the production of cars. Its workers can produce three times as many cars as Malaysia, but only one and a half times as many toys. A country has a comparative advantage in a product when it has a lower opportunity cost in that product than other countries. In our example, the opportunity cost of one car in America is lower than in Malaysia, 20 toys as opposed to 40 toys. Malaysia's comparative advantage is in the production of toys. It can produce two-thirds as many toys as the USA but only a third as many cars and it has a lower opportunity cost in the production of toys.

Table 3 shows the situation if the USA concentrates mainly on car production, devoting 8 workers to car production and 2 to toy production, while Malaysia specialises completely in toy production.

Specialisation in this context has also caused total output to rise. Both countries will benefit from trade if the exchange rate lies between their respective opportunity cost ratios. This is shown in Table 4, where it is assumed that the exchange rate is 1 car for 30 toys and the USA exports 13 cars. Both countries are better off.

Limitations in applying the theory of comparative advantage

While the theory of comparative advantage demonstrates that if there are differences in relative productivity, both developed and developing countries can benefit from increased trade, its application does have its limitations.

- It is often expressed, as here, in terms of a few countries and a few products. Of course, in the real world, there are many countries, many products and situations are always changing, it is, therefore, more difficult to work out where comparative advantages lie.
- It ignores transport costs.
- It assumes free trade.
- It fails to account for externalities associated with the development of particular industrial sectors, for example high technology industries.

Trade barriers

In spite of the economic arguments for freer trade as an aid to development, both developed and developing countries use a range of techniques to protect their domestic markets. These include the following.

- Quotas – these are actual limits on exports or imports of specified products.
- Exchange controls – especially in relation to **hard currencies**.
- Embargoes – prohibitions often used for political reasons.
- Tariffs – import or export taxes.

The use of these measures is often supported by a range of arguments put forward by both developed and developing countries for imposing restrictions on free trade. These include arguments for raising revenue, protecting the whole industrial base of the country, protecting infant industries and dealing with balance of payments problems.

A further barrier to trade is that presented by trade blocs such as the EU and ASEAN (the Association of South East Asian Nations), who encourage trade between members but often place barriers in the way of trade with other countries.

Trade conflicts

Whereas the application of comparative and absolute cost theory provides a powerful case for freer trade, which should benefit both developed and developing countries, there are enormous conflicts between countries and trading blocs limiting agreements over freer trade. The EU and the USA are keen to open markets for their exporters but they are much more reluctant to open their own markets and many developing countries feel discriminated against.

The World Trade Organisation

The main body with a role overseeing world trade and promoting freer trade is the World Trade Organisation (WTO), which was formed in 1995 replacing the General Agreement on Tariffs and Trade (GATT). It seeks to reduce tariffs and other restrictions on international trade and provides a means by which countries can settle their trade disputes.

The WTO, which currently has 136 member countries, seeks to promote trade liberalisation through a series of negotiations (which are often referred to as rounds). For example, the Uruguay Round achieved agreement to reduce trade barriers in textiles. Recently, it admitted China as a new member after a number of years of discussion and conflict.

The role of the WTO has been criticised by developing countries, who argue that industrialised countries are favoured. For example, tariffs on tobacco have been reduced to 4 per cent, while tariffs on tobacco products remain at 40 per cent. Developing countries argue that the differential has nothing to do with health concerns but is concerned with keeping industrial processing, where higher profits are made, in the west.

They also claim that in certain circumstances the WTO, by allowing industrial countries to impose restrictions to prevent **dumping**, is often merely enabling them to protect jobs in sensitive industries where it would prove politically unpopular to allow them to decline.

Summary

Free international trade provides a number of potential benefits to both developed and developing countries. Most importantly, free trade can lead to higher levels of output, in turn leading to increased income and employment levels for all. However, it can also pose problems for countries, especially if they cannot trade on equal terms.

Countries impose a range of import restrictions, including tariffs and quotas in order to protect their economies and industries. The WTO is meant to encourage freer trade but many developing countries believe that it acts to protect the interests of the most powerful countries, especially the USA.

Quickie

How does comparative cost theory provide a rational for developing countries to remove barriers to international trade?

Y ou should understand that development economics is very complex and it should follow that simple one-size-fits-all solutions to development issues are not likely to work and, as will be shown in section 5b.11, have probably increased poverty and suffering.

Those countries which have had the most sustained growth, such as China and South Korea, have adopted a range of measures which have involved both government and private sector development and activity. Both have developed comprehensive policies, which have included economic, social and political objectives to promote development. In the past, some countries have tended to or been forced to focus on strategies which target particular sectors of the economy.

Edexcel require you to know about sectoral development in agriculture, industry and tourism.

Agriculture

High levels of employment in the agricultural sector are associated with low levels of economic development – in the world's poorest countries, the bulk of the population work on the land. If countries develop, agricultural productivity usually rises but the relative importance of agriculture tends to decline. Moreover, it has already been noted that dependence on one or two primary products places developing countries in a very vulnerable position.

For these reasons, some countries have ignored the importance of agriculture and concentrated on developing the industrial sector. This attitude was commonplace in the 30 years following World War II, and has been shown to be mistaken because of the following:

- agricultural resources are some countries' most valuable resources
- an emphasis on industrialisation and neglect of rural areas has accelerated urbanisation, creating a new set of negative externalities
- ignoring agriculture can lead to a fall in domestic food production, resulting in higher imports of foreign food and so using up limited foreign currency
- those living in rural areas are often those in greatest need in terms of access to clean water, medical supplies and education.

Agricultural development can make a positive contribution to the development process since growth in agricultural productivity can contribute to the creation of more wealth. In turn, this can provide for locally financed infrastructure improvements and an emerging market for agricultural capital and relatively low technology consumer goods.

Agricultural improvements can also provide the basis for industrial developments which give developing countries more opportunity to benefit from the added value of manufacturing. Clearly it would be in the interest of many countries not just to produce and sell coffee beans to the developed world but also to process those beans and sell on the final product.

Synoptic links

The section draws directly on all the work you have done so far, looking at:
- application of micro and macro theory to development, AS sections 1.13–1.16 and 3.5–3.11
- economic growth theory, AS sections 3.15 and 3.23.

In spite of the obvious advantages, there are a number of constraints which have to be overcome if agricultural productivity is to be increased, including:

- cultural and social issues
- unequal land holdings
- developed countries imposing limitations
- subsidies.

Cultural and social issues

In many countries, especially with a history of slavery, working on the land has low status and even small increases in prosperity can fuel the desire to live in cities. Similarly, the better-off may prefer to consume imports of foreign produced food rather than rely on local consumption.

Unequal land holdings

In some countries gross inequalities in income and wealth derive from very unequal land holdings. Redistributing land from the rich to the poor can be a prerequisite for agricultural development. However, this involves great social change and the potential for conflict is huge, as can be seen today in Zimbabwe.

Developed countries imposing limitations

In is in the interest of developed countries to encourage the production and export of primary crops and to limit the ability of third world countries to use their own resources to manufacture goods for export to the developed countries.

Subsidies

Even worse, the USA and EU pay subsidies to their farmers to produce primary crops which can be grown in developing countries. The USA spends more on subsidies to its own cotton farmers than it does on aid to Africa, which forces down the world price of cotton below that which enables African producers to survive.

Improving agricultural productivity

In the major university text on development, *Economic Development* (Addison-Wesley), M. P. Todaro argues that improving productivity in the agriculture sector of developing countries has three necessary conditions.

- Land reform – Latin America has too many large landlords, whereas patterns of ownership in south-east Asia are much more fragmented. **Collectivisation** and co-operative developments offer potential for both increasing productivity and ensuring that the benefits are more widely distributed.

Definition

Collectivisation is forcing individual farmers to form larger agricultural holdings to gain economies of scale and other productivity gains.

- Supportive policies – Todaro argues that governments need to develop farmer-friendly rural institutions, involving the availability of credit, seed and fertiliser supplies, effective communications and access to water. Many of these are low technology solutions.
- Integrated development – it is argued that agriculture improvements must be accompanied by other developments to ensure that those living in rural areas have access to education, decent housing, and medical services.

Industrial development

The linear development theorists and those focusing upon sectoral change have all emphasised the importance of the development of a manufacturing sector to provide a possible way of achieving the following:
- reducing the outflows of foreign exchange to pay for imported manufactured goods
- generating foreign exchange earnings to improve the balance of payments and provide funds for further investment
- providing employment opportunities to meeting the growing demand for jobs.

Interestingly, the first two bullets provide the basis for two alternative strategies which have been used in developing countries since World War II.

Import substitution

Import substitution has developed especially in response to the non-availability of supplies from the developed world in times of war. Many developing countries invested heavily in developing their own capacity to produce relatively low technology consumer goods.

In order to do this, they used tariffs to protect their infant industries from cheaper foreign imports. In theory, the successful development of these industries would contribute to improved living standards, more employment opportunities and generate funds for investment in intermediate and capital goods.

These strategies appear to have met with limited success as governments tended to be reluctant to reduce tariff barriers. This and the creation of local monopolies have often meant that there were fewer incentives to make production more efficient. Consequently, countries such as Brazil, Pakistan and Argentina that tried this strategy found that after some initial economic growth, progress slowed and they did not move on to the next stages of industrial development.

Other factors contributing to this failure to develop include the following.
- Dependence on second-rate, hand-me-down technology from the developed world. For example, Ladas were built using machinery formally used to produce an earlier outdated Fiat model.

Research task

Produce a development strategy for a country of your choice.

- Raising expectations and globalisation has meant that many people in developing countries demand globally marketed products, rather then domestically produced substitutes which are often perceived to be inferior goods. An example would be a locally produced cola compared with Coca-Cola.
- Failure to address other issues contributing to poverty and lack of development such as disempowerment, access to clean water, medical supplies and education.

Export led growth

Some countries in east Asia adopted a different strategy modelled on the success of the Japanese, who transformed their economy from a backward primary producer to a world leader in the production of motor vehicles and a wide range of electronic goods.

The Japanese protected domestic producers by using import controls but encouraged competition between producers in their domestic markets. Successful companies were rewarded with import licenses to import the most up-to-date and appropriate technologies from more developed countries.

Although it is an oversimplification, it is said that the Japanese government helped identify those industries which were likely to grow fastest over the succeeding 10 to 20 years. Economic planning was then undertaken to support the required technological developments. So, in the 1950s and 1960s, companies such as Honda and Suzuki targeted the perceived world market for small motorbikes and similar products. They invested heavily in modern technology and by producing for world rather than domestic markets they were able to exploit technical economies of scale. They were more efficient than competitors in the developed world and have become world leaders in this kind of production. This model has been applied to electronics manufacture and ICT with great success.

Other east Asian countries have developed variants upon this strategy which appears to have been successful, especially when linked to the high domestic savings ratios identified in section 5b.4. This kind of approach, coupled with undemocratic and autocratic governments, has resulted in high levels of economic growth in countries like Singapore, Taiwan, South Korea and the most successful developing country of all – China.

Tourism

Growing incomes in developed countries, coupled with falling relative prices of air travel have given rise to another development strategy – tourism. The impact of this approach has been very mixed. On the positive side:
- tourism creates jobs
- tourist spending can provide markets for producers of artefacts and other support services.

However, there are a number of drawbacks to adopting the tourist approach.

- Tourists bring foreign tastes and expectations and in many cases expect the food and service levels that they are used to in their home country. In the worst scenario, as in Antigua in the West Indies, it is estimated that 95 cents of every tourist dollar spent immediately leaves the local economy to pay for imported foodstuffs, energy supplies and as profit to the foreign owners of hotels.
- Tourists pose a threat to fragile ecosystems such as coral reefs, and air transport is very damaging to the ozone layer.
- Tourists can represent a very visible demonstration of the inequalities between developing and developed world, and this can lead to social unrest.

Nonetheless, some countries such as Cuba and the Maldives consider that their beaches and cultures offer one of the few opportunities to earn foreign currency to help develop other sectors of their economies. Cuba has adopted a variant of the east Asian model by encouraging competition between differently managed state-owned travel companies and uses import controls to try to ensure that tourist needs are sourced locally.

There is also a high level of state intervention in the Maldives in which foreign investors are allowed to develop a local tourist infrastructure which is very sensitive to the local ecology.

Hot potato

Tourists should pay special tax – do you agree?

Summary

These three approaches to development offer different chances of success. Import substitution is now largely discredited. Tourism only contributes positively to development if it occurs within a highly regulated framework. Export led strategies appear most promising if accompanied by other strategies to tackle poverty and disempowerment. The success of these requires the co-operation of developed countries, which is not always forthcoming.

Puzzler

Choose a country which has adopted one of these strategies. What have been the costs and what have been the benefits?

5b.11 Sources of external finance

Synoptic links

This section is devoted to exploring the costs and benefits to developing countries of different types of external finance and links most closely to sections 5b.9 and 5b.10, both of which identified the importance of finding ways of financing greater investment in order to stimulate developing economies and provide much needed improvements in infrastructure, health-care and education.

Definition

Transfer pricing relates to internal trading within different parts of MNCs in which resource might be sold very cheaply from a developing to a developed country but thereafter they are traded internally at much higher prices.

External finance is crucial to development in many countries. The two main forms of external finance are as follows:

- investment by multinational companies (MNCs)
- foreign aid.

Finally, consideration is given to how countries and international institutions are responding to the slow and often negative progress made by most countries over the last two decades in reducing poverty and promoting development.

Multinational investment

Some 500 companies control nearly 25 per cent of the total value of the world's economy and provide an important source of inward investment to both developed and developing countries with most going to the former.

The incentives for MNCs to investment in developing countries include access to the following:

- the extraction and export of raw materials and agricultural produce
- growing domestic markets, for example China today
- cheap, non-unionised labour, especially in south-east Asia.

The possible benefits to the developing country include:

- technology transfer, that is access to modern production techniques and new skills
- job creation
- investment in infrastructure.

The record of MNCs in promoting development is very mixed. They have been responsible for the mining and extraction of raw materials from poor countries that have received very little in return. They can be very powerful and capable of extracting very favourable terms for investment in particular countries, such as freedom from local taxation, and in some cases their activities can be very destabilising for the developing countries, for example oil exploration in Columbia and Ecuador. They use **transfer pricing** as a technique for understating the profits made from activities in particular countries.

On the other hand, external finance is required. The extraction of resources is often beyond the means of poorer countries and some MNCs are more ethically inclined than others. When governments are strong enough to negotiate wide ranging agreements with MNCs, they can help ensure that they share more fairly in the profits of the particular activity, that local people are trained to take senior as well as lower level jobs, and that other ethical considerations are included.

Foreign aid

Foreign aid, or to give it its proper name 'official development assistance' or ODA, comes in two forms: bilateral assistance, which is given from a developed country to a developing country, and multilateral assistance, which comes from an agency such as the EU or the World Bank. Three characteristics apply to this form of assistance:

- it is undertaken by the official sector
- tackling development is the principle objective
- it is given on 'concessional terms', which are meant to ensure that the interest rate and length of time for the repayment of loans is less demanding than would be the case of commercial loans.

The effectiveness of foreign aid is another major area of debate among development economists.

Bilateral aid

There is little evidence to suggest that the bulk of bilateral aid is given with the notion of benefit to the developing country. The granting of aid is often linked directly to political considerations rather than any assessment of relative need in different countries. In the days of the Cold War between the USA and the Soviet Union, each would tend to give aid in return for political support. Today, Arab countries friendly to the USA are more likely to receive aid than those who are not.

Alternatively, there may be economic motives, ranging from the notion that economic development will result in the growth of potential export markets to the narrow self-interest in which aid is tied to purchases of goods and services from donor countries. The effect of this is that most aid given by the USA and UK is spent in the USA and UK on American and British produced products or services.

These political and economic considerations mean that those countries in most need to aid such as those in Sub-Saharan Africa tend to receive less than some better-off countries

Multilateral Aid

Multilateral aid, by which countries join together to provide aid and support to developing nations, can potentially be more helpful to developing countries. The main sources of multinational aid include:

- the UN
- the World Bank
- the International Monetary Fund (IMF).

The UN

The UN is responsible for both emergency aid and assistance to promote long term development. Its intervention has been very significant in supplying food to Ethiopia, which appears to have prevented a repetition of the mass starvation seen in Ethiopia in the mid 1980s. However, UN responses can be slow, especially as it is necessary to obtain the agreement of most member states.

The IMF and the World Bank

The IMF was set up as a result of the Bretton Woods agreement after World War II in an attempt to prevent a repeat of the financial crises that had marred international trade in the pre-war period. It is specifically designed to help countries through periods of balance of payment difficulties in order to avoid competitive devaluations. The leading economies each contributed to a fund which each could then draw upon if needed.

The World Bank was also created following the Bretton Woods agreement, and the leading economic powers agreed to contribute to a fund which developing countries could draw upon to help fund growth and development. Both organisations have effectively been run and organised by the USA, and in the 1980s and 1990s pursued right wing economic policies associated with President Regan and UK Prime Minister, Margaret Thatcher.

The activities of the World Bank and the IMF in the 1990s have brought enormous discredit to both these organisations. They are blamed by Nobel Prize Winning economist, Joseph Stiglitz, for exacerbating problems of poverty in Africa, Latin American and the former Soviet bloc by insisting on various forms of conditionality to aid packages and measures designed to free developing countries from the crippling problem of debt. Aid and help with rescheduling debt have been tied to the imposition of free market ideas, forcing countries to open capital markets to foreign competition, to privatise state owned organisations and to instigate internal austerity programmes as a means of combating inflation and balance of payments programmes.

Definition

Structural adjustment is the euphamistic term given to the act of forcing developing countries to adopt free market policies.

These policies, given the generic title of '**structural adjustment**', have been applied on the presumption that market based solutions work and that market failure is unlikely. Yet, as has already been demonstrated, markets in developing countries are much more likely to be imperfect or even missing.

One of the results of reducing government intervention has been failures in capital markets, resulting in the bankruptcy and closure of firms in Argentina. When the Russian government carried through privatisation programmes there was massive fraud by criminal elements. These examples of government failure have caused civil unrest in a number of countries, including Argentina and Indonesia, and have resulted in falling living standards in most of the ex-communist countries who have been forced to take rapid measures to liberalise their economies.

Those countries who have challenged the World Bank prescriptions for development have tended to do better than countries that accepted structural adjustment packages. Thus, South Korea and Malaysia appear to have recovered more quickly from the crash in eastern Asia of the late 1990s than those countries, such as Thailand, who were more compliant with the World Bank.

The World Bank and IMF have also been responsible for programmes which are designed to resolve problems of indebtedness.

Current developments

There is general consensus among economists today that if development is to occur, countries need to adopt comprehensive polices to tackle different aspects of underdevelopment. Narrow strategies aimed at the development of a particular sector are unlikely to work.

The application of free market ideology has been shown to be just as shortsighted as the prescriptions of collectivisation and state domination that are characteristic of Communist approaches to development. Countries in which there is little democracy, or in which the bulk of the population are excluded from access to sufficient food, clean water and health care, are not likely to make progress.

These considerations are reflected in the UN's Millennium Development Goals, reproduced in Figure 1. These stress the importance of targeting poverty. The new stress is on partnership including organisations such as the World Bank and clear targets have been set for achieving each of these goals

It is also unlikely that poorer countries will able to develop without the support and cooperation of the developed nations. However, the current political situation, especially the instability in the Middle East, is likely to mean that political rather than humanitarian considerations may well continue to act as constraints upon development.

Web link

To gauge the progress in meeting the eight Millenium Development Goals visit www.heinemann.co.uk/hotlinks and click on this section.

Millennium Development Goals

"We will spare no effort to free our fellow men, women, and children from the abject and dehumanizing conditions of extreme poverty, to which more than a billion of them are currently subjected."
United Nations Millennium Declaration – September 2000

1. Eradicate extreme poverty and hunger
2. Achieve universal primary education
3. Promote gender equality and empower women
4. Reduce child mortality
5. Improve maternal health
6. Combat HIV/AIDS, malaria, and other diseases
7. Ensure environmental sustainability
8. Develop a global partnership for development

Figure 1 Millennium Development Goals

Quickie

Which of the eight Millenium Deveopment Goals are economic?

Puzzler

Why is it so hard to judge the positive impact of MNCs on developing countries?

Activities

Activity 1

In the mid 1990s, aid totalling 300 million yen (£1.9 million) was given to Malawi for the purchase of Argentinean maize by two Japanese companies. Only 79 million yen (£0.5 million) was spent on maize; the rest went towards transport and insurance costs. So just 3000 metric tonnes of maize was actually delivered. Yet if Malawi had been able to buy the maize within the southern Africa region, the same money could have bought more than three times as much – 10,000 tonnes of maize.

Tied aid can skew development projects towards commercial considerations. Secondly, it can exclude the apparent beneficiaries – whose participation and support is essential for the eventual success of a development project – from the decision-making process for which the aid is granted. Thirdly, it favours capital-intensive over smaller, more poverty focused projects, and fourthly, it can lead to the provision of inappropriate goods, services and advice. Moreover, aid tying is inefficient. It can increase the costs of goods and services by up to 30%, as there is often no or little competition for contracts.

The UK Government announced that all its aid would be untied from 1 April 2001 and will raise its aid budget to 0.4% of GDP by 2005-6. On 25 April 2001, the High Level Meeting of the Development Assistance Committee of the OECD endorsed a recommendation on untying aid to the Least Developed Countries. This is the first international agreement on untying and is an important first step towards ending the practice. However, it excludes technical co-operation and food aid and, as such, represents only a fraction of development spending.

The Danish government, whose development aid, at around 1% of GNP, makes it the world's most generous donor, argues that it is only through ensuring benefits domestically as well as in developing countries that their electorates are willing to support high levels of development aid at all.

Source: DFID and Action Aid websites.

Boost your grade

Note that the UN target for aid contributions is 0.7% of GDP. This is currently only observed by four nations. The UK government has a stated commitment to move towards this level in the Budget 2003 document. The US government gives the most in absolute terms but only 0.11% of GDP in 2002.

	Untied aid	Tied aid	Total	% Untied	% Tied	Aid, % GDP
Australia	134	92	226	59.3	40.7	0.25
Canada	236	509	745	31.7	68.3	0.22
Denmark	635	46	681	93.3	6.7	1.03
Finland	139	20	159	87.5	12.5	0.32
France	1178	161	1768	66.6	9.1	0.32
Germany	1370	249	1619	84.6	15.4	0.27
Italy	39	458	496	7.8	92.2	0.15
Japan	7200	1557	8878	81.1	17.5	0.23
Norway	695	8	703	98.9	1.1	0.83
Sweden	824	33	953	86.5	3.5	0.81
UK	964	63	1027	93.9	6.1	0.32

Source: OECD, DAC accounts 2002.

Table 1 Bilateral official development assistance, 2001 $mn

a) Define 'tied aid' and 'official development assistance.'
b) Explain the significance of foreign aid as a source of external finance for development.
c) Assess the case for untying all bilateral government aid.

Activity 2

	Agriculture, % of GDP		Agricultural employment, % labour force		Urban population, % of total	
	1970	1999	1980	1998	1970	1999
Indonesia	45	19	56	45	17	40
Philippines	30	18	52	40	33	58
Rwanda	66	46	93	–	3	6
Myanmar	38	60	67	63	23	27

Source: World Bank Development Indicators 2001.

Table 2 Agricultural dependency and urbanisation

a) How might a country benefit from the process of urbanisation?
b) What problems are countries such as Indonesia and the Philippines likely to experience from such a rapid process of urbanisation?
c) Assess the effects of agricultural dependency on nations such as Rwanda and Myanmar.

Activity 3

	GDP per capita 1999 ($ PPP)	GDP average annual % growth 1965-99	Population average annual % growth 1965-99	Gini index	Life expectancy at birth Male 1999	Life expectancy at birth Female 1999
Congo, Dem. Rep.	–	-0.4	3.1	–	45	47
Hungary	11,050	2.1	0.0	0.244	66	75
Italy	22,000	2.8	0.3	0.273	75	82
Mozambique	810	3.0	2.2	0.396	42	44
Peru	4480	2.0	2.3	0.462	66	71
UK	22,220	2.2	0.3	0.361	75	80
Venezuela	5420	2.1	2.8	0.488	70	76

Source: World Bank Development Indicators 2001.

Table 3 Development indicators

a) What effect is the rapid rate of population growth in countries such as Peru likely to have on the standards of living?
b) What are the problems with using the data on GDP per capita to examine the differences in living standards between the nations in the table?

Answers

Activity 1

a) Tied aid is bilateral government aid that is given on the condition that it is spent in a particular way, normally on the exports of the donor nation. Official development assistance, meanwhile, refers to grants and loans with a concessional rate of interest. To qualify, a loan from one government to another must have a discount of at least 25% below available market rates of interest. It also includes grants of technical co-operation and assistance.

b) Foreign aid can provide an important injection of investment finance that helps a developing nation grow, or might offset decline. The **Harrod–Domar model** of economic growth suggests that countries need to build up their domestic savings ratios to foster investment, however, this may be unrealistic in the case of developing nations. Aid can fill this savings gap, at least in the short run. For some countries it is critical to the prevention of significant social and economic problems, for example, aid flows amounted to 21% of Zambian and 20% of Rwandan GDP in 1999. In years of poor harvests or political turmoil it may be a real lifeline; in 1995 aid flows were equivalent to 95% of the Rwandan GDP.

c) For:

- It would allow the recipient to use the money freely (use the Malawi example of the inefficiency of uncompetitive tendering). They may be able to buy more for the money from another country.
- It would force the developed world companies relying on uncompetitive government-sponsored contracts to become more efficient.
- The government and people in the nation close to the problems may have a better idea of exactly what is needed.

Against:

- Many nations might not be willing to give so much aid if it is untied (use Table 1 and quote the Danish argument).
- Tying the aid might allow more control to be held by the donor over how the funds are spent and avoid money being lost as a result of corruption.
- Are there more important problems to sort out first such as debt-relief and removing protectionist barriers against developing nations' exports?

Activity 2

a) The Lewis model of structural change suggests that many developing nations suffer from under-employment in rural areas. Workers would have a higher marginal productivity by moving to urban, basic industry. This might encourage a more diversified economy that is less susceptible to shocks. Urbanisation will also allow economies of scale and scope to be realised so that the provision of basic infrastructure such as roads and power networks becomes economically viable.

Definition

The Harrod–Domar model suggests that the rate of economic growth of a nation will be equal to the savings ratio divided by the capital-output ratio. The savings ratio is the % of GDP that is saved. The capital-output ratio measures the efficiency of the capital in the nation.

b) The fact that the increase in the urban population exceeds the fall in the agricultural share of the labour force might suggest that many of the new urban population are *unemployed* (use data from Table 2). Other problems include:
   - lack of access to clean water in shanty towns
   - greater inequality
   - inequality and population density may lead to increased crime
   - growing informal sectors.

c) Erratic supply coupled with price inelastic market demand and supply for agricultural products will produce enormous price volatility. This will mean income volatility for farmers. They may be unable to plan ahead and be less inclined to invest. Primary export earnings are volatile and debt may occur from balance of payments problems. This might also destabilise the exchange rate leading to further macroeconomic problems. (see Figure 1).

Activity 3

a) If the average annual population growth exceeds the growth of real GDP then the real GDP per capita (average economic standards of living) will decline. This will have occurred in the Democratic Republic of Congo, Peru and Venezuela 1965-99. Social resources such as hospitals and schools become over-stretched, because the funds available to the government will not be growing as fast as the number of people needing access to those facilities. If the growing population is a product of a high birth rate it may also lead to a higher **dependency ratio**.

b)
   - It is a 'mean' average that does not show the degree of inequality of the income distribution. This makes the GDP per capita less accurate as a true reflection of the income of a citizen in that country. (use Gini index data from Table 3)
   - It does not take social factors into account that impact on living standards; health, education, political freedom, environment, cultural amenities. The **Human Development Index** attempts to monitor this. (use life expectancy data from Table 3)
   - It will not include subsistence farming (Mozambique) or take into account fully the size of the grey economy of a nation (Italy).

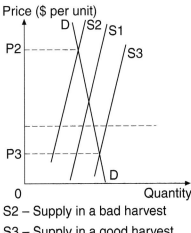

S2 – Supply in a bad harvest
S3 – Supply in a good harvest
P2-P3 – Potential price from one season to the next

Figure 1 Price instability

Definitions

The **dependency ratio** measures the economically inactive population as a proportion of the total working population (employed + unemployed). Economically inactive dependants include children, the elderly/retired and housewives.

The **Human Development Index** is calculated by the United Nations Development Programme. It measures longevity, knowledge and resources as components of living standards. One third of the index is given to real GDP per capita, one third to life expectancy and the final third to literacy rates and school enrolment.

Exam guidance and practice

Exam guidance

Exam hint

Read the questions before each passage to make better use of your time. You could use different coloured pens to annotate the passages as you read them, to highlight sections that are relevant for particular questions.

Exam hint

Remember that the data and prose has been deliberately selected for the questions set. It is unlikely that there will be irrelevant material. It is often a useful exercise to consider whether each table or excerpt provides any suitable source material for each question. This will maximise your 'application' marks.

Boost your grade

Watch out for the keyword in the question. Many candidates write good analytical answers that demonstrate clear understanding but fail to evaluate their argument. This might limit their maximum score to 12 on a question worth 20 marks. 'Assess, to what extent and examine' are all evaluative keywords.

Exam guidance

Unit 5b is worth 15% of the overall A-level grade (30% of the A2 marks).

You must attempt ONE of two data response questions with a time constraint of one and a half hours. Most candidates find this a little less of a problem than in Unit 4. Question selection is clearly vital here and it is certainly advisable to spend *up to the first 15 minutes* reading the passages to make the appropriate choice. There will probably be four questions totalling 60 marks on each data response. Try and ensure that you allocate your time according to the marks for each question, for example, a 20 mark question should take about a third of your writing time, or about 25 minutes, if you spend the full 15 minutes reading the passages.

It is useful to bear the four assessment objectives in mind when constructing your answers; *knowledge, application, analysis* and *evaluation.* The knowledge component will make up 15% of the paper and you will gain these marks by demonstrating relevant understanding of the specific content of the question. The application marks are also 15% of the paper and you can gain these by using relevant examples to support your argument, either through examples that you have learned or by using relevant information/quotes from the passage. The higher order skills of analysis and evaluation are worth 30% and 40% respectively of the total marks on the unit. For the analysis component, you must develop your argument through extended chains of economic reasoning. Evaluative content can be demonstrated in several ways; by differentiating short and long run effects, by assessing the magnitude of the effect under discussion, by providing a counter-argument or exposing the weak assumptions behind an argument or by weighing up the strengths of the points raised on both sides of an argument and forming a judgement.

For example, in a question asking you to examine the effects of international trade on the Zambian economy, you might explain that export earnings from copper sales act as an injection and are a component of aggregate demand (*knowledge* and *application*). This could then be developed by explaining how the multiplier effects of this injection boost incomes and employment in the non-tradable sectors of the Zambian economy, as well as in the copper industry and then illustrate your argument with an aggregate demand and supply diagram showing the AD shifting to the right and generating economic growth (*analysis*). You could then examine this argument by explaining that since the Zambian economy suffers from a sectoral imbalance in their dependency on the primary sector they do not have very well-developed consumer goods industries and therefore a large amount of the income earned by the people working in the copper industry will be spent on imports and will not generate significant multiplier effects in the domestic economy. The copper mining companies may be multinationals that repatriate their profits into developed world financial institutions rather than saving them in Zambia. This might limit the funds

available in Zambian banks to provide capital for investment and constrain
future growth possibilities (*evaluation*).

Exam practice

	GDP, $ mns		Agriculture, % of GDP		Industry, % of GDP		Services, % of GDP	
	1990	1999	1990	1999	1990	1999	1990	1999
Central African Republic	1488	1053	48	55	20	20	33	25
Congo, Dem. Rep.	9348	5584	30	58	28	17	42	25
Germany	1,770,368	2,111,940	1	1	33	28	64	71
Hungary	33,056	48,436	15	6	39	34	46	61
Poland	61,197	155,166	8	3	48	31	44	65
Uganda	4304	6411	57	44	11	18	32	38
UK	987,641	1,441,787	2	1	31	25	67	74

Source: World Bank Development Indicators 2001.

Table 1 Sectoral share of output in a number of countries

a) Compare the growth performances of these nations over the 1990s. What
   factors might explain the trends?   (15 marks)
b) Suggest reasons why the structure of these economies have changed over
   the period.   (15 marks)

Some hints

Group the nations into 3 distinct categories to simplify the analysis rather
than talking individually about each. The most logical groups would be the
three African nations, the two transition economies of Hungary and Poland
and the developed economies of Germany and the UK. However, it is a good
idea to be careful about making generalisations. Uganda has clearly grown
while the other two African nations have shrunk (largely as a by-product of
civil wars). Use *comparative* language as this is specified in the question, for
example, the transition nations grew *faster* on average over the 1990s than
the other nations shown, in the move away from their command economic
systems (largely attributable to significant foreign direct investment flows
into Hungary and Poland).

Manipulate the data rather than just repeating the table, for example, you
could calculate the rates of growth 1990-1999. You might point out that the
data could be misleading if the exchange rates of the nations against the
US$ have moved significantly out of line with the purchasing power of these
nations over the period shown.

Further reading

5b.2

F. Nixson, *Development Economics*, 2nd edn., Heinemann, 2001, Chapters 1 and 2.

5b.3

C. Bamford and S. Grant, *The UK Economy in a Global Context*, Heinemann, 2000, Chapter 7.

S. Grant, *Economic Growth and Business Cycles*, Heinemann, 1999, Chapters 2–5.

F. Nixson, *Development Economics*, 2nd edn., Heinemann, 2001, Chapter 7.

5b.4

S. Grant, *Economic Growth and Business Cycles*, Heinemann, 1999, Chapter 3.

F. Nixson, *Development Economics*, 2nd edn., Heinemann, 2001, Chapter 3.

5b.5

F. Nixson, *Development Economics*, 2nd edn., Heinemann, 2001, Chapter 7.

5b.6

F. Nixson, *Development Economics*, 2nd edn., Heinemann, 2001, Chapters 4 and 9.

5b.7

F. Nixson, *Development Economics*, 2nd edn., Heinemann, 2001, Chapters 5 and 7.

5b.8

S. Grant, *Economic Growth and Business Cycles*, Heinemann, 1999, Chapter 4.

F. Nixson, *Development Economics*, 2nd edn., Heinemann, 2001, Chapters 6 and 7.

5b.9

F. Nixson, *Development Economics*, 2nd edn., Heinemann, 2001, Chapter 8.

5b.10

S. Grant, *Economic Growth and Business Cycles*, Heinemann, 1999, Chapter 4.

F. Nixson, *Development Economics*, 2nd edn., Heinemann, 2001, Chapters 3 and 7.

5b.11

F. Nixson, *Development Economics*, 2nd edn., Heinemann, 2001, Chapters 1, 9 and 10.

PART 6

THE UK IN THE GLOBAL ECONOMY

Introduction to the UK in the global economy

This module develops and extends the knowledge and understanding you gained in AS Module 3, 'Managing the economy'. It also introduces new areas of study with particular emphasis being placed on international trade and exchange rate issues.

Coverage of the module

The module covers:

- globalisation
- international trade
- protectionism
- the balance of payments
- international competitiveness
- exchange rate systems
- European Monetary Union (EMU)
- foreign direct investment (FDI)
- government spending and taxation
- macroeconomic performance.

You will already have some background knowledge on some of these areas from your AS studies. At A2 level, you will explore them in more depth and, as the title of the module suggests, in a global context. You will apply additional theories and concepts, including the law of comparative advantage, monetary union and the Phillips curve. You will also be able to make considerable use of AD and AS analysis and your understanding of the effectiveness of fiscal, monetary and supply-side policies will prove to be very useful.

At A2 level, the skills of analysis and evaluation are very important. The sections reflect this emphasis, frequently analysing and assessing different views on economic relationships, causes of economic problems and appropriate government policies.

The exam

This module is assessed in a unit paper lasting one hour and 45 minutes. The exam counts for 20 per cent of your total A-level mark and consists of one structured essay question chosen from three and one data response question chosen from two.

Maximising your grade

You can do well in this module if you:

- show an awareness of recent changes in the UK economy
- recognise the potential benefits and costs of international trade
- appreciate the links between the UK economy and other economies
- apply relevant economic concepts to analysing macroeconomic issues

- make judgements about the causes, consequences and remedies to economic problems
- write clearly.

You should have an awareness of changes in government policies and trends in economic growth, inflation, unemployment, the current account position and the pattern and nature of international trade over the last ten years. You need to know how to interpret trends in data, to assess information critically and to decide on appropriate policies to tackle particular economic problems.

You must select the essay question carefully. Make sure that you can do well on both parts of the question. Once you have selected the question, spend 5 minutes planning your answer. Then answer it directly, supporting your answer with relevant economic theory, awareness of recent events and well-supported evaluative comments.

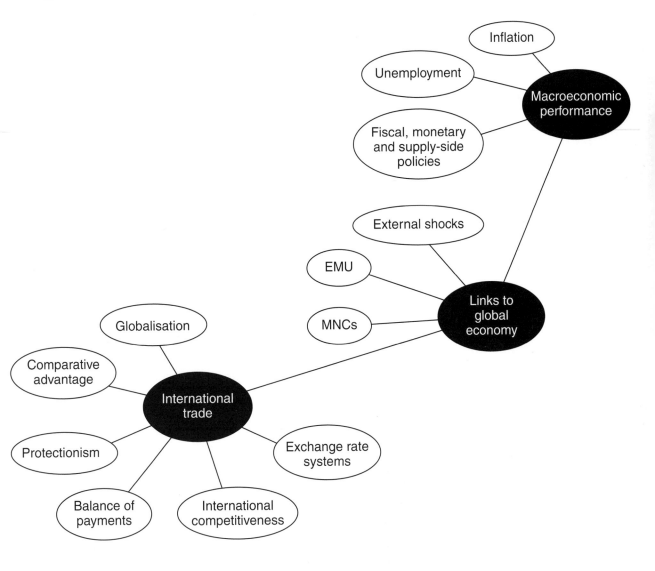

Globalisation

6.2

The UK is operating in a global economy. Advances in technology and reductions in transport costs are enabling UK consumers to access markets throughout the world. UK firms are selling their products throughout the world and locating separate parts of their production processes in a range of countries. However, as the demonstrations which regularly occur at meetings of the World Trade Organisation and other international organisations show, some people are concerned about the effects of globalisation.

The meaning of globalisation

Globalisation is the development of the world into one marketplace. National barriers are being broken down in terms of where firms make their products and where people buy their goods and services.

Countries have always traded with each other, but now the scale of the movement of goods, services, ideas and capital investment between countries is increasing rapidly. The production processes and patterns of consumption are becoming more and more integrated. Consumers in, for example, China, France and Nigeria buy more of the same products such as Manchester United football strips and Coca-Cola. Parts of products, including cars and toys, are being assembled in a number of industrialised and developing countries.

Features of globalisation

Globalisation is manifesting itself through the rapid increase in international trade, which is growing faster than world output, and an increase in FDI (the movement of physical capital between countries).

Other periods – for example, the end of the nineteenth and start of the twentieth centuries – have witnessed rapid increases in international trade and international capital movements, but this time these have also been accompanied by the growth of **multinational companies (MNCs)**. These are increasingly thinking and operating globally, not only owning plants in different countries but also engaging in the fragmentation of production. This involves MNCs spreading different stages of production around the world, sometimes using their own plants and sometimes a combination of their own plants and other firms' plants. So when the managers of MNCs plan their production processes, they do not simply consider producing a product in one location. Instead, they think transnationally – they consider assembling parts in a range of countries and they use a decentralised management structure.

There has also been an increase in the number of countries producing manufactured goods for export.

Synoptic links

This section builds on the knowledge and understanding of international trade you gain in AS sections 3.14 and 3.22.

Research task

Using the ONS Monthly Digest of Statistics, analyse the extent to which China has become an increasingly important trading partner for the UK.

Definition

Multinational companies (MNCs) are companies that produce products in several different countries.

Causes of globalisation

Globalisation is occurring as a result of the following.

- Improved communication – advances in information and computer technology are increasing the ease with which consumers can find out about and buy products from other countries and the ease with which producers can co-ordinate production throughout the world. For example, consumers in the UK now regularly use the Internet to order CDs, books and so on from the USA and other countries. Managers of UK MNCs keep in touch with their staff in other countries using a range of information and computer technology, including e-mail and teleconferencing.
- Reduced transport costs – over time, with the development of containerisation and increasing use of larger ships and plans, transport costs have been falling.
- Trade liberalisation – since World War II, the barriers to the free movement of goods, services and capital have been reducing.
- Increased competition in manufactured goods – this is coming from developing countries, particularly from the **newly industrialised countries (NICs)** of south-east Asia such as South Korea and Singapore.
- The rise in skill levels throughout the world – this is enabling MNCs to assemble products and parts of products not only in industrialised countries but also in developing countries.

Definitions

Newly industrialised countries (NICS) are countries or economies that have experienced a rapid rate of growth of their manufacturing sector – most noticeably, the Asian tigers.

Consequences of globalisation

Globalisation is changing the nature of international trade. An increasingly high percentage of international trade consists of the exchange of similar products from the same industries (for example, different makes of computers from China to the USA and from the USA to China). A smaller percentage consists of different products from different industries (for example, textiles from India to France and cars from France to India). At the start of the twentieth century, manufactured goods were being exported from Europe and the USA to developing countries in return for raw materials. Now, at the start of the twenty-first century, Europe and the USA are still exporting manufactured goods to developing countries – but in return for manufactured goods.

More and more firms are thinking globally. As has already been noted, advances in technology and transport are enabling firms to target consumers throughout the world and to operate in a range of countries. FDI is increasing. MNCs are seeking out the lowest cost countries in which to locate production and parts of the production process. Indeed, some are now being referred to as transnational companies, as they have substantial operations in a large number of countries and have a decentralised management structure.

Globalisation is increasing the susceptibility of countries to external crises. The increased integration of economies means that the problems in one part of the world quickly spread to other countries. This was seen during the East

Asian Crisis of 1997–99. The difficulties faced by financial institutions and other companies in Japan, Thailand, Indonesia and other east Asian countries slowed down world growth, reduced aggregate demand in the West and caused problems for US and European firms and banks with links to the Far East.

The more integrated nature of the world economy is increasing the role of international organisations in overseeing world trade, including the World Trade Organisation (WTO) and the International Monetary Fund (IMF). It seeks to reduce tariffs and other restrictions on international trade, and provides a means by which countries can settle their trade disputes. The IMF was established in 1947 with the main aim of encouraging world trade. It acts as an international bank offering assistance to countries in financial difficulties and was discussed in section 5b.11.

Globalisation is also changing countries' comparative advantage (see section 6.3). The rise in the level of competition coming particularly from the newly industrialised countries is causing a shift in resources in Europe and the USA.

Price differences between countries are being reduced. A market is said to be completely integrated when identical products sell at the same price in different countries.

Thinking like an economist

Analyse the effects that globalisation is likely to bring about in demand for labour in industrialised countries and in developing countries.

Quickies

1 What is causing globalisation to occur?
2 Explain two possible advantages and two possible disadvantages of globalisation for UK consumers.
3 What is meant by 'firms thinking transnationally'?
4 What factors could slow down globalisation?

Puzzler

Will globalisation lead to greater prosperity or greater inequality?

I n section 5b.9, the nature of comparative advantage was examined. In this section, the effects of globalisation on comparative advantage are discussed. The benefits and costs of international trade are also considered.

Globalisation and comparative advantage

As noted in section 6.2, globalisation is changing countries' comparative advantage. Developing countries are becoming more efficient at producing manufactured goods. Their comparative advantage at the moment is mainly in manufacturing industries that make use of low-skilled labour. They have a large supply of low-skilled workers, which means their wage rates are lower.

In the past, this did not result in a comparative advantage because although wages were low, so was productivity and, as a result, unit wage costs were high. However, now with rises in productivity, particularly in NIEs, unit wage costs have been falling. Some commentators have expressed concern that this will result in a rise in unemployment and a fall in wages in industrialised countries. Their fear is that MNCs will locate more of their processes in developing countries, and that developing countries' firms will gain a larger share of the market for manufactured goods.

However, this is only part of the picture. It is not so much that industrialised countries are facing a fall in demand for their output, but that a shift in demand from some products towards other products has resulted from changes in relative efficiencies. Resources will have to shift to reflect these changes and this process is already underway.

Average wages are not falling in most industrialised countries, but the wages of unskilled workers are falling relative to skilled workers. Industries producing goods and services requiring high-skilled labour are experiencing rises in demand, while some relying on low-skilled labour are facing lower demand. In the case of the UK, some processes are being relocated to lower production cost countries, but at the same time FDI is being attracted by the high-skilled labour force of the country.

Therefore, while jobs requiring low skill levels are declining, jobs requiring high skill levels are increasing. To ease the shift in resources, educational and vocational qualifications need to rise.

Of course, the situation is always changing, and economies and their citizens have to be adaptable. Currently, the UK has a comparative advantage in, for example, oil, financial services, business services and scientific instruments. However, in a few years' time, with skill levels rising throughout the world and patterns of demand and supply changing, this may alter.

Synoptic link

It is important that before you start this section you should reread A2 section 5b.9 to ensure that you have a good grasp of comparative advantage.

Benefits and costs of international trade

If countries specialise and trade, total output should be greater than it would be otherwise. The resulting rise in living standards is the main benefit claimed for free international trade.

Consumers can benefit from the lower prices and higher quality that result from the higher level of competition that arises from countries trading internationally. They also enjoy a greater variety of products – including a few not made in their own countries.

Although firms will face greater competition in their domestic markets, they will also have access to larger markets in which to sell their products (enabling them to take greater advantage of economies of scale) and from which to buy raw materials.

However, despite all these advantages and increasing trade liberalisation, restrictions on exports and, more particularly, imports still exist. Concern that certain undesirable products may be imported, that the continued existence of new and strategic industries may be threatened and that other countries may not engage in fair competition are among the explanations given by the government for such restrictions. These points are examined in more detail in A2 section 6.5.

International trade provides countries with challenges. Competition from other countries and access to their markets results in some industries contracting and some expanding. This requires the shifting of resources, which can be unsettling and may be difficult to achieve due to, for example, occupational immobility of labour.

Thinking like an economist

Explain three benefits a UK insurance company could gain from engaging in international trade.

Quickies

1   Why is productivity rising in NIEs?
2   Why does the UK no longer have a comparative advantage in textiles?
3   What is the main benefit of international trade?
4   Which firms benefit from international trade?

Puzzler

Why did James Dyson relocate his vacuum-manufacturing firm from Swindon to Malaysia?

F ree trade occurs when there are no restrictions imposed on the movement of goods and services into and out of countries. In contrast, **protectionism** refers to the deliberate restriction of the free movement of goods and services between countries and trade blocs. A government engages in protectionism when it introduces measures to protect its own industries from competition from the industries of other countries.

Methods of protection

Tariffs

Tariffs (which can also be called customs duties or import duties) are taxes on imported products. They can be imposed with the intention of raising revenue and/or discouraging domestic consumers from buying imported products. For example, the EU's common external tariff, which is a tax on imports coming into the EU from countries outside, does raise revenue but its main purpose is to encourage EU member countries to trade with each other.

Tariffs can be *ad valorem* (percentage taxes) or specific (fixed sum taxes). The effect of imposing a tariff is to raise the price to domestic consumers and, in the absence of any retaliation, shift demand from imports to domestically produced products.

Figure 1 shows the effect of a specific tariff. Before the country engages in international trade, the price is P and the quantity purchased is Q, all of which comes from domestic suppliers. When the country engages in international trade, the number of producers in the market increases significantly. The increase in competition drives price down to P1.

The quantity demanded, meanwhile, extends to Q1. Of this amount, QX is now bought from domestic suppliers and QX–Q1 from foreign firms. So domestic supply falls from Q to QX.

The imposition of a tariff also causes the world supply to decrease to WS1. It raises the price to P2 and causes the quantity to be purchased on the domestic market to fall to Q2. Domestic supply rises to QY and imports fall to QY–Q2. Domestic producers gain but this is at the expense of domestic suppliers.

Finally, consumer surplus falls by the area *a–e*. Domestic producer surplus rises by *a* and the governmant gains tax revenue of *c* and *d*. There is a net welfare loss of *b* and *e*.

Non-tariff measures

Non-tariff measures include the following.

- Quotas – a quota is a limit on the supply of a good or service. It can be imposed on exports. For example, a developing country may seek to limit the export of food during a period of food shortages. However, quotas on imports are more common. For example, a quota may place a restriction on the imports of cars to, say, 40,000 a year. The effect of a quota is to

Synoptic link

Import restrictions were discussed in AS section 3.22. This section explores tariffs and quotas in more depth and discusses a range of other measures.

Definitions

Protectionism is the restriction on the free movement of products between countries.

Tariffs are a tax on imports.

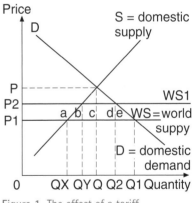

Figure 1 The effect of a tariff

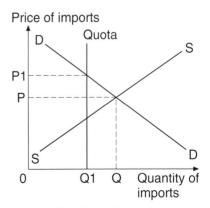

Figure 2 The effect of a quota

reduce supply. This is likely to push up price. Foreign firms will experience a reduction in the quantity they can sell, but they may benefit from the higher price if demand for their products is inelastic and if the quotas are not operated via the selling of import licences.

- Voluntary export restraint or restriction (VER) – this measure is similar to a quota, but this time the limit on imports arises from a voluntary agreement between the exporting and importing countries. A country may agree to restrict its exports in return for a similar limit being put on the exports of the importing country or to avoid more damaging import restrictions being imposed on its products. VERs have been used frequently by the EU and the USA. For example, the EU entered into several VERs with Japan, which restricted the sale of Japanese cars.

- Exchange control – a government or an area may seek to reduce imports by limiting the amount of foreign exchange made available to those wishing to import goods and services or to invest or to travel abroad. This measure was used by a number of European countries, including the UK, in the 1960s and 1970s and is still found in some developing countries.

- Embargoes – an embargo is a ban on the export or import of a product and/or a ban on trade with a particular country. For example, a country may ban the export of arms to a country with a poor human rights record and may prohibit the importation of hard core pornography. They are also likely to break off trading relations with a country during a military conflict.

- Import deposit schemes – the UK made use of import deposit schemes in the 1960s. These schemes involve requiring importers to deposit a given sum of money with a government before they can import products. The intention is to increase the cost, in terms of time and money, of importing.

- Time delaying customs procedures – these are designed to have a similar effect as import deposit schemes. If it takes time to complete long and complex customs forms, it will be more expensive to import products.

- Quality standards – a government may use quantity standards as a means of limiting imports. They may set high and complex requirements with the intention of raising the costs for foreign firms seeking to export to the country.

- Government purchasing policies – a government may try to reduce imports by favouring domestic firms when it places orders, even when the domestic firms are producing at a higher cost or lower quality.

- Subsidies – subsidies given to domestic firms may be used as an indirect way of protecting them. The subsidies may enable relatively high cost domestic firms to undercut more efficient foreign firms in the domestic market.

Puzzler

Are quality standards always a form of unfair competition?

Several arguments can be put forward for imposing restrictions on free trade. These include:

- raising revenue
- protecting the whole industrial base of the country
- protecting particular industries
- recently, protecting domestic standards of, for example, food safety, environment and labour market conditions.

Raising revenue

The imposition of tariffs enables governments to raise revenue. This is no longer a major motive behind industrial countries imposing import duties, but the revenue received by some developing countries is a significant proportion of their tax revenue.

Protecting the whole industrial base

There are many arguments, which will be addressed in turn. The first is protecting domestic employment. This argument was used by a number of countries in the 1930s, when countries in the West were going through a depression. It was thought that if a country imposed import restrictions, it would mean that its citizens would purchase more domestic products and thereby raise domestic employment. This concentration on domestic employment at the expense of other countries led to such measures being referred to as 'beggar my neighbour' policies. However, imposing import restrictions is likely to result in a reduction in other countries' abilities to buy the country's exports and may provoke retaliation. So the country's exports may decline and any jobs created by imports may be offset by jobs lost due to the fall in exports. Indeed, the level of unemployment may rise if the imposition of tariffs results in a trade war with countries raising their tariffs higher and higher – building 'tariff walls' around their countries. There will also be a welfare loss resulting from countries not being able to specialise to any great extent in those products that give them a comparative advantage.

The next argument involves improving the country's balance of payments position. One reaction to a situation where expenditure on imports exceeds revenue from exports is to place restrictions on imports. The intention is to switch domestic expenditure from imports to expenditure on domestic products. However, the same risks and disadvantages apply to this argument as to the one above – that is, it may provoke a price war and it reduces the degree of specialisation. In addition, just imposing import restrictions in the absence of any other policy measures does not solve the cause of the balance of payments deficit. If domestic consumers are purchasing imports because their quality is higher, for example, they may still continue to buy imports even after the restrictions have been imposed.

Another method involves protecting the country's industries from 'unfair low wage competition' from abroad. This would involve putting restrictions on

Synoptic link

This section explores the arguments for and against the imposition of the methods of protectionism you examined in A2 section 6.4.

imports from certain countries. Some argue that if the wages paid to workers in developing countries are very low, then firms in industrial countries will not be able to compete unless they reduce wages to unacceptably low levels. However, low wages do not always mean low unit wage costs. Due to a lack of capital equipment and education, labour productivity in a number of countries is low.

Being able to sell products without restrictions to industrial countries may enable income levels to rise in developing countries. This may result in a rise in their levels of investment, education, wages and purchases of products from industrial countries.

The competition from low wage countries may also reflect the fact that those countries have a comparative advantage in low-skilled, labour intensive industries – in which case, unemployment in certain industries may rise but the rise in unemployment may be a temporary situation if that labour can move into the industries in which the country does have a comparative advantage.

Where the case for imposing restrictions has more justification is where wages are being held below the equilibrium rates, the working conditions are poor and child or slave labour is employed.

Another argument requires the country to maintain a diversified industrial base. Import restrictions may be imposed on a range of products in order to ensure that a number of domestic industries survive. The intention would be to avoid the risks that arise with a high level of specialisation. For example, if a developing country's employment and income is dependent on a few industries, there is a risk that world fluctuations in demand and supply side problems can result in significant falls in economic activity.

Finally, restrictions may be imposed to improve the terms of trade. The terms of trade refers to the relationship between a country's export and import prices and is measured by calculating:

$$\frac{\text{Index of export prices} \times 100}{\text{Index of export prices}}$$

If a country is a dominant buyer of a product or products (monopsonist or oligopsonist) then placing restrictions on imports may force the sellers to lower their prices in order to remain competitive on the domestic market. If this occurs the country will be able to purchase its imports more cheaply. The fall in the price of imports will improve the terms of trade.

Protecting particular industries

One argument for protecting particular industries is to prevent dumping. Dumping occurs when firms sell their products at less than cost price. Foreign firms may engage in dumping because government subsidies permit them to sell at very low prices or because they are seeking to raise profits by price discriminating. In the latter case, the initial reason for exporting products at a low price may be to dispose of stocks of the good. In this case, consumers in the importing country will benefit. However, their longer-term objective may be to drive out domestic producers and gain a strong market position. In this case, consumers are likely to lose out as a result of the reduction in choice and the higher prices the exporters feel able to charge.

Another argument is to enable **infant industries** to grow. Infant industries (which are also called sunrise industries) are newly established industries. The firms in such industries may find it difficult to develop because their average costs may be higher than their well-established foreign competitors. However, if they are given protection in their early years, they may be able to grow and thereby take greater advantage of economies of scale, lower their average costs and become competitive. At this stage the protection could be removed. The infant industry argument is thought to be particularly strong in the case of high technology industries, which have high fixed costs and a potential comparative advantage. However, there is a risk that the industries may become dependent on protection.

Protecting industries can also permit declining industries to go out of business gradually. Declining industries (also called sunset industries) are likely to be industries that no longer have a comparative advantage. However, if they go out of business quickly there may be a sudden and large increase in unemployment. Protection may enable an industry to contract gradually, thereby allowing time for resources, including labour, to move to other industries.

Protecting certain industries may enable them to regain their comparative advantage. Industries may have lost their comparative advantage due to a lack of investment. A case may be made to protect them temporarily while additional investment is made.

Finally, it may be advantageous to protect strategic industries. This is more of a political than an economic argument. Many countries believe it is important to have a degree of self-sufficiency in certain industries – including arms and agriculture in case disputes or military conflicts cut off supplies.

Protecting domestic standards

Countries have traditionally placed restrictions, including embargoes, on demerit goods – for example, drugs and pornography. However, in recent years domestic regulations on food safety, labour conditions and environmental standards have increasingly been acting as trade restrictions.

Although countries may be keen on free trade in theory, in practice many are reluctant to compromise domestic policy in sensitive areas such as genetically modified foods. As mentioned in Part 1 in the AS book, economies are becoming more closely connected through trade and investment, so a government policy can have a discriminatory impact on foreign firms. For example, the EU has banned all hormone-treated beef, largely because of public concern about food safety. This has hit US farmers in particular, as there is widespread use of hormones in US beef farming.

Thinking like an economist

Analyse the effect of a US firm dumping products in the UK on UK consumers.

Definition

An **Infant industry** is a newly established industry that has not yet grown large enough to take full advantage of the available economies of scale.

Making connections

Identify three internal economies of scale that a newly established car company is likely to be able to take advantage of.

Trade barriers are being reduced within trade blocs but trade barriers still exist between different trade blocs. The existence of these barriers sometimes gives rise to trade wars. There is pressure, however, being placed on trade blocs and individual countries to liberalise their international trade.

Trade blocs

The breakdown of trade barriers has actually occurred mainly within groups of countries operating as trade blocs. There are four main types of trade blocs with increasing degrees of integration:

- free trade areas
- customs unions
- common markets
- Economic and Monetary Union.

Synoptic links

This section builds on A2 sections 6.4 and 6.5 and is also linked to section 6.10.

Free trade areas

Countries within a free trade area remove restrictions between each other but are free to operate whatever trade restrictions they wish on non-members. The members have to make some provision, usually via maintaining customs points, to prevent imports to the area coming in via the country with the lowest tariffs.

Examples of free trade areas include the North American Free Trade Agreement (NAFTA) consisting of:

- Canada
- the USA
- Mexico.

The ASEAN (Association of South East Asian Nations) consisting of:

- Brunei
- Indonesia
- Malaysia
- the Philippines
- Singapore
- Thailand.

Customs unions

The members of a customs union not only remove trade restrictions between each other but also agree to operate the same import restrictions on non-member countries. An example is MERCOSUR, which consists of Brazil, Argentina, Paraguay and Uruguay, and operates a common external tariff.

Common markets

These not only have no import restrictions between member countries and a common external tariff, but also permit the free movement of labour and capital between its members. In 1986, the Single Market Act was signed which moved what was then the EC, but has since become the EU, towards a single market.

Economic and Monetary Union (EMU)

This takes integration several stages further by introducing a single currency, similar labour market policies and some degree of tax harmonisation. The Maastricht Treaty of 1992 started the move of the EU towards EMU.

Trade blocs and conflicts

As the EU has become more integrated and powerful economic force, it has come into more conflict with the USA and NAFTA. The USA complains particularly about the EU's protection of its farming and film industries .

In 1997 and 1998, the USA protested to the WTO about the privileged market access given to the export of bananas from former British and French colonies in Africa, the Caribbean and Pacific under the Lome convention at the expense of cheaper Latin American bananas.

In 1999, it imposed retaliatory tariffs of more than US$190 million on a range of European goods after the EU failed to comply with a WTO ruling requiring it to restructure its banana import regime to prevent the discrimination against Latin American exporters.

The EU, in turn, is concerned about the noise levels caused by US aeroplanes, about hormone-treated beef and about genetically modified food. At the start of the 2000s, a trade dispute broke out over the EU's ban on US hormone-treated beef.

So while the EU and the USA are keen to open markets for their exporters, they are much more reluctant in practice to open their own markets. Countries outside trade blocs, particularly developing countries, feel discriminated against. They do not obtain the benefits of belonging to a trade bloc, but have restrictions imposed on their products by the EU, the USA and other countries.

Pressure for trade liberalisation

The key pressure to remove restrictions on the movement of goods and services across national borders is recognition of the benefits that free trade can bring.

If countries specialise and trade, total output, and hence living standards, should be greater. Consumers can benefit from the lower prices, higher quality and greater variety that result from the higher level of competition that arises from countries trading internationally.

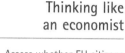

Thinking like an economist

Assess whether EU citizens would benefit from the EU giving some non-EU goods greater access to its market.

Bananas at war

Making connections

Explain the likely effect of trade liberalisation on productive and allocative efficiency.

Although firms will face greater competition in their domestic markets, they will also have access to larger markets in which to sell their products (enabling them to take greater advantage of economies of scale) and from which to buy raw materials.

Import restrictions reduce competitive pressure and can lead to a misallocation of resources. The Common Agricultural Policy (CAP) of the EU has come in for particular criticism. CAP consists of a series of measures to promote and regulate agriculture in the EU. These include production subsidies, investment grants, direct income payments and minimum prices.

CAP sets prices for a range of agricultural products including butter, cereals and meat above the world equilibrium price. Figure 1 shows the effect of setting a minimum price of butter above the market price.

To maintain price at this artificially high level, two main measures are used. The interventionist agency of CAP buys up the surplus created and an import tax (tariff) is placed on produce from outside the EU. Some of the surplus is destroyed, some stored and some is exported at low, subsidised prices. The import tax is set so that the price of non-EU produce is above that of the minimum price.

CAP creates unfair competition with developing countries. Tariffs imposed on developing countries' agricultural products makes it difficult for them to compete. The EU is the second largest exporter of agricultural products in the world but it does not have a comparative advantage in the vast majority of these products.

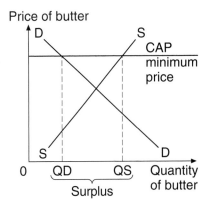

Figure 1 The effect of setting a minimum price

Quickies

1 Distinguish between a free trade area and a customs union.
2 In what sense may protectionism impose a cost on a country or trade area?
3 What is the role of the WTO?
4 In what sense does the CAP distort comparative advantage?

Exam hint

In answering essay questions on the arguments for and against protectionism, make sure you focus on the arguments – do not devote too much time just describing the methods of protection.

6.7 The balance of payments

The sections of the balance of payments were introduced in AS sections 3.2 and 3.14. AS Section 3.22 gave an outline of possible policy measures that could be used to correct a balance of payments deficit. This section examines in more depth the UK's international trade performance and three policy measures to correct a deficit.

Synoptic links

AS sections 3.2, 3.14 and 3.22 examined the format of the balance of payments, current account deficits and surpluses and policies to improve the balance of payments. Before you examine these issues in more depth, it would be beneficial to reread these AS sections.

The sections of the balance of payments

As noted in AS sections 3.2 and 3.14, the balance of payments account consists of a number of sub-groups. These are:

- the current account
- the capital account
- the financial account
- the international investment position.

The current account is influenced by:

- the international competitiveness of the goods and services produced
- the amount of income earned and paid on overseas investments and financial assets and liabilities.

The financial account covers the flow of investment into and out of the UK – including direct investment, a significant amount of which is carried out by multinational companies.

Balance of payments disequilibrium

A country that lacks international competitiveness may experience a deficit on its current account. It will earn less from the sale of its exports of goods and services than it spends on imports of goods and services if its products are more expensive and/or of a lower quality than its rivals.

The UK usually has a deficit on its current account. As its trade in services and its investment income are usually in surplus, this suggests that the UK has a competitive weakness in its trade in goods.

Export performance

International trade is significant for the UK. The country exports approximately 32 per cent of all the goods it produces and imports approximately 36 per cent of all the goods it consumes.

In terms of export intensity (the ratio of exports to domestic production), the UK has a similar record to other EU countries. However, this masks a decline in its performance in manufactured goods. This is partly because of the contribution of the oil industry to UK exports.

Import penetration

When the UK economy is growing, it tends to suck in imports. Since World War II, UK imports of primary products, such as food and tobacco, have declined in importance, while imports of finished manufactured products, for example TVs, cars and washing machines, have increased. **Import penetration** has increased more in the UK than in most other industrial economies and more rapidly than its export intensity ratios.

Definition

Import penetration is the ratio of imports to domestic consumption.

Causes of a poor trade performance

These include:

- Inflexibility – some countries produce products that are not in high and increasing world demand. Market conditions change and if resources are not reallocated quickly and smoothly, a country may find itself producing inappropriate products for its own consumers and for foreign buyers.
- High relative prices – if a country's prices are high relative to its competitors, it will lose some of its market share. A key influence here is unit labour costs, since a country with high unit labour costs is likely to have high prices.
- High income elasticity of demand for imports – for example, the UK's income elasticity of demand is high and currently higher than the income elasticity of demand for UK exports. This means that when world income rises, UK imports increase by more than UK exports.
- Poor quality – in terms of, for example, design, reliability, lifespan or inclusion of new technology. This in turn is influenced by research and development, technology and labour skills. This is linked to income elasticity of demand (YED). A country which produces low quality products is likely to have high YED for imports and low YED for exports.
- Poor marketing and sales – this includes advertising, delivery dates, packaging and after sales service.

Balance of payments policy measures

If a country continues to have large deficits on its current account, its government may decide to take action to increase its export revenue and/or reduce its import expenditure. There are a number of measures which it might consider taking, including:
- exchange rate adjustment
- demand management
- supply-side policies.

Exchange rate adjustment

A country may seek to reduce the value of its currency. If it is operating a fixed exchange rate, it will **devalue** its currency. If, however, it is operating a

Definition

Devaluation is the reduction of a fixed exchange rate from one value to a lower value by the government.

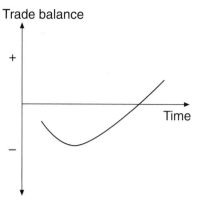

Trade balance

Figure 1 The J curve effect

floating or managed exchange rate, it will try to bring about a depreciation in the exchange rate.

This could be achieved by lowering the rate of interest and/or selling the currency. A lower value of the currency will cause export prices to fall in terms of foreign countries' currencies and import prices to rise in terms of the domestic currency.

The immediate effect may be to worsen the balance in trade in goods and services. This is because in the short run demand for exports and imports may be inelastic as it takes time for firms and consumers to recognise the price changes and to change their orders. In the longer run, it will be hoped that the trade position will improve. This tendency is known as the **J curve effect** and is illustrated in Figure 1.

However whether the position does improve or not will depend on:

- The price elasticities of demand for exports and imports – the **Marshall-Lerner condition** states that for a devaluation to be successful in improving the trade position, the combined price elasticities of demand for exports and imports must be greater than one.
- The reaction of other countries – if other countries reduce the value of their currencies, the effect will be negated.
- Import restrictions – if other countries increase their import restrictions, the devaluation may not be successful in increasing the volume of exports.
- Elasticity of supply – if demand for exports rises as a result of the fall in their price, it is important that more can be produced. So, reducing the exchange rate may not be considered to be an appropriate measure to take at a time of full or near full employment.
- Low propensity to import – if a high proportion of the extra income resulting from higher export earnings is spent on imports, the beneficial effect on the trade position will be reduced.

Reducing the value of the exchange rate is likely to increase aggregate demand. Such an increase may benefit employment and output in the short run. It may, however, generate inflationary pressure via both higher aggregate demand and higher import prices. A lower rate of interest is also likely to increase aggregate demand and may result in a government failing to achieve its inflation target.

Independent depreciation is not a policy option for a member of the single currency.

Demand management

Demand management involves the government manipulating aggregate demand to achieve its macroeconomic objectives. To correct a balance of payments deficit, the government may introduce fiscal and monetary measures designed to reduce total domestic spending.

Deflationary measures include higher taxation, lower government spending and/or higher interest rates. The intention is that people will buy fewer of all goods and services, including imported products. The lower demand may also put extra pressure on domestic firms to increase their sales abroad. Such deflationary measures are more likely to be adopted when an economy is experiencing higher levels of spending and supply constraints.

However, there is the risk that the resulting fall in aggregate demand may cause unemployment. In addition, if there are other causes of the deficit such as the poor quality of domestically produced products, the problem is likely to reappear.

Supply-side policies

If the cause of the deficit is thought to be a lack of competitiveness, a government may seek to improve economic performance through supply-side policies. These are measures which seek to increase aggregate supply by improving the quality and quantity of economic resources.

If the productive potential of the economy is increased through a rise in the quantity of resources, the country will be more able to satisfy its population's increasing demand for goods and services. Improved quality of resources, through, for example, increased research and development, higher investment and improved training, should reduce costs of production, increase innovation and raise the quality of the products produced. These should all make the products more attractive to both home and foreign consumers.

Indeed, to remain internationally competitive, it is important that a country's product and labour markets are able to respond quickly and fully to changes in comparative advantage. Supply-side policies are likely to play a key role in achieving such flexibility.

Quickies

1   Why does the UK usually have a current account deficit?
2   Why is a fall in the value of the currency unlikely to cause an immediate improvement in the country's trade position?
3   In what circumstances may a fall in the value of the currency increase the country's export revenue?
4   Explain how an increase in income tax may improve the country's trade in goods and services balance.

Puzzler

Will a rise in the rate of interest always increase the value of exports?

International competitiveness, multinational companies and foreign direct investment

Synoptic links

See AS section 3.22 and A2 section 5b.11 for links to this section.

Definition

Foreign direct investment refers to the setting up of foreign subsidiaries or the acquisition of a lasting management interest in a foreign company (more than 10% of the voting shares in that company).

Making connections

What is the connection between FDI and the current account position?

The UK is a main recipient of inward **foreign direct investment (FDI)** in the EU, although its share has fallen since 1999. The presence of foreign multinational companies in the country can bring a number of advantages including the introduction of new technology. Such advantages should help to raise the country's international competitiveness.

Foreign direct investment

UK MNCs invest abroad and foreign multinational companies invest in the UK. This investment includes:

- the establishment of new plants
- the expansion of existing plants
- the purchase of existing plants and firms.

MNCs seek the highest return on their capital. So, the amount of foreign direct investment attracted by a country is influenced by the productivity and flexibility of its workers, its tax rates, the stability of its economic policies, its rate of economic growth, the size of its market and the perception of its future economic prospects.

The UK is currently an attractive location for FDI because of the following.

- Government grants – especially for MNCs setting up in the poorer regions of the UK.
- It has a flexible labour force.
- It has a time zone advantage in financial services.
- Its membership of the EU – setting up in the UK gives, for example, a Japanese or US multinational company access to the EU market without having to pay the common external tariff. However, some economists (as noted in Part 3 of the AS book) believe that if the UK continues to stay out of the single currency, FDI may be reduced.
- The use of the English language – this is the main language of the Internet and is frequently used in international business. In addition, it is obviously spoken by Americans and is the most popular foreign language learnt by the Japanese and South Koreans.

Effects of foreign direct investment

The initial effect of FDI is an inflow of investment, which will appear as a credit item in the financial account. However, in the longer run, money will flow out of the country in the form of investment income (profit, interest and dividends), which will appear in the current account. The goods and services that the multinational company sells abroad will count in the country's exports. The net effect on imports is rather more uncertain. Some goods and services that had previously been bought abroad from the MNCs may now be purchased from their plants in the home country. However, the MNC may purchase some of their raw materials and services from their home countries.

MNCs may cause a rise in employment. This is one of the key reasons that governments give grants to MNCs to set up in their countries. They hope that the MNCs will increase employment directly by taking on workers and indirectly by increasing economic activity and demand in the area in which they are based. However, some of those employed by the MNCs, particularly in top management posts, may be bought over from the home country. Even more significantly, if the competition from MNCs leads to domestic firms going out of business, they will not be creating employment, merely replacing jobs.

MNCs, especially in developing countries, can help to spread knowledge and understanding of recent technological advances. A high proportion of MNCs are high-tech, capital intensive firms.

They can bring in new ideas about management techniques. The establishment of Japanese and South Korean MNCs in a range of countries has resulted in their host countries reviewing their management styles. Their output counts in the home country's GDP and, in many cases, their contribution to output and growth is significant.

MNCs tend to have high labour productivity. This is mainly because of high capital/labour ratios. This may encourage domestically owned firms to raise their productivity levels and may reduce inflationary tendencies.

A rise in tax revenue may occur, but some MNCs try to reduce their tax payments by moving revenue around their plants in different countries in order to minimise their payments.

Finally, FDI may cause pollution levels to rise. This is particularly the case in developing countries where MNCs may locate in order to get round tighter environmental regulations at home. MNCs may also be attracted by less strict labour market policies in terms of working hours, health and safety, minimum wages and lowest working age.

International competitiveness

International competitiveness can be defined as the ability of a country's firms to compete successfully in international markets and thereby permit the country to continue to grow.

Sometimes, referring to a country as being internationally competitive is taken to mean that it can produce products more cheaply than most other countries. However, it is more commonly understood by economists in a wider context to include competitiveness in terms of quality and marketing.

Indicators of international competitiveness

In assessing how internationally competitive an economy is, economists examine a range of indicators, which include the following.

- Growth rates – competitive economies tend to grow faster than non-competitive ones, because their products are in high world demand.

Thinking like an economist

What effect may the presence of MNCs in a country have on the country's employment?

Research task

Assess the impact that MNCs are having in your area.

Making connections

Explain the connection between a country's international competitiveness and its economic growth rate.

- Productivity levels – higher productivity levels increase the country's productive capacity and allow long-term growth to occur.
- Unit labour costs – this is obviously linked to productivity levels. If output per worker rises more rapidly than wages and other labour costs, unit labour costs will fall.
- Share of exports in world trade – it is becoming increasingly difficult for an industrial country to maintain its share of world trade in the face of increasing competition from a number of developing countries, particularly the NIEs.
- Balance of trade in goods and services – this is linked to the point above. A competitive country is not likely to have a large deficit on its trade in goods and services balance.
- Investment as a proportion of GDP – investment is seen as an important cause of economic growth.
- Education and training – as with investment, these are thought to be very important indicators. A country with high quality education and training is likely to have a flexible, high-skilled and highly productive labour force.
- Investment in research and development – high levels of expenditure on research and development are likely to develop and encourage the implementation of new technology.
- Communications and infrastructure – good communications and infrastructure will increase the efficiency of firms by lowering their costs and increasing their speed of response to changes in market conditions.
- Industrial relations – good industrial relations increase the quantity and quality of output.
- Composite indicators – each year, the Swiss-based International Institute for Management Development (IMD) publishes a global league table for international competitiveness. This ranks 46 countries on 259 criteria designed to measure factors providing a good business environment. These include economic performance, infrastructure, the role of government, management, the financial system and technological competence. Two-thirds of the criteria are based on statistical data and one-third comes from an opinion survey of more than 4000 business executives worldwide. So far, the USA has always come top of the league table.

Changes in international competitiveness

There are a number of key factors which may raise a country's international competitiveness. One is a fall in the value of the currency. This will make the country's products relatively more competitive. Another is changes in relative inflation rates. If the country's products rise in price less than their competitors' price levels, its products will again become more competitive. A rise in productivity will improve a country's international competitiveness.

The UK's international competitiveness

The UK's position in the IMD league table fluctuates but in recent years, the trend has been upwards. On certain of the criteria used to measure competitiveness, the UK has been performing well in recent years. These include economic growth (where the trend economic growth rate has improved), a reduction in strikes and high levels of FDI. However, investment and productivity levels still remain below some of the UK's main competitors and the high value of the pound has been putting pressure on the price competitiveness of exporters.

Government measures to promote competitiveness

These include:

- maintaining price stability and general economic stability
- promoting FDI
- increasing the quality and quantity of education and training
- encouraging investment.

New classical economists also favour privatisation and deregulation as they believe that these measures increase the efficiency with which industries work.

Quickies

1 Why do governments seek to attract FDI?
2 Identify two disadvantages of capital inflows from MNCs.
3 What is meant by 'a country increasing its international competitiveness'?
4 In what ways might increased investment raise a country's international competitiveness?

Puzzler

How would you judge whether China is becoming more internationally competitive?

Exchange rate systems

A country or area can operate a **fixed, managed** or **floating exchange rate** system. Whatever exchange rate system a country or area chooses to operate, it will have both advantages and disadvantages. The UK and the **euro area** are currently operating floating exchange rates.

Synoptic links

At AS level, it is important that you understand the effects of exchange rate changes (sections 3.18 and 3.22). For A2, you have to explore exchange rates in more depth, including assessing the relative merits of different exchange rate systems.

Definitions

The **euro area** includes the countries that have adopted the euro as their currency. The area currently consists of Austria, Belgium, Finland, France, Germany, Greece, the Republic of Ireland, Italy, Luxembourg, the Netherlands, Portugal and Spain.

A **fixed exchange rate** is an exchange rate fixed against other currencies that is maintained by the government.

A **floating exchange rate** is an exchange rate determined by market forces.

A **managed exchange rate** is an exchange rate system in which a government allows the exchange rate to move within margins.

Parity means the price of one currency in terms of another currency or group of currencies.

A fixed exchange rate

This is one where the **parity** (exchange value, for example, £1 = $1.5) of the currency is pegged against other currencies. If the parity comes under threat by market forces, the central bank, acting on behalf of the government, will step in to maintain the value by buying or selling the currency and/or changing its rate of interest. For example, Figure 1 shows an exchange rate set at £1 = 5 Yen. If demand for the country's exports, demand for the country's currency increases, the government would intervene by selling its currency and/or reducing its interest rate. Figure 2 shows the effects of these events.

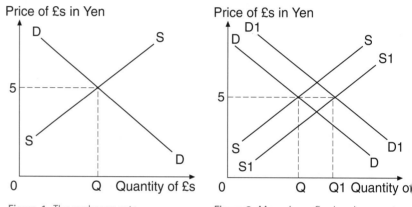

Figure 1 The exchange rate

Figure 2 Managing a fixed exchange rate

A managed exchange rate

A government may not set a particular parity but it may seek to influence the general direction of exchange rate movements in order to prevent changes that are too large and perhaps to prevent the rate rising too high or low. Again, its central bank would influence the value of the exchange rate by buying and selling the currency and changing its interest rate.

Floating exchange rate

This is one determined by market forces. If demand for the currency rises, this will raise the exchange rate whereas if the supply of the currency increases, the exchange rate will fall in value.

Advantages and disadvantages of a fixed exchange rate

The main advantage claimed for a fixed exchange rate is the certainty it provides to traders, investors and consumers. A firm buying raw materials from abroad will know how much it will have to pay in terms of foreign currency. A firm selling products abroad will know how much it will receive in terms of its own currency. Investors will know the cost of, and expected return from, their investment, and consumers going on holiday abroad will know how much they will have to pay.

A fixed exchange rate may also impose discipline on government policy. For example, if the country is experiencing inflation, a government could not rely on the exchange rate falling to restore its international competitiveness; it would have to tackle the causes of the inflation.

Making connections

Identify an opportunity cost of operating a fixed exchange rate.

To maintain the parity, however, other policy objectives may have to be sacrificed. For instance, if the exchange rate is under downward pressure, the government may raise its interest rate, which could slow down economic growth and cause a rise in unemployment.

There is also no guarantee that the parity set will be at the long run equilibrium level. If it is set too high, this will put its firms at a competitive disadvantage, since exports will be relatively high in price while its imports will be relatively low in price. In this case, the rate would not be sustainable and the value of the currency would have to be reduced.

In addition, reserves of foreign currency have to be kept in case the central bank has to intervene to increase demand for the currency. This involves an opportunity cost – the foreign currency could be put to alternative uses.

Advantages and disadvantages of a floating exchange rate

Operating a floating exchange rate means that the exchange rate no longer becomes a policy objective. The government does not have to sacrifice other objectives and does not have to keep foreign currency to maintain it.

Also, in theory, a floating exchange rate should move automatically to ensure a balance of payments equilibrium. For example, if demand for the country's exports fall, demand for the currency will fall and supply will rise. This will cause the exchange rate to fall, making exports cheaper and imports more expensive.

In practice, however, the balance of payments position is influenced not just by demand for exports and imports. A country may have a deficit on the current account of its balance of payments, but speculation may actually lead to a rise in the exchange rate.

A floating exchange rate can create uncertainty with traders and investors being unsure how much the currency will be worth in the future. Some may seek to offset this uncertainty by agreeing a price in advance, but this involves a cost. The degree of uncertainty will be influenced by the extent of the fluctuations in the currency.

Factors affecting exchange rates

A number of factors influence the value of a floating exchange rate and put upward or downward pressure on a fixed and managed exchange rate, including:

- relative inflation rates
- income levels
- relative quality
- relative interest rates
- levels of foreign direct investment
- speculative capital flows.

Relative inflation rates

A country that is experiencing an inflation rate above that of its competitors is also likely to experience a decrease in demand for its exports and a rise in demand for imports. This would cause demand for the currency to fall and supply of the currency to rise. These changes would put downward pressure on a fixed exchange rate. Figure 3 shows the effect on a floating exchange rate.

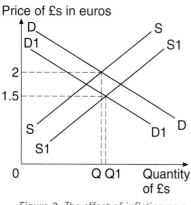

Figure 3 The effect of inflation on a country's floating exchange rate

Income levels

Rises in income levels abroad will tend to increase a country's exchange rate. This is because foreigners will have more income to spend on the country's exports.

Relative quality

If a country's products rise in quality relative to its competitors, demand for its products both at home and abroad will increase. This will cause a rise in the floating exchange rate and put upward pressure on a fixed exchange rate. Improvements in marketing and after-sales service will have a similar effect.

Relative interest rates

If a country's interest rate rises relative to other countries' interest rates, it is likely to attract an inflow of funds from abroad into its financial institutions. This will increase demand for the currency and raise the exchange rate or put upward pressure on it.

Levels of foreign direct investment

A country that attracts more investment from foreign MNCs than its own MNCs invest abroad will experience an increase in demand for its currency and upward pressure on its exchange rate.

Making connections

Explain why a fall in the exchange rate may create inflation.

Speculative capital flows

A high percentage of the dealing in foreign exchange markets is now accounted for by speculation. Speculators buy and sell currency, hoping to make a profit from movements in interest rates and exchange rates. Speculation can have a stabilising or a destabilising effect on exchange rates. The rate will be driven down even further if speculators respond to a falling exchange rate by selling some of their holdings of the currency. However, if they think the rate will soon start to rise, they will purchase the currency, thereby preventing a large fall. Speculation is something of a self-fulfilling principle; by their action, speculators bring about what they expect to happen.

Exchange rates as a policy instrument

A government may alter the value of a fixed exchange rate or influence the value of a managed or floating exchange rate in pursuit of its aims.

A rise in the exchange rate will raise the price of the country's exports in terms of foreign currencies and reduce the price of imports in terms of the domestic currency. This will put downward pressure on inflation. This is because the price of imported raw materials will fall, thereby reducing the cost of production and the price of imported finished products that count in the calculation of the country's inflation. In addition, domestic firms, facing cheaper imported rival products at home and facing the prospect of their products becoming more expensive abroad, will be under pressure to cut their costs in order to keep their prices low.

In contrast, in a bid to improve the balance of payments and raise employment and output, a government may seek to reduce the value of its currency. A fall in the exchange rate reduces the price of exports and raises the price of imports. The change in prices will affect demand. If demand for exports is elastic, the revenue earned from selling exports will rise and import expenditure will fall. This would improve the balance of payments position and increase aggregate demand.

Quickies

1   Identify three factors that could cause a fall in a country's exchange rate.
2   Why may a government seek to alter the country's exchange rate?

Puzzler

Should currency speculation be outlawed?

European Monetary Union

Synoptic links

In AS sections 3.18 and 3.22, you examined monetary policy and the role and effects of changes in interest rates and the exchange rate. This section builds on that understanding in the context of a single European monetary policy.

The European Central Bank

European Monetary Union is part of Economic and Monetary Union (EMU). As its name suggests, it is concerned with member countries operating the same monetary policy. This involves having the same currency and the same interest rate.

The European single currency

The European single currency, the euro, is currently operated under a floating exchange rate system. However, the European Central Bank (ECB) reserves the right to intervene if it considers it to be necessary. In addition, the changes to its interest rate, which it makes mainly to control inflation, have an impact on the value of the euro.

The single currency came into existence on 1 January 1999 with coins and banknotes starting to circulate on 1 January 2002. It started with eleven members (Greece joined later). This group is variously referred to as the euro area, euroland or the euro zone. Denmark, Sweden and the UK chose not to join at the start. The ten countries due to join the EU in 2004 are planning to adopt the single currency as soon as they are able to meet the criteria for joining. These were set down in the Maastricht Treaty and are referred to as the convergence criteria.

Convergence criteria

To join the single currency (sometimes referred to as joining EMU), a country has to show that its economy is operating at a similar stage of the economic cycle as the rest of the members. The specific criteria are as follows:

- the government budget must not exceed 3 per cent of GDP
- government debt should not be above 60 per cent of GDP
- the inflation rate should not exceed the average of the three members with the lowest inflation rates by more than 1.5 percentage points
- long-term interest rates should not be more than 2 percentage points above the average of the three members with the lowest inflation rate
- the country must have a stable exchange rate.

Those members in the single currency have to continue to meet the limits on the fiscal deficits.

UK government's criteria

Chancellor of the Exchequer, Gordon Brown, has set down five conditions that must be met before the 2003 UK government will consider entry to the single currency.

- There must be sustainable convergence between the UK economy and the economies of the euro area countries.
- There must be flexibility within the euro area for coping with economic change.

- Entry must be beneficial for promoting foreign direct investment in the UK.
- Entry must benefit UK financial services.
- Entry must be good for jobs and growth.

On 9 June 2003, Gordon Brown said that the UK economy was not yet ready for entry, since, while the fourth condition had been met, the other conditions had not yet been achieved.

He also announced an action plan to prepare businesses, the housing and labour markets for entry and that, in preparation, the Bank of England's inflation target was to be changed from 2.5 per cent, as measured by RPIX, to the ECB's target of 'close to but below 2 per cent', as measured by the Harmonised Index of Consumer Prices.

Research task

Investigate whether the UK currently meets the convergence criteria set by the EU.

Effects of belonging to the single currency

Joining the single currency would have a number of effects for the UK, some potentially beneficial and some potentially harmful.

Benefits

The benefits of joining the single currency are as follows.

- There would be a reduction in transaction costs. UK firms and consumers would no longer have to spend money and time converting pounds into euros.
- The exchange rate risk with the euro areas would be eliminated. For example, UK firms would no longer be caught out by unexpected changes in the value of the pound against the euro.
- There would be increased transparency. This is thought to be an important advantage. Having one currency makes it easier for firms and consumers to compare prices throughout the EU. Consumers and firms will not have to spend time and effort converting prices into pounds before they decide which are the best offers. Competition should increase and price discrimination should decrease – for example, if the price difference in car radios in EU countries and the UK should fall. In 1999, car radios were 36 per cent higher in price in London than in Rome.
- There would be increased influence within the EU. Being part of the single currency would give the UK more say in the future direction of the EU. It would also make the EU a stronger economic power.
- There would be lower interest rates. Since its inception, the EU has had a lower rate of interest than the UK. A lower interest rate may stimulate investment and growth in the UK.
- There would be increased FDI. Some claim that membership of the euro would attract more MNCs to set up in the UK. It is argued that the UK would become a more attractive location because of the reduced transaction costs and reduced exchange rate uncertainty.

Costs

There would be transitional costs, which are the costs of changing over from using the pound to using the euro. For example, firms would have to convert their IT systems, show for a period of time prices in both pounds and euros, and train staff. However, transitional costs are one-off costs and are not a major consideration in deciding whether to join the single currency or not.

More significant are the disadvantages that may be longer lasting – including reduction in independence of macroeconomic policy. The ECB sets the rate of interest in the euro area. In addition to no longer being able to operate its own interest rate, the UK government would lose the exchange rate as a policy tool and would have constraints imposed on its use of fiscal policy.

The EU argues that a limit has to be placed on the budget deficits that governments can operate in a single currency to ensure price stability and economic growth. If a government, or group of governments, operate large budget deficits, they will add to aggregate demand and possibly the money supply. This is likely to put downward pressure on the euro that may generate inflationary pressure and result in a higher rate of interest for all member countries. Some, however, argue that the requirement is too harsh and needs to be reformed. A budget deficit over 3 per cent may not be significant if it results from capital spending or if it stimulates higher employment and incomes.

Another disadvantage might be an asymmetric policy sensitivity. The UK economy differs from the rest of the EU in three main ways, which may mean that it would be affected more significantly than other members by changes in policy. These three differences are:

- More UK borrowing is undertaken on variable interest rate terms than in most EU countries. So if the euro area's interest rate were to rise, this would affect UK home buyers and firms more than those in other EU countries. However, there is an increasing tendency for loans to be taken out on fixed interest rate terms.
- The UK trades more with the USA than other EU countries and is therefore affected more than the other countries by changes in the level of economic activity in the USA and changes in the value of the dollar.
- The UK is also still a major exporter of oil, so its economy is influenced more (and in a different way) by changes in the world price of oil than other EU countries that import oil.

The effects of staying out

The UK government has not yet decided on entry. Staying out of an arrangement that most of the EU members have joined may have a number of effects on the UK economy, including the following.

- A tendency for its exchange rate to be high because of its higher interest rate.

Thinking like an economist

A country joins the single currency. Analyse the possible effect this may have on the efficiency of the country's firms.

- A risk of loss of FDI. The euro area has formed a large market that may prove more attractive to FDI than the UK. This may particularly be the case if companies decide to locate close to each other to benefit from external economies of scale. Currently, FDI is very important for the UK. Indeed, the UK is the third largest recipient of FDI, after the USA and China.
- A risk that some of the UK's financial institutions may move to the euro area to be closer to the main financial dealings.

Quickies

1. Which countries are currently members of the single currency?
2. Identify three of the criteria the government has set for UK entry into the single currency.
3. Explain how membership of the single currency reduces a country's economic sovereignty.
4. Why is it thought necessary for members of the single currency to limit any budget deficit?

Puzzler

Does membership of the single currency increase economic performance?

External shocks

I n AS section 3.11, you read how demand-side and supply-side shocks can affect an economy. With globalisation, economies are becoming more susceptible to external shocks. These unanticipated events, starting in other countries, can have significant effects on an economy. Governments seek to offset these effects both in the short run and the long run. Their ability to do so can, however, be affected by membership of trade blocs.

Synoptic link

This section explores in more depth the topic of external shocks that was introduced in AS section 3.11.

Susceptibility to external shocks

A country will be more susceptible to external shocks the more it engages in international trade. The UK, for example, is a relatively open economy. Its main trading partners are Germany, the USA, France and the Netherlands. As a result, it is particularly badly hit by adverse events in these economies. Some economies, including the USA, Germany, Japan and the UK are such large economies, however, that their performance has a significant influence on economies throughout the world.

As economies are not the same, they may react in different ways to external shocks. For instance the UK, being an oil producer, is likely to be less adversely affected by a rise in oil prices than Japan, which imports all of its oil.

The effects of external shocks

The terrorist attack on the World Trade Centre on 11 September 2001 contributed to a slowdown in world economic growth. Demand for air travel and tourism fell dramatically. Consumer and business confidence declined. Share prices fell and a number of investment projects were cancelled.

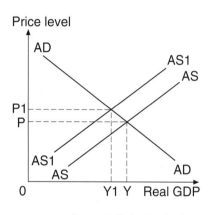

Figure 1   A rise in oil prices

The build up to and duration of the second Gulf War also generated uncertainty. Such uncertainty, again, had an adverse effect on world stock markets and investment. In mid 2003, the deflationary spiral in Germany began to affect first Austria, Belgium and the Netherlands, and then the other parts of the EU. Austria was particularly badly affected as more than a third of its exports are purchased by Germany.

Adverse external shocks can reduce the growth of a country's output to below its trend economic growth rate and may even lead to a recession. Figure 1 shows a fall in output resulting from a rise in oil prices and Figure 2 shows a fall in output resulting from a reduction in exports.

The response to an external shock

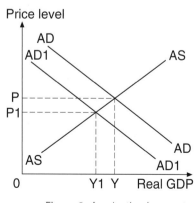

Figure 2   A reduction in exports

Government authorities seek to compensate for external shocks in a variety of ways. If there is an economic downturn in a major economy, such as Germany, UK authorities are likely to implement expansionary fiscal and monetary measures. Tax rates might be cut and government spending might be raised. In recent years, though, the main policy used in the UK has been interest rate changes.

In setting the rate of interest, the Monetary Policy Committee (MPC) of the Bank of England takes into account not only domestic indicators of future economic performance but also indicators of world economic activity. If the MPC considers that the UK economy will experience deflationary pressure as a result of a slowdown in German activity, it is likely to seek to offset this effect by cutting the rate of interest.

Changes in the rate of interest tend to have more of an impact in the UK than in many other economies. This is because more people borrow on the basis of variable interest rates and the housing market plays a more prominent role than in many other countries.

The response to an external shock in the euro area

If the euro area countries are at a similar stage of the economic cycle and are operating similar economies, it is relatively straightforward for the European authorities to take the appropriate action. The ECB could respond to, for instance, a stock market crash in the Far East by cutting its interest rate and, if it was thought necessary, by engineering a fall in the value of the euro.

While there has been some convergence between the euro area countries, differences still exist in their levels of economic activity and so they are likely to be affected by an external shock in rather different ways. In such circumstances, a cut in interest rate may be too much for the stronger economies and too little for the weaker economies.

As members of the euro area, the independent action that member government authorities can take is limited. They have given up control over interest rates to the ECB and do not have national currencies whose value they can alter. Their ability to increase their government spending by borrowing is restricted by membership of the Stability and Growth Pact.

Long-term response to external shocks

A government can seek to make its economy less vulnerable to external shocks in a number of ways. One is to increase the wage flexibility, employment flexibility and the skills of its work force. The more flexible the economy's work force is, the more quickly and smoothly it can adjust to external shocks. The Labour government has put particular emphasis on trying to reduce long-term unemployment and raise the skill levels of the work force so that the labour market is better able to adapt to changing economic conditions. It has met with some success and the UK labour market is now noticeably more flexible than that of the euro area.

A government may also try to make its economy less dependent on one particular product or trade with one or a few economies. In recent years, for instance, the USA has reduced the amount of energy used in its production processes. This has meant that changes in the price of oil now have less impact on US aggregate demand and economic activity. A number of developing countries are trying to diversify the destination of their export markets and sources of imports so that they are less adversely affected by a downturn in one economy.

Quickies

1   What measures might a country's authorities take to offset the effects of a global slowdown?
2   What effect would an economic recession in Japan be likely to have on world output?
3   Identify two reasons why the UK and Japan are likely to respond differently to an external shock.
4   How does membership of the euro area affect a national government's ability to respond to an external shock?

Puzzler

What effect did the Sars outbreak in 2003 have on the world economy?

C hanges in the level and distribution of public expenditure can have a significant impact on households, firms and the economy as a whole. Public expenditure compared to tax revenue gives the government's budget balance.

Forms of public expenditure

Public expenditure can also be referred to as government spending. It includes spending by both central and local government and public corporations, and can be divided into:

- capital expenditure – on hospitals, schools and roads and so on
- current spending – on the running of public services (including teachers' pay and the purchase of medicines to be used in the NHS)
- **transfer payments** – money transferred from tax payers to recipients of benefits (for example, pensioners and the unemployed)
- debt interest payments – payments made to the holders of government debt (for example, holders of National Savings Certificates).

Capital and current expenditure are sometimes referred to as real or exhaustive expenditure, as they make use of resources directly. When the government builds a new school, it is paying for the use of the land, materials and other resources.

On the other hand, transfer payments and debt interest are non-exhaustive forms of expenditure. In their case, the government is not buying the use of resources, but enabling others to do so and it is the recipients of the benefits and interest that will determine the use of resources.

Forms of government spending

The four most important areas of government spending are social security payments, health, education and debt interest.

The amount and proportion spent on different items is influenced by a number of factors. For example, spending on social security, while influenced by benefit rates, is much more significantly affected by economic activity. It rises during periods of increasing unemployment and falls during periods of falling unemployment.

Expenditure on health and education is affected by government priorities, government policies (for example, the replacement of student grants with loans) and changes in the age composition of the population among other factors. The UK's ageing population is putting upward pressure on government spending.

Debt interest payments are affected by the level of government debt and the rate of interest. Spending on other categories is influenced by a number of factors. For instance, spending on defence rose in 2003 due to the second Gulf War.

Public expenditure and the budget

Synoptic link

This section draws on the knowledge and understanding you gained in AS section 3.17. Before starting this section check your understanding of public expenditure (government spending).

Definition

Transfer payments refers to money transferred from one person or group to another which is not in return for any good or service.

Thinking like an economist

Education and health care have positive income elasticity of demand. Explain what this means and its significance for the government's budget position.

The 2003 Labour government has introduced a comprehensive spending review that decides how much departments can spend over the next three years.

Effects of higher public expenditure financed by borrowing

It is generally thought that higher government spending will lead to a multiple increase in aggregate demand. However, new classical economists argue that an increase in government spending financed by borrowing will not always cause aggregate demand and economic activity to increase. This is because they believe it can lead to crowding out, which means that the extra government spending does not add to total expenditure, it merely replaces some private sector spending.

The thinking is that the higher borrowing used to finance the increased spending pushes up demand for scarce funds and thereby raises the rate of interest. The higher rate of interest discourages private sector consumption and investment. It may also cause a rise in the exchange rate, which will further reduce demand for the country's output.

However, Keynesians argue that increased government spending can cause a rise in public sector spending – crowding in. They believe that higher government spending will encourage firms to increase their output, either because the government is buying directly from them or because the recipients of benefits will buy more from them. The higher incomes that arise will result in increased savings, which can finance the borrowing.

Effects of higher public expenditure financed by higher taxation

It might be expected that higher government spending financed by taxation would have a neutral effect on aggregate demand. In practice, this is rarely the case. This is because the recipients of government spending often spend a relatively high proportion of their disposable income while tax payers, especially high tax payers, tend to spend a lower proportion of their income. So higher public expenditure will tend to increase aggregate demand. If the economy is initially operating below its full capacity output, higher aggregate demand should raise output and employment. It may also have an inflationary impact if output rises close to full capacity.

Changes in the distribution of public expenditure

Even if the level of public expenditure does not change, the government can use its spending to influence economic activity and affect the distribution of income. Increased government spending on unemployment benefits and assistance to areas of high unemployment and decreased compensatory spending on higher education and government offices based in prosperous areas is likely to make income more evenly distributed. It is also likely to increase aggregate demand. Of course, reduced government spending on higher education may have an adverse effect on aggregate supply and the economy's long-term economic prospects.

The Budget

The Budget is presented annually by the Chancellor of the Exchequer, usually in March. To calculate the country's budget position, tax revenue and government spending are compared. A budget surplus arises when tax revenue exceeds government spending. A budget deficit occurs when government expenditure exceeds tax revenue. A budget deficit will increase demand in the economy, as the government is injecting more spending into the economy than it is withdrawing from it.

A government has to borrow to cover a budget deficit. The size of a country's **public sector net borrowing (PSNB)** is influenced by the level of economic activity and government policy measures to influence that activity. If a country is experiencing a recession, there is a likely to be a need for the government to borrow as its tax revenue will be relatively low and its expenditure on benefits and measures to stimulate the economy relatively high.

Definition

Public sector net borrowing (PSNB) is the excess of public expenditure over revenue.

EU policy and member governments' budget positions

The EU influences member countries' budget positions in a number of ways. The fundamental way is that all member countries are expected to avoid 'excessive' budget deficits. The Stability and Growth Pact states the medium-term objective for the budget positions of countries in the single currency should be close to balance or in surplus. Countries are allowed to react to normal cyclical fluctuations but are required to keep to the budget deficit limit of 3 per cent of GDP, except in exceptional circumstances.

Quickies

1 Distinguish between exhaustive and non-exhaustive government spending.
2 Identify three possible reasons why the government may increase its spending on health.
3 Why might higher government spending not increase aggregate demand?
4 Is housing benefit a universal or a means-tested benefit?

Puzzler

What effect would a reduction in child benefit and an increase in child tax credit have on the distribution of income?

Taxation and public expenditure

Taxes have a significant impact on households, firms and the economy as a whole. In assessing this impact it is important to consider the types of taxes imposed, the qualities of a good tax and the relative merits of direct and indirect taxes.

Types of taxes

Most tax revenue in the UK comes from income tax, followed by value added tax (VAT).

- Income tax is a direct and progressive tax; as income rises, both the amount and the percentage that a person pays in tax rises.
- VAT is an indirect and largely regressive tax. It is imposed on the sale of goods and services at different rates.

The standard rate of VAT is 17.5 per cent, but a few items, including sanitary protection, are taxed at 5 per cent. Some products – for example, most foods, children's clothing, prescription medicines, books and newspapers – are zero-rated. This means that the firms selling the products cannot charge VAT but can reclaim any VAT paid on their inputs. Others, including education, finance and health services, are VAT exempt. In this case, the firms do not charge VAT but cannot claim back any VAT they have paid.

Other taxes include excise duty, capital gains tax and inheritance tax.

- Excise duty is an indirect tax imposed on specific products – for example, alcohol, petrol and tobacco. The rate varies depending on the product.
- Capital gains tax is a tax on the increase in the value (difference between purchase and selling price) on items such as shares, second homes and paintings. A large number of assets are exempt, including agricultural property, private motor cars and winnings from gambling.
- Inheritance tax is a tax on transfers of wealth above a certain amount.

Qualities of a good tax

Four qualities of a good tax were identified by the eighteenth-century economist Adam Smith. He argued that a good tax should be equitable, certain, convenient and economical.

- Equitable – this means that the amount of tax a person or firm pays should be fair. Economists now discuss horizontal and vertical equity. Horizontal equity occurs when people or firms with the same income and financial circumstances pay the same amount of tax. Vertical equity occurs when the amount that people and firms pay is based on their ability to pay, so that the rich pay more than the poor. Some economists argue that taxes should be based not on the **ability to pay principle** but on the **benefit principle**. The latter suggests that people should pay taxes related to the benefit they receive from public expenditure. It would be relatively easy to apply this principle in connection with services that can be provided privately and that do not have significant externalities.

Synoptic link

This section draws on the knowledge and understanding you gained on AS section 3.17.

Prescription medicines are an example of a zero-rated product

Definitions

The **ability to pay principle** is the rule that people with higher incomes should pay more in tax.

The **benefit principle** is the rule that the amount people pay in tax should be related to the benefit they derive from public expenditure.

It is more difficult to apply when it is hard to estimate who benefits and to what extent they benefit.

- Certain – this means that it should be clear to people and firms how much tax they will have to pay.
- Convenient – the tax should be easy for taxpayers to pay and for the government to collect.
- Economical – an economical tax is one that, relative to the revenue raised, is cheap for people or firms to pay and for the government to collect.

Since Adam Smith's time, economists have added two additional criteria – flexible and efficient.

- Flexible means that it must be possible for the tax to be changed relatively quickly in the light of changing market conditions.
- An efficient tax is one that increases efficiency in markets. An example of an efficient tax is a **Pigouvian tax** (see section 6.14).

Exam hint

When considering the impact of taxation on fairness (equity), make sure you discuss both the ability to pay and the benefit principles.

Definition

A **Pigouvian tax** is a tax designed to correct a negative externality.

Direct and indirect taxes

In the last two decades, there has been a shift in the UK and other EU countries from reliance on direct to indirect taxes. In the UK, income tax rates have been cut while excise duty rates have increased.

Direct taxes are progressive and, depending on their rates, contain a degree of equity. They also help to make the distribution of income more equal. In addition, they help to stabilise economic activity; revenue from direct taxes rises automatically during an economic boom when incomes and profits increase and falls automatically during a recession.

However, governments have reduced their reliance on direct taxes, mainly because they believe they can act as a disincentive to work and effort. The argument is that high marginal rates of income tax may discourage some workers from working overtime, some from taking promotion and some marginal workers from entering the labour force. It is also thought that high marginal rates of corporation tax discourage entrepreneurs from expanding their firms and high marginal tax rates on savings reduce the incentive to save. There can also be the problem of savings effectively being taxed twice – once when the income is earned and again when it is saved.

Furthermore, direct taxes can take some time to change. For example, changes in income tax rates can take some time to implement, since PAYE (pay as you earn) codes have to be adjusted. Changes in indirect tax can usually be implemented more quickly. It is also claimed that indirect taxes have less of a disincentive effect, since they are based on spending rather than earning and, in part, because they are thought to be less obvious to the payers. They are also difficult to evade.

Taxes can also be used to influence the consumption of particular products. For example, demerit goods can be taxed highly. Indirect taxes, as well as direct taxes, have a stabilising effect, since spending rises in line with the trade cycle. Indirect taxes, however, tend to be regressive. The zero rating of

VAT on some products reduces the regressive effect but some claim that, overall, VAT takes a higher proportion of the income of the poor. It is also argued that the coverage of excise duty results in horizontal inequity. For example, two families of the same size and with the same income will pay different amounts of tax if one family enjoys walking and reading (which are not taxed) and the other enjoys driving and drinking alcohol (which are taxed).

Indirect taxes can be inflationary if a rise in indirect tax stimulates a further rise in prices. This is thought to be a particular risk with taxes on petrol that feed through to increased costs of production.

Indirect taxes also reduce consumer surplus and distort the pattern of consumption. Indirect taxes may be introduced to eliminate negative externalities. However, unless negative externalities can be measured accurately, there is a danger that indirect taxes will result in a less efficient allocation of resources.

Thinking like an economist

Analyse the arguments for and against cutting tax on wine.

Hypothecated taxes

A hypothecated tax is one that is raised, or raised in part, for a specific purpose. So the revenue, or some of the revenue, is 'ring fenced'. In November 1999, the Chancellor of the Exchequer, Gordon Brown, announced that some of the revenue raised from tobacco duty would be earmarked for the National Health Service to spend directly on fighting smoking-related diseases. It was the first time he had specifically earmarked revenue for public spending, although later that month he also said that any further increases in petrol and diesel duties would be spent on improving public transport.

Hypothecation gives consumers some choice, can give some idea of how much people are prepared to pay for a particular service and can be used to take money from those creating negative externalities to compensate those who suffer as a result.

However, hypothecation reduces the Chancellor's flexibility in changing tax revenue and government spending to influence economic activity. The revenue earned is itself also subject to changes in economic activity. It is debatable whether many people would want spending on the NHS to fall during a recession, for example. Additionally, there is the question of financing categories of government spending that are less popular than education and health and, if adopted on a large scale, the technical problems of aggregating individual preferences.

Research task

Check the details of the most recent budget to discover which tax rates have changed and why.

Quickies

1 What effect would a shift from direct to indirect taxes be likely to have on the distribution of income?
2 Is income tax based on the ability to pay principle or the benefit principle?

C hanges in public expenditure and taxation have effects on particular markets and the economy as the whole. Some of these effects are intentional, but others are not.

Fiscal policy

Microeonomic effects

A government may raise fuel and vehicle excise duty in an attempt to reduce the growth of road use and thus reduce negative externalities – including pollution, damage to wildlife habitats and congestion. Such a move, however, is also likely to raise firms' costs of production. Indeed, an indirect tax is equivalent to a rise in costs of production and shifts the supply curve to the left. Transport is a significant cost for many firms. Firms may find it difficult to switch from using road to rail to move their products and raw materials.

A government may make cuts in income tax to increase incentives in the labour market. However, it is difficult to predict what effect a cut in income tax will have on the number of hours worked. This is because:

- some workers will not be able to change the number of hours they work
- some may chose to work more hours
- some may work less, because they can potentially stay on the same wage and therefore enjoy more leisure time.

Imposing different taxes and different rates of taxes on products influences the pattern of consumer expenditure. Again, this is sometimes intentional (see below) and sometimes it is not. For example, while shaving equipment does not have VAT imposed on it because shaving is regarded as an essential activity, sanitary protection carries a 5 per cent rate of VAT.

Public expenditure also has microeconomic effects. For instance, the government may give a subsidy to encourage the production of a particular industry. A subsidy shifts the supply curve to the left and lowers price, as shown in Figure 1. Throughout the world, one of the most heavily subsidised industries is agriculture.

Synoptic link

This section draws on the knowledge and understanding of fiscal policy, the budget and aggregate demand you gained in AS section 3.17.

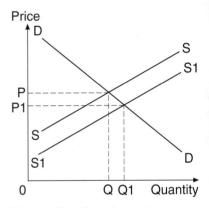

Figure 1 The effect of a subsidy

Pigouvian tax

The Pigouvian tax is named after Arthur Pigou (1877–1959), who wrote extensively about economic welfare. It has the prime aim of not raising income but correcting a negative externality. The tax is imposed to turn the external cost into a private cost and thereby achieve allocative efficiency. However, for the tax to be efficient it must be possible to measure the external costs accurately. Figure 2 shows that the tax does improve the allocation of resources.

Sin taxes are a form of Pigouvian tax. They are designed to discourage unhealthy living. As well as possibly harming those who partake of them, smoking and drinking alcohol generate negative externalities.

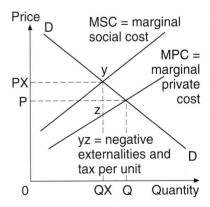

Figure 2 A Pigouvian tax

Definitions

Reflationary fiscal policy involves increases in public expenditure and cuts in taxation designed to increase aggregate demand.

Deflationary fiscal policy involves decreases in public expenditure and increases in taxation designed to decrease aggregate demand.

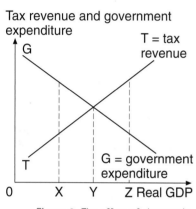

Figure 3 The effect of changes in economic activity on tax revenue and goverment spending

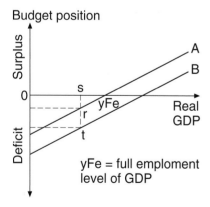

Figure 4 The full employment budget

Fiscal stance

Fiscal policy can have a significant impact on aggregate demand. Fiscal stance refers to whether the government is seeking to raise or lower aggregate demand through its fiscal policy measures. A **reflationary**, or expansionary, **fiscal policy** is one that is increasing demand. A **deflationary**, or contractionary, **fiscal policy** aims to reduce aggregate demand.

However, it is harder to assess a government's fiscal stance than might initially appear to be the case. A government may be trying to raise aggregate demand, but may end up with a budget surplus. This is because the budget position is influenced not only by government policy, but also by changes in the level of economic activity.

Figure 3 shows how tax revenue rises and government expenditure falls with real GDP. At income level **X**, there is a cyclical deficit. At income level **Y**, there is a balanced budget. At income level **Z**, there is a cyclical surplus.

A number of forms of government expenditure and taxation adjust automatically with economic activity to dampen down the fluctuations. These are referred to as automatic stabilisers. For example, spending on Jobseeker's Allowance falls when economic activity picks up. Of course, some forms of government expenditure and taxation are not automatic stabilisers. For example, spending on child benefit is not linked to the economic cycle.

Full employment budget position

To try to assess how a budget's position is influenced by cyclical fluctuations, economists sometimes make use of the full employment budget concept. This plots the budget position that would occur taking into account only cyclical factors achieving a balanced position at full employment – shown in Figure 4 by line A. Then the government's actual budget position is plotted on line B.

If GDP is at *s*, there is budget deficit of *st*. Of this, *sr* is the cyclical deficit component and *rt* is the structural deficit. A structural deficit arises from government policy on taxation and spending. It is the result of government spending being too high relative to tax revenue over the whole economic cycle.

Reflationary and deflationary fiscal policy

A government may implement a reflationary fiscal policy by increasing public expenditure and cutting taxation during a recession. If the economy is overheating, the government may implement a deflationary fiscal policy by reducing its level of spending and/or raising taxes. However, this may not be that easy, as households and firms get used to higher levels of government spending and do not like tax rises.

Seeking to influence the level of aggregate demand in the economy is sometimes referred to as demand management. Governments do this to create greater stability. They try to act counter-cyclically, injecting extra demand when private sector demand is thought to be too low and reducing its own demand when private sector demand is thought to be too high.

In the past, governments frequently engaged in fine-tuning. This involved short-term changes in government spending and/or taxation with the aim of achieving a precise level of aggregate demand. However, they now accept that fiscal policy cannot be used so precisely, so they may be said to engage in coarse-tuning, which is less frequent changes in policy designed to move the economy in the right direction.

Public sector net borrowing

The public sector net borrowing (PSNB) is the excess of public expenditure over tax revenue. It arises when the government has a budget deficit. To finance such a gap between expenditure and revenue, the government will borrow either from the banking sector (high street banks or the Bank of England) or the non-bank private sector (households, insurance companies and so on). The government borrows by selling – for example, government bonds and National Savings certificates on which it pays interest. A negative PSNB means that revenue exceeds expenditure. This would enable a government to repay past debt.

Thinking like an economist

Analyse the effect of a rise in public expenditure coming into effect just as the economy starts to enter an economic boom.

Exam hint

Be careful not to confuse a budget deficit and a balance of payments deficit.

Hot potato

A tax should be imposed on high-fat foods. Do you agree?

Quickies

1 Explain two reasons why a government's budget position may move from a deficit into a surplus.
2 What is meant by 'crowding out'?
3 Distinguish between a structural and a cyclical deficit.
4 Explain the relationship between the PSNB and the economic cycle.

Puzzler

What might be the consequence of a government confusing a cyclical surplus with a structural surplus?

Fiscal, monetary and supply-side policies

Synoptic links

Before starting this section, it would be useful to recap on the understanding you gained of fiscal, monetary and supply-side policies in AS sections 3.17, 3.18 and 3.19, particularly focusing on the effectiveness of the policies.

Definition

Fiscal relates to the use of government spending and taxation to influence macroeconomic variables.

Definition

The multiplier relates to the relationship between an initial change in aggregate demand and the final change in GDP.

You have already assessed the effectiveness of **fiscal**, monetary and supply-side policies at AS level. This section explores some of the problems a government may encounter in seeking to achieve its policy objectives.

Views on government policy

Keynesians believe that markets do not work efficiently. They think that market failure is a real problem. They also think that governments have the appropriate knowledge, skills and tools to intervene and improve the performance of the economy. In contrast, new classical economists argue that markets work efficiently and that there is a real risk that government intervention will make the situation worse. They believe that governments should:

■ remove any past policies, laws and regulations that are hampering the smooth working of free market forces

■ keep taxation low

■ concentrate on creating a low inflationary climate, which will provide the basis for achieving the other three macroeconomic objectives.

Poor quality of information

If a government lacks information or has inaccurate information, it may make the wrong policy decisions. For example, if the Bank of England wrongly believes that aggregate demand will rise too rapidly in the future, it may raise interest rates now. If the economy is actually on the brink of a recession, this will reinforce the downturn in demand. If a government estimates the extent of negative externalities inaccurately and imposes a tax on this basis, it will reduce economic welfare.

The government employs a high number of economists who supply it with analysis and advice. The government also receives advice from other economists working in academia, the media and industry. Some of these economists now use very sophisticated models, but the accuracy of these models is influenced by the information and theories fed into them and how the predictions are interpreted.

In assessing the expected effect of changes in government policies on the economy, economists make use of the concept of **the multiplier**. This is the relationship between an initial change in aggregate demand and the final change in income. For example, the government may increase its spending by raising the state pension. Pensioners receiving more money will spend some of the extra. The shopkeepers who benefit from the rise in spending will, in turn, spend some of the extra revenue they receive and so on. The size of the multiplier can be measured as either:

$$\frac{\text{Final change in GDP}}{\text{Initial change in AD}} \quad \text{or} \quad \frac{1}{1 - \text{proportion of extra income which is spent}}$$

For example, if people spend 80 per cent (or 0.8) of their extra income, the multiplier would be:

$$\frac{1}{1-0.8} = \frac{1}{0.2} = 5$$

Keynesians believe that it is possible to calculate the multiplier reasonably accurately, while new classical economists think it is not. So the latter group believe it is difficult for a government to assess, in advance, the effect that changes in government spending and taxation will have. New classical economists also argue that markets provide higher quality information and provide it more quickly.

In a free market, in theory at least, an increase in demand will result in a rise in price which will automatically inform producers that they should expand production of the product.

Economic theory

The policies adopted are influenced by the economic theories followed by politicians and their economic advisers. However, there are disagreements as to which are the appropriate theories to follow.

For example, there are different theories on the relationship between inflation and the money supply. Monetarists argue that inflation is caused by excessive increases in the money supply, while Keynesians argue that increases in the money supply is the consequence and not the cause of inflation.

Time lags

By the time some government policies take effect, the situation that caused them to be implemented may have changed. For example, a government may cut income tax to increase consumer spending but by the time the tax rates are changed, the economy may be entering a boom period. The three main time lags involved with government policy are:

- recognition lag – this refers to the time it takes for a government to recognise there is a problem
- implementation lag – it can take time for a government to decide on the appropriate policy measure and implement it
- behavioural lag – this is the time it takes for people and firms to change their behaviour in the light of government policies. For example, a government may cut income tax but people may take time to adjust their spending.

Unexpected responses

Economics is a social science. It deals with people, and people and the firms they run do not always react in the way the government expects or wants.

Thinking like an economist

A government implements expansionary fiscal policy. Analyse the possible effect on the economy of underestimating the size of the multiplier.

Making connections

What factors influence how much people spend?

For example, the Japanese government, in 1998, cut interest rates and income tax hoping to stimulate a rise in aggregate demand. However, this failed to materialise because consumers and firms were pessimistic about the future and so actually saved more.

Economists have also noted that targeting can itself alter the behaviour of what is being targeted. This phenomenon was identified in **Goodhart's law**, which states that any measure of the money supply behaves differently when it is targeted.

Complexity

The world is a complex, increasingly integrated and constantly changing place. Economic growth of a country can be knocked off trend by sudden and unexpected events abroad such as the East Asian crisis of 1997–99.

Conflicts of objectives

Policy instruments simultaneously affect a number of objectives. So a rise in income tax designed to reduce inflation may also contribute to a rise in unemployment. However, it is interesting to note here that new classical economists argue that policy objectives do not need to conflict. They think that if the government keeps inflation low, largely by avoiding the temptation to increase aggregate demand, the other three objectives will be achieved.

There is increasing agreement that supply-side policies can, in the long run, help a government to achieve all of its major objectives. The new economic paradigm also holds out the promise of increasing the ease with which all four major objectives can be achieved simultaneously.

Government self-interest

The recommendations and decisions made by politicians and civil servants may be influenced by their own self-interest. For example, a government may receive advice from economists that now would not be an appropriate time to cut income tax. However, if it is approaching a general election, it may go ahead with such a change. Ministers and civil servants might resist cuts in the spending of their department for fear that a smaller department will reduce their status and, in the case of civil servants, their pay.

Economists also recognise the risk of **regulatory capture**. This arises when regulators of industries become unduly influenced by the managers of the industries they are regulating, perhaps because of their frequent contacts with the managers, or perhaps because of the superior knowledge of the managers and in some cases because of perks offered.

Rigidities

As noted earlier, while market conditions are constantly changing, it is difficult to change some aspects of government policy. For example, laws take time to change. Some forms of public expenditure are difficult to change. Once a government has started to build a hospital, it is difficult and costly to stop. If governments are reluctant to admit their mistakes, they may continue to spend money on a project that does not have long-term viability.

However, where consumers and firms need to make long-term plans, frequent and large changes in government policies can cause problems. For example, a decision to remove grants to firms that have located in a depressed region three years after they were first announced may put the viability of those firms in question. A doubling of the rate of interest would also cause major problems for those with mortgages.

Policy constraints

Membership of international organisations and increasing globalisation limit the autonomy of national government policy. The UK government cannot impose tariffs on EU members, and its rate of interest cannot be significantly out of line with that of the EU and the USA.

Quickies

1   Why might a change in government spending cause a greater change in GDP than anticipated?
2   Why does it take time for government policies to have an effect on the economy?
3   Why might a rise in income tax not reduce consumer spending?
4   Why do frequent changes in government policies tend to reduce private sector investment?

Puzzler

Have the AS and A2 examinations introduced in 2000 improved educational standards?

The causes of unemployment

U nemployment can be caused by demand-side factors and supply-side factors. People may be without jobs because of a lack of aggregate demand. They may also be unemployed because they lack information about job vacancies, the incentive to work, the appropriate skills and/or the ability to move to where vacancies exist.

Synoptic link

This section builds on AS Section 3.12. Before starting this section, check your understanding of the causes of unemployment.

Definition

Cyclical unemployment is unemployment arising from a lack of aggregate demand.

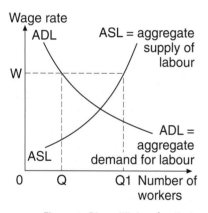

Figure 1 Disequilibrium (cyclical unemployment)

Thinking like an economist

Analyse the likely effect on UK unemployment of an economic boom in the USA.

Demand-side causes

Cyclical unemployment, or demand-deficient unemployment, is linked to the business cycle since it begins to develop during a downturn in economic activity and can grow to very high levels during a recession.

Another term that is sometimes applied to cyclical unemployment is disequilibrium unemployment. This term emphasises the fact that cyclical unemployment arises when there is disequilibrium in the labour market, with the aggregate supply of labour exceeding the aggregate demand for labour at the going wage. Figure 1 shows that the number of people wanting to work at the wage rate W is Q1, while the number of workers firms want to employ is Q, resulting in unemployment of Q–Q1.

When aggregate demand for labour falls, the real wage may not fall because workers are likely to resist cuts in wages. Indeed, if the wage rate did fall it may actually make the situation worse. This is because a fall in wages is likely to reduce demand for goods and services that, in turn, will cause a further fall in demand for labour – in other words, there is a risk that a downward spiral may develop.

Keynesians favour trying to reduce cyclical unemployment by raising aggregate demand via increases in government spending and/or cuts in taxation or interest rates.

Supply-side causes

Unemployment may also arise because of supply-side problems. There may not be a lack of vacancies, but those people out of work may not be able or willing to fill the vacancies for a number of reasons. Economists identify a number of types of unemployment related to supply-side problems – the main three being voluntary, frictional and structural.

Voluntary unemployment

Voluntary unemployment occurs when there are vacancies, but the unemployed do not take them up because they are not prepared to work for the going wage rate. New classical economists argue that if unemployment benefit is high, some of the unemployed may take their time looking for a good job and some may decide they are better off being unemployed.

Frictional unemployment

Frictional unemployment includes workers who are between jobs and young people seeking their first job. What determines how long these people are out of work is principally the mobility of labour. The more geographically and occupationally immobile workers are, the longer they are likely to be out of work.

There are three particular forms of frictional unemployment.

- Seasonal unemployment – the seasonally unemployed are people who are out of work for a short period because of falls in demand that occur at particular times of the year. For example, the hotel and catering industry and the construction industries tend to employ fewer workers in the winter than in the summer.
- Casual unemployment – some people work on an occasional basis, most noticeably actors.
- Search unemployment – this is a form of frictional unemployment that economists pay particular attention to and which is related to voluntary unemployment. Some people who are out of work do not necessarily accept the first job on offer. Instead, they spend time searching for a congenial and well-paid job. The length of time people are prepared to remain unemployed is influenced by the savings they have, the level of benefits they receive and how society views unemployment.

Structural unemployment

Structural unemployment is usually more significant than frictional unemployment as it is often more long run. Again, a key factor is immobility of labour, both geographical and occupational. At any time, it is likely that some industries will be declining and some will be expanding. This will require workers to move from one industry to another. However, some of those workers may lack the necessary skills or may find it difficult to move from where they currently live to where the expanding industries are.

The main forms of structural unemployment are as follows.

- Regional unemployment – this arises when declining and expanding industries are in different parts of the country. For example, some of the towns and cities in the south of the UK have shortages of labour, while some of the towns and cities in the north have significantly higher than average unemployment.
- Technological unemployment – this occurs when the introduction of new technology reduces demand for workers in particular jobs and industries. For example, the development of cash points and electronic banking have reduced the demand for bank cashiers. However, as well as reducing demand for workers in certain industries and occupations, technological change can also result in an increase in demand for workers employed in

Definition

Frictional unemployment is unemployment arising because workers are in between jobs.

Definition

Structural unemployment is unemployment arising from changes in demand and supply that cause a change in the structure of the economy's base and a change in demand for labour.

other occupations and industries. For example, in recent years the mobile phone industry has expanded, taking workers on to, for instance, develop and market phones that incorporate facilities that give access to the Internet and transmit pictures.

- International unemployment – on a world scale, changes in comparative advantage can lead to changes in the demand for labour in terms of quantity and type in different countries. For example, while demand for British steel has declined in the last two decades, demand for steel from Brazil has increased as Brazil has become more efficient in its production.

Supply-side problems and government policy

To reduce voluntary, frictional and structural unemployment, economists recommend measures that make work more attractive to the unemployed and that make the unemployed more attractive to employers – in other words, measures that increase the incentives to work, the ability of the unemployed to work, the skills of the unemployed, and the occupational and geographical mobility of the unemployed.

In recent years, particular attention has been paid to increasing the flexibility of the labour market. Firms are likely to take on more workers if it becomes cheaper and easier to hire and fire staff. The unemployed are also more likely to gain employment if they are willing to take on temporary work, are prepared to vary the hours they work, and are willing and able to adapt to new technology and new tasks.

	Unemployment rates			
	EU	Euro area	UK	USA
2000	7.8	8.4	5.5	4.0
2001	7.4	8.0	5.1	4.8
2002	7.6	8.3	5.1	5.8
2003	7.9	8.7	5.2	5.7

Table 1 Unemployment rates

EU unemployment performance

Table 1 shows that unemployment is higher in the EU than the USA. It also shows that output in the euro area exceeds both that of the USA and the UK. The USA and the UK have more flexible labour markets than those in the euro area.

If wages do not adjust fully and quickly to changes in demand, unemployment is likely to result. Figure 2 shows aggregate demand for labour falling from **ADL** to **ADL1**. If the wage rate does not fall, unemployment of **QX–Q** will result.

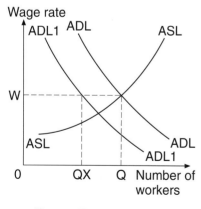

Figure 2 The labour market failing to clear

Wages in the euro area are relatively inflexible for a number of reasons. One is that wages are determined on the basis of national, collective bargaining to a much greater extent than in the UK and the USA. This can prevent wages reflecting different demand pressures in different areas. If wages are the same in both depressed and in prosperous areas, there will be little incentive for workers to move to the prosperous regions and for capital to move to the depressed regions.

It is thought that unions in a number of the euro area countries have been pushing up wage rates above their equilibrium levels. Unions in Germany have been particularly militant in pursuit of wage rises and while unions in France represent only a relatively small proportion of the labour force, they exert a considerable influence on the political determination of minimum wage and the length of the working week.

There is also rigidity in employment relationships. If employers believe that it will be difficult to sack workers should demand fall, they may be reluctant to take on many workers when demand is high. Employment protection in many EU countries makes sacking workers a costly and lengthy process, with employers having to consult with unions and local and national authorities. In contrast, in the USA, where there is less government intervention in labour markets, a fall in demand tends to result initially in a greater rise in unemployment but then a greater decrease.

Generous unemployment benefits and some state employment can reduce labour market flexibility. Unemployment benefits are higher in most EU countries than in the USA and eligibility rules are laxer. It may be claimed that this reduces the incentive for the unemployed to search for work and to be prepared to accept offers of employment at the going wage rate. The labour market can also be distorted by more generous pay and conditions in state employment than in private sector employment. In France, for instance, civil servants can claim a full pension after 37 years employment compared to 40 years for their private sector colleagues.

Quickies

1 Distinguish between frictional and structural unemployment.
2 What factors influence the level of voluntary unemployment?
3 Why might the aggregate supply of labour be greater than the aggregate demand for labour?
4 Why might a more flexible labour force reduce unemployment?

Puzzler

Why may workers be less keen than employers on flexible labour markets?

The consequences of unemployment

The consequences of unemployment are influenced by the rate of unemployment and the duration of unemployment. Obviously, a high rate of unemployment lasting for a long period of time will have more harmful effects than a low rate of a short duration. The consequences of unemployment can be considered in terms of the effects on economic performance and on individuals.

Effects on economic performance

The most obvious cost of unemployment to an economy is the opportunity cost of lost output. If, for example, 2 million people are out of work, the output they could have produced is lost for all time. When a country has unemployed workers, it is not using all its resources and so is not producing the maximum output it is capable of (not reaching its potential output). In this case, there is an output gap.

Figure 1 shows that an increase in unemployment would make an economy even less productively efficient. Output of capital goods falls from A to A1 and the output of consumer goods from B to B1.

Unemployment has implications for fiscal policy. It tends automatically to push the government's budget position towards deficit. This is because it reduces tax revenue while increasing government spending. With income and spending levels being below those that would exist with full employment, tax revenue from income tax, corporation tax, VAT and excise duties is below its potential level. The existence of unemployment necessitates government spending on unemployment benefit (Jobseeker's Allowance) and on other benefits, including income support and housing benefit.

Government spending may also have to rise to deal with problems associated with unemployment – including health and crime. People tend to experience worse physical and mental health when they are out of work. High levels of long-term unemployment may lead to social unrest, as was witnessed in some parts of the UK, including Liverpool, at the start of the 1990s. Unemployment is not evenly spread. It falls most heavily on unskilled, male workers from ethnic minorities. There is also some evidence of a link between the level of unemployment and crime. When young men are out of work, they may feel alienated from society and turn to crime to gain a higher income and perhaps even a certain form of status.

Additionally, unemployment reduces potential demand for firms' products. This, in turn, reduces potential profit levels and may discourage investment.

Cost of unemployment to the individual

The main cost of unemployment falls on those who are unemployed. There is obviously a financial cost. A few people may be cushioned from the effects of unemployment if they have sufficient savings and are not out of work for

Synoptic link

This section builds on the understanding you gained about the consequences of unemployment in AS section 3.12.

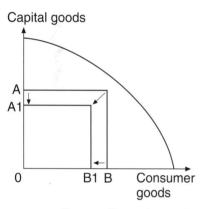

Figure 1 How an increase in unemployment makes an economy less productively efficient

Thinking like an economist

Use an AD/AS diagram to analyse the effect of unemployment on an economy.

long. However, most unemployed people experience a fall in income and often a fall in their self-esteem.

Unemployment usually involves financial costs. When people are out of work they may spend more time at home. This will increase, for example, their heating and lighting costs. Applying for jobs and going for interviews also involves paying out money.

The longer people are out of work, the more de-skilled they become. This is because they miss out on training and updating. They may also lose the work habit. Both of these effects make it more difficult for them to gain employment. Some unemployed people can become so dispirited that they give up looking for work. These people are sometimes referred to as **discouraged workers**.

Additionally, being unemployed places a strain on personal relationships. Indeed, in some cases it contributes to physical violence in the home and to divorce rates.

Benefits of unemployment

Being unemployed may enable some people to reappraise their skills and ambitions, and to gain a more rewarding job. Some people leave their jobs voluntarily in order to search for a better job.

The existence of unemployed workers enables firms to expand relatively quickly. Short-term unemployment may indicate a flexible labour force, with workers moving between jobs as demand and supply conditions change. Firms may also find that the existence of unemployed workers will keep wage rises down and make workers more willing to accept new production methods. From the economy's point of view, the existence of unemployment may keep inflationary pressures down.

However, most politicians and economists believe that the costs of unemployment, particularly long-term unemployment, outweigh any benefits.

Thinking like an economist

Explain why being unemployed tends to reduce a person's physical and mental health.

Definition

Discouraged workers are people who have given up looking for work.

Quickies

1 Explain three ways in which higher unemployment may increase government spending.
2 What effect would a decrease in unemployment be likely to have on the government's budget position?
3 Explain why a person's chances of gaining a job reduce the longer he or she is out of work.
4 In what ways will a reduction in unemployment improve a country's economic performance?

The causes of inflation

The causes of inflation can be divided into cost-push and demand-pull. In recent years inflation in the UK has been low and stable. In the early 2000s, the UK was experiencing an inflation rate below the EU's average rate.

Synoptic links

This section builds on AS sections 3.2, 3.3 and 3.13. Before you work through this section review your understanding of the meaning, measurement and causes of inflation.

Definition

A **wage-price spiral** is a rise in wages which triggers off rises in the price level and in turn leads to higher wage claims.

Thinking like an economist

Why do increases in the price of oil have a significant impact on the rate of inflation?

Cost-push inflation

Cost-push inflation occurs when higher costs of production shift the aggregate supply curve to the left and trigger off a series of rises in the price level. The causes of cost-push inflation can be broken down as follows:

- a rise in wages
- higher raw material costs
- an increase in profit margins.

If workers in key industries get a pay rise, it is likely to encourage workers in other industries to press for pay rises. Higher wages, not matched by equal increases in productivity, will reduce profits and encourage firms to pass on at least some of the cost in the form of higher prices. In turn, the higher prices will be likely to stimulate workers to press for higher money wages in order to maintain their real wages. A **wage-price spiral** may be set in motion, with prices continuing to rise. In the UK, changes in wages are a significant factor since they account for approximately two-thirds of total costs.

Higher import prices could result from a fall in the exchange rate. The higher prices of finished imported goods and services would directly increase the RPI and other measures of inflation. In addition, the higher cost of imported raw materials will raise costs of production that may be passed on to consumers in the form of higher prices. Domestic producers, facing less fierce price competition from overseas, may be more inclined to raise prices.

If workers respond to the rise in the price level by demanding and receiving higher wages, prices will rise still higher. These higher prices will reduce the country's international price competitiveness. The resulting fall in demand for exports may reduce the exchange rate further. This will once more raise the general price level and encourage workers to press for wage rises.

Higher raw material costs may also result from shortages due to, for example, a failure of a crop, or a hurricane or from producers forming a cartel and exerting their increased market power. It is also possible that profit-push inflation may occur with prices being forced up as a result of firms raising their profit margins.

Demand-pull inflation

Demand-pull inflation may occur for a number of reasons. One is a consumer boom. When consumers are very optimistic about the future, they are likely to spend more. If the higher aggregate demand occurs when the economy is approaching or at full employment, the price level will be pulled up.

Another possible cause is demand for exports increasing when the economy is at or near full capacity. If more exports are not offset by more imports, there will be more income coming into the country with fewer goods and services on which to spend the income.

Demand-pull inflation may also be initiated by an increase in government spending. One of the reasons governments impose taxation is to try to ensure that spending does not cause inflation. For example, a government may believe that its economy is capable of producing £120 billion worth of products. It estimates that, in the absence of taxation, private sector spending will be £110 billion. If it wants to spend £40 billion, it will reduce private sector spending via taxation by £30 billion to ensure that total spending does not exceed £120 billion.

Of course, in practice, it is difficult to get these estimates right. There is also the problem of time lag. A government may decide to increase its spending when private sector spending is low. However, by the time public sector spending is increased, the economy might have picked up anyway and the extra government spending may result in an excess of aggregate demand and hence demand-pull inflation.

Monetarists argue that the key cause of excessive increases in aggregate demand is excessive increases in the money supply – too much money chasing too few goods.

Thinking like an economist

Explain why an increase in government spending on training is less likely to lead to inflation than an increase in government spending on pensions.

Recent trends in inflation

Recent years have witnessed a period of low inflation in many countries. It is thought there are a number of reasons why inflation is remaining low in the UK including the following:
- advances in information technology, which are raising productivity levels, reducing costs of production and increasing competition by lowering barriers to entry globalisation which is increasing competition in many markets
- reduced expectations of inflation – having experienced a number of years of low inflation, consumers, workers and firms no longer expect high inflation and so do not act in ways which create inflation
- privatisation and regulation of utility firms, which are driving down utility prices
- high value of sterling which lowers import prices, reduces costs of production and puts pressure on UK firms to keep their costs low
- more flexible labour markets, which permit output to change more rapidly and smoothly to meet changes in demand.

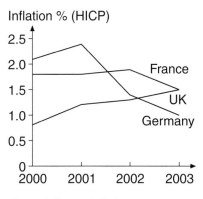

Figure 1 Recent inflation rates

Inflation in the EU

Inflation rates in the EU have also been relatively low. There have, however, been variations with inflation being higher than the EU average in, for

	2001	2002
Austria	2.3	1.7
Belgium	2.4	1.6
Denmark	2.2	2.4
Finland	2.6	2.0
France	1.8	1.9
Germany	2.1	1.3
Ireland	4.0	4.7
Italy	2.4	2.6
Netherlands	5.1	3.9
Portugal	4.4	3.7
Spain	2.8	3.6
Sweden	2.7	2.0
UK	1.2	1.3
EU	2.3	2.1
Euro area	2.4	2.2

Table 1 Inflation rates as measured by the Harmonised Index of Consumer Prices (%)

example, Ireland and the Netherlands and lower in Belgium and Germany, as shown in the Table 1.

The objectives for monetary policy for the euro area were set out in the Maastricht Treaty. The key objective is to maintain price stability. Subject to that objective, the EU wants monetary policy to foster sustainable economic growth and high employment.

The European Central Bank's inflation target is an inflation rate close to but below 2 per cent. The ECB did not always achieve its initial inflation target. Between 2000 and 2003, inflation was above 2 per cent on a number of occasions, but not significantly so.

One of the main criticisms of European Monetary Policy has not been that inflation has been too high but that the policy has tended to be too deflationary. It is thought that on several occasions the ECB has resisted cutting interest rates when there was no real risk of the inflation rate rising and when such a cut would have been beneficial for stimulating economic activity in a number of member states.

Another criticism made is based on the 'one-size-fits-all' nature of European Monetary Policy. The interest rate decided by the ECB applies to all the countries in the euro area. There is a risk that an interest rate that may be appropriate for the area as a whole may be inappropriate for some individual countries. Those member countries with overheating economies and high inflation will have low real rates of interest when they need high real interest rates, while economies with high levels of unemployment and low inflation will have high real interest rates. If all the economies were operating at a similar point on the economic cycle, having the same rate of interest would not be a problem. In practice, though, there are still significant differences in euro area countries.

Quickies

1   An increase in the money supply results in inflation. Would this be an example of cost-push or demand-pull inflation?
2   Using AD and AS diagrams, explain why cost-push inflation may be considered more detrimental to an economy than demand-pull inflation.
3   Identify two possible causes of demand-pull inflation.
4   Explain in what circumstances an increase in aggregate demand may not result in a rise in the price level.

Puzzler

Why is it often difficult to determine the initial cause of inflation?

The effects of inflation will depend on a number of key factors. These include its level, its stability or otherwise, whether it has been correctly anticipated or not, its rate in comparison to other countries' inflation rates and how the government responds to it. An accelerating inflation rate above that of rival countries and above the expected rate is likely to cause more harm than a low, stable and fully anticipated rate. It is possible to consider the impact of inflation on individuals and on the economy as a whole.

Effects on individuals

Some people tend to gain (for example, borrowers) and some tend to lose (for example, lenders) as a result of inflation. This is because the nominal rate of inflation does not usually keep pace with inflation, which means that the real rate of interest falls. If, for example, the nominal rate of interest is 6 per cent and inflation is 2 per cent, the real rate of interest is 4 per cent. If, then, the inflation rate rises to 5 per cent but the nominal interest rate only rises to 8 per cent, the real rate of interest will fall to 3 per cent. There have even been times when the real rate of interest has been negative. In such circumstances, lending will make people worse off.

One of the main reasons that people borrow large sums of money is to buy a house. Mortgage holders are often beneficiaries of inflation. This is because while the real interest rate they pay back is usually reduced by inflation, the real value of their houses tends to rise, since the price of houses increases by more than the rate of inflation.

Inflation also usually redistributes income from those workers with weak bargaining power towards those with strong bargaining power. Those workers who can gain wage rises above the rate of inflation will experience increases in real income, while those whose wages do not keep pace with inflation will suffer a fall in real income. People on state benefits may also experience a fall in real income because, for instance, Jobseeker's Allowance may not be raised in line with inflation.

Unanticipated inflation will create uncertainty and some confusion. People will not know, for instance, whether it is better to take out a fixed or variable rate mortgage and what wage rise to ask for. Inflation also generates inflationary noise, with distorted information being sent out about relative prices. As people will be unsure whether price rises are in line with inflation or not, they may make inefficient choices. In addition, taxpayers will lose if the government does not adjust tax margins in line with inflation. In such circumstances, taxpayers will be dragged into higher tax brackets when their nominal incomes rise.

Effects on the balance of payments

As discussed at AS level, if a country has an inflation rate above that of its main competitors, its products will become less price competitive. This fall in

Synoptic link

This section builds on AS section 3.13. Before you start this section check your understanding of the consequences of inflation.

Thinking like an economist

What are the economic arguments for and against index-linking state pensions?

international price competitiveness is likely to result in a rise in imports and a fall in exports, and thus a deterioration in the current account balance.

The balance of payments may also be affected in other ways. If the country is experiencing high and accelerating inflation, portfolio and direct investment into it may also be discouraged.

Additionally, government policy measures to reduce inflation may harm the balance of payments. For instance, if the Bank of England raises the rate of interest to reduce aggregate demand, this may raise the country's exchange rate. A higher exchange rate increases the price of exports and reduces the price of imports. If demand for exports and imports is price elastic, a higher exchange rate will cause export revenue to fall and import expenditure to rise.

Effects on output

A low level of anticipated demand-pull inflation may cause a rise in output in the short run. This is because the higher aggregate demand and the higher prices are likely to encourage firms to raise their production. However, inflation can have a detrimental effect on national output.

Hyperinflation is particularly harmful to economic activity. When the price level is rising rapidly, it can be difficult for an economy to operate. In Germany in the 1920s, for example, inflation reached phenomenal levels. Money became worthless and people asked to be paid in a range of items, including cigarettes, which they believed would prove to be more acceptable when it came to paying for goods and services. Barter also made a comeback with people directly exchanging goods and services. The disruption caused to the economy and people's lives led to political unrest and assisted Hitler's rise to power.

A rate of inflation well below hyperinflation levels but still considered high and unstable may also have a detrimental effect on output. This is because it will increase firms' costs, create uncertainty and it may decrease aggregate demand.

Inflation raises firms' costs

This happens in a number of ways. Firstly, inflation can impose menu costs. Firms have to spend money changing their prices in, for example, catalogues and advertisements.

Firms also experience shoe leather costs – the extra time and effort they have to spend moving money into and out of financial institutions such as banks. If money is losing its value at a high rate it cannot be left idle. So firms receiving payments are likely to try to gain interest on the money, even if they are going to pay it out in a few days time. Staff time has to be used in assessing where the highest interest is being paid and moving the money around.

There are also other financial costs to firms as a result of inflation. Extra time and effort has to be taken in searching round for the lowest prices of raw materials, adjusting accounts, estimating appropriate prices and negotiating with unions about wage rises.

Inflation increases uncertainty

Unanticipated and accelerating inflation makes it particularly difficult for firms to plan ahead and this may discourage them from investing. As with the balance of payments position, output may also be harmed by short-term government measures to reduce inflation. This is particularly the case if the measures are of a deflationary nature.

Inflation reduces aggregate demand

Even without such policies, inflation may reduce aggregate demand. This is because the uncertainty it generates may reduce consumption and investment and because the effect it may have on international competitiveness may reduce net exports. As well as reducing aggregate demand, a fall in investment will have an adverse effect on economic growth.

Effects on employment

If a low and stable rate of inflation is accompanied by an increase in output, unemployment may fall. However, there are a number of reasons for thinking that inflation may have an adverse effect on employment. These reasons have been touched on earlier. If inflation makes the country's products less price competitive, raises firms' costs and creates uncertainty, output is likely to fall and may therefore cause unemployment.

Again, some government measures implemented to reduce inflation may have a harmful effect on employment. Deflationary fiscal and monetary policy measures may reduce output and thus increase unemployment. However, some longer-term measures, designed to reduce inflation by increasing aggregate supply, may have a beneficial effect on employment. For instance, increasing and improving education and training is likely to improve the skills, occupational mobility and therefore employability of labour.

Making connections

Explain why government measures to reduce unemployment may increase inflation.

Quickies

1 In what circumstances will the real rate of interest be negative?
2 Identify three groups who are likely to suffer as a result of unanticipated inflation.

Puzzler

Is unemployment or inflation currently imposing greater costs on the UK economy?

Thinking like an economist

Discuss how a fall in the rate of inflation may improve a country's economic performance.

Phillips curves

Phillips curves are used by economists to analyse the relationships between unemployment and inflation, and to assess the impact of changes in government policy on inflation and unemployment. In this section you will assess different views on the likely shape of the **Phillips curve**. You will also develop the ability to plot Phillips curves to assess current relationships between unemployment and inflation in the UK and other economies.

Synoptic links

This section draws on your understanding of aggregate demand and aggregate supply analysis, the causes of inflation and policy conflicts (see AS sections 3.5–3.8, 3.12–3.13 and 3.20–3.21).

Definition

Phillips curve is a graph showing the relationship between unemployment and inflation.

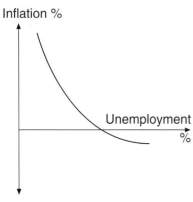

Figure 1 The short run Phillips curve

Figure 2 Phillips curve for the USA in the 1960s

Origin of the short run Phillips curve

The Phillips curve is named after Bill Phillips, a New Zealander, who started his working life as an engineer. After World War II he moved to the UK to study sociology at the London School of Economics (LSE). During his course, he became interested in economics and, in particular, in studying the effect of changes in unemployment rates on money wages.

Phillips stayed on at the LSE, and studied unemployment rates and wage increases for the period 1861–1913. He found an inverse, non-linear relationship between unemployment rates and wage increases. This means that as unemployment falls, rises in money increase but not at a proportionate rate – they accelerate. When unemployment falls to low levels money wages rise rapidly, whereas when unemployment rises to high levels, workers resist cuts in money wages.

Development of the short run Phillips curve

The Phillips curve was developed in 1960 by two US economists, Paul Samuelson and Robert Solow, with changes in money wages being taken as an indicator of inflation to show the expected relationship between unemployment and inflation. Figure 1 shows the inverse relationship between unemployment and inflation.

When demand for labour rises, unemployment is likely to fall. The increased competition for workers is likely to bid up wage rates. Higher pay for workers can increase the price level via increased costs of production and higher aggregate demand as the workers spend their wages.

Economists had drawn up Phillips curves for most countries by the mid-1960s (see Figure 2 as an example). In this period, the short run Phillips curve was interpreted by economists and politicians to suggest that policy makers could trade off inflation and unemployment to reach a desired combination. For example, a reduction in unemployment from, say, 6 per cent to 4 per cent might have to be 'bought' at the price of a rise in inflation from, for example, 3 per cent to 5 per cent.

Changes in the relationship between unemployment and inflation

In the late 1960s and 1970s, the Phillips curve faced criticism. Some economists argued that the relationship it predicted still existed, but that the curve had shifted to the right, indicating that a higher level of unemployment would be combined with any level of inflation. They suggested that in the 1970s and 1980s workers had got used to higher levels of unemployment and so did not modify wage claims to the same extent when unemployment rose (see Figure 3).

Long run Phillips curve

Milton Friedman, the most famous **monetarist** economist, went further. He questioned the accuracy, in the long run, of the traditional Phillips curve in predicting the effect of changes in aggregate demand on the level of unemployment and inflation. He argued that while a Phillips curve relationship may exist in the short run between unemployment and inflation, in the long run, changes in aggregate demand would influence inflation but leave output and unemployment unaffected. The **long run Phillips curve** he developed is also sometimes referred to as the expectations-augmented Phillips curve (see Figure 4).

Explanation of the long run Phillips curve

Figure 4 shows the economy initially operating on the short run Phillips curve 1 (**SPC1**) with 0 per cent inflation and 5 per cent unemployment.

An increase in aggregate demand may, in the short run, encourage firms to expand their output and take on more workers. Unemployment falls and the economy is at point *a*. However, the rise in demand for goods and services and the resources to produce them will result in inflation.

The economy now moves to point *b*. When producers and workers realise that inflation has eroded their real profits and wage levels, they adjust their behaviour. This, combined with some workers leaving their jobs because of the fall in real wages, causes unemployment to return to the **NAIRU** level.

NAIRU is the level of unemployment which exists when the aggregate demand for labour is equal to the aggregate supply of labour at the going wage rate. It is consistent with the level of unemployment at which there is no upward pressure on the wage rate and inflation.

NAIRU consists of voluntary, frictional and structural unemployment. These are the people who are out of work because they are unaware of vacancies, unsuited to take up the vacancies or are unwilling to take up the vacancies.

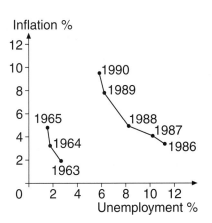

Figure 3 The rightward shift of the short run Phillips curve in the UK in the 1980s

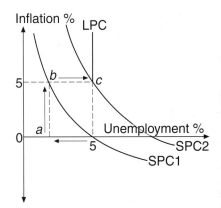

Figure 4 The long run Phillips curve

Definitions

Monetarists are a group of economists who believe that increases in the money supply in excess of increases in output will cause inflation.

Long run Phillips curve (LPC) is a curve that indicates that there is no long run trade off between unemployment and inflation.

NAIRU (the non-accelerating inflation rate of unemployment) is the level of unemployment that exists when the labour market is in equilibrium.

After the return of the NAIRU level the economy moves to point **c** on the LPC, where there is no trade-off between unemployment and inflation. However, the economy is also on a higher level short run Phillips curve since now expectations of inflation have been built into the system. Producers and workers have experienced 5 per cent inflation and so will base their future prices and wage claims on the assumption that the price level will continue to rise. Any future increase in aggregate demand not accompanied by an increase in long run aggregate supply will result in an acceleration in inflation.

Policy implications of the long run Phillips curve

The long run Phillips curve implies that there is no trade-off between unemployment and inflation in the long run and that governments are powerless to reduce unemployment by implementing expansionary fiscal and monetary policy.

The view that government attempts to reduce unemployment by increasing aggregate demand would not succeed in lowering unemployment but would increase inflation was expressed by James Callaghan, the Labour prime minister, in a speech to the Labour Party Conference in 1976. The Conservative government, which came to power in 1979, subscribed to this view, and the Conservative administrations of the 1980s and 1990s did not attempt to reduce unemployment by increasing aggregate demand.

Relationship between Phillips curves and aggregate demand and supply

The long run Phillips curve is related to the long run aggregate supply curve. An increase in aggregate demand, caused by, for example, a rise in government spending, will in the short run increase real GDP and raise the price level. In the long run, there will be a decrease in short run aggregate supply due to the rise in production costs that occur when output is produced beyond the productive potential level.

Figure 5, which uses an aggregate demand curve, an aggregate supply curve and Phillips curves, shows how an increase in aggregate demand results in higher inflation but unchanged unemployment in the long run.

Recent relationship between unemployment and inflation

The late 1990s and early 2000s witnessed falls in both the unemployment rate and the inflation rate in the USA, the UK and a number of other European countries. Economic relationships appear to have changed in this period. Falling unemployment was not putting upward pressure on the

> 'It used to be thought that a nation could just spend its way out of recession and increase employment by cutting taxes and boosting government spending. I tell you in all candour that that option no longer exists. In so far as it existed in the past, it had always led to a bigger dose of inflation followed by a higher level of unemployment.'
> James Callaghan

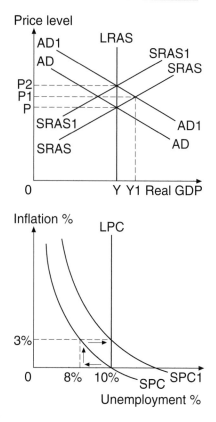

Figure 5 The long run relationship between unemployment and inflation

inflation rate. There were a number of reasons advanced to explain why inflationary pressure may have fallen. These included:

- changes in labour markets for example, reduced trade union power and increased labour market flexibility
- advances in technology which reduce unit costs
- increased competition from abroad forcing firms to keep down rises in prices.

Figure 6 shows an almost horizontal Phillips curve for the UK for the period 1993 and 2001. As the economy approached full employment, inflation remained low.

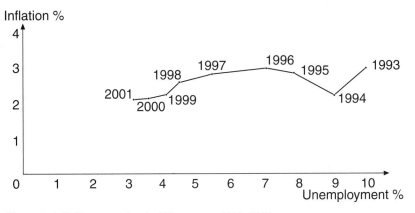

Figure 6 A Phillips curve for the UK economy 1993–2001

A horizontal Phillips curve is an ideal situation for a government, as it means that it can achieve both low unemployment and low inflation – that is, there is no policy conflict.

Quickies

1   Why might a fall in unemployment cause an increase in inflation?
2   In what sense does the short run Phillips curve indicate a policy conflict?
3   Why, in the long run, may there be no trade off between unemployment and inflation?
4   What could cause the long run Phillips curve to shift to the left?

Activities

Activity 1

	Budget deficit % of GDP		Unemployment rates %		Real GDP growth %	
	2000	2002	2000	2002	2000	2002
UK	4.0	−1.2	4.7	5.4	3.1	1.6
Germany	1.1	−3.6	7.8	8.2	2.9	0.2
France	−1.3	−3.1	9.6	8.8	4.2	1.2
Italy	−0.6	−2.4	10.6	9.0	3.1	0.4
Spain	−0.6	−0.1	13.9	11.4	4.2	2.0

Source: IMF World Economic Outlook April 2003.

Table 1 Budget positions

Pitfalls to avoid

The budget deficit records the annual excess of government expenditure over the tax revenue collected. A positive figure indicates that the budget was in surplus. The UK Treasury 'Golden rule' states that the current spending budget must be balanced over the course of the economic cycle.

a) Suggest reasons for the general deterioration in the fiscal positions of the European nations shown in Table 1.

b) What is the likely impact of a significant budget deficit on an economy?

c) How might membership of the Euro constrain a government's macroeconomic policy freedom?

Activity 2

Regional trading bloc	Value of exports within trading bloc $mn				% of total exports traded within the bloc			
	1970	1980	1990	1999	1970	1980	1990	1999
APEC	58,663	357,697	901,560	1,904,911	57.8	57.9	68.3	71.9
EU	76,451	456,857	981,260	1,376,314	59.5	60.8	65.9	62.6
NAFTA	22,078	102,218	226,273	581,162	36.0	33.6	41.4	54.6
MERCOSUR	451	3424	4127	15,313	9.4	11.6	8.9	20.5
ECOWAS	86	692	1533	2687	2.9	10.1	7.8	12.2

Source: World Bank Development Indicators 2001.

Table 2 Trade blocs

a) Suggest three reasons for the significant rise in the value of exports shown in Table 2.

b) What evidence does Table 2 provide for the increasing importance of regional trading blocs in recent years?

c) Assess the potential disadvantages associated with the growth of regional trading blocs?

Activity 3

	Foreign direct investment $ mn		Portfolio investment (bonds) $ mn		Portfolio investment (equities) $ mn		Net capital flows $ mn
	1990	1999	1990	1999	1990	1999	1999
Argentina	1836	23,929	-857	8000	13	404	32,296
Brazil	989	32,296	129	2683	0	1961	22,793
Mexico	2634	11,786	661	5621	563	1129	8244
China	3487	38,753	-48	660	0	3732	40,632
Indonesia	1093	-2745	26	-1458	312	1273	-8416
Korea, Rep.	788	9333	151	-1414	518	12,426	6409
Mozambique	9	384	0	0	0	0	374
Sudan	0	371	0	0	0	0	371

Source: World Bank.

Table 3 Capital flows

a) What is meant by 'foreign direct investment'?
b) What does Table 3 suggest about the extent of globalisation of investment flows?
c) How might the table be used to illustrate the negative side of global capital flows?
d) Evaluate the effects of foreign direct investment on a nation.

Activity 4

	1996	1997	1998	1999	2000	2001
The UK real effective exchange rate, 1990 = 100	96.0	114.4	121.7	123.8	130.6	130.3
Current account balance $bn	-13.6	-2.8	-8.0	-31.9	-29.1	-23.6

Source: IMF World Economic Outlook April 2003.

Table 4 The exchange rate and current account position

a) What is meant by the 'real effective exchange rate'?
b) What factors might account for the appreciation of the £ over the period shown?
c) How might the strength of the currency be used to explain the movement of the UK current account of the balance of payments?

Activity 1

a) The UK and Germany moved from a significant budget surplus in 2000 to a budget deficit in 2002. However, the Spanish budget deficit shrank, so the question is not entirely accurate. The key point is the decrease in the growth rates of these economies (use the data to show this). This reduces the tax revenues from income taxes and corporation taxes particularly, and would also mean higher benefit payments such as income support (link to unemployment data). The UK also decided to increase expenditure significantly on public services.

b) A budget deficit is an expansionary fiscal policy that stimulates aggregate demand, through government spending and/or indirectly through lower taxation allowing greater consumer expenditure. The multiplier then acts on this injected demand to magnify the final impact on GDP. If the economy has spare capacity, it is likely to generate more output and employment, but if the economy is close to full employment then the extra demand is likely to be inflationary. Government spending on capital projects and supply-side policies or direct tax cuts might also raise the aggregate supply of the economy.

c) Macroeconomic demand management can be separated into monetary and fiscal policies. Membership of the Euro would remove control of interest rates, the exchange rate and the rate of growth of the money supply from an individual nation and give it to the European Central Bank. However, technically the Bank of England has been operationally independent of the government in handling monetary policy since May 1997. The 'Growth and Stability Pact' limits the size of the budget deficit that a Euro nation is allowed to 3% of GDP, so this constrains the overall fiscal position, although some nations have recently exceeded the constraint.

Activity 2

a) ▪ The figures are not adjusted for inflation.
   ▪ Economic growth has raised incomes and demand for other nations imports.
   ▪ Trade barriers have been removed.

b) The share of trade conducted within these trade blocs has risen, as well as the large increase in the value of trade conducted. This means that trade with non-trading bloc nations has not risen as fast as that with the trading bloc. Data on the share of total world exports would be needed to prove the growing importance of trading blocs.

c) ▪ Trade diversion – this may cause allocative inefficiency by shifting trade from efficient non-member nations to less efficient members of the trading bloc who do not face tariff-barriers.
   ▪ Raise prices above world market levels.
   ▪ Reduce tariff revenues.
   ▪ Structural unemployment if the trade protection a domestic industry received from import competition is removed.

Exam hint

Remember that this is the synoptic unit so material from AS unit 3 can come in useful in question 1b. You could illustrate the effects described by using an AD/AS diagram with a Keynesian LRAS curve.

Boost your grade

APEC Asian Pacific Economic Co-operation, founded 1989, consists of 21 Pacific-rim nations.
NAFTA North American Free Trade Area, founded 1994, USA, Canada and Mexico.
MERCOSUR Southern Cone Common Market, founded 1991, Argentina, Brazil, Paraguay and Uruguay.
ECOWAS Economic Community of West African States, founded 1975, 16 west African nations.

Activity 3

a) Foreign direct investment refers to the setting up of foreign subsidiaries or the acquisition of a lasting management interest in a foreign company (more than 10% of the voting shares in that company).

b) The size of the investment flows, both direct and portfolio, has significantly increased to the South American and Asian countries shown. Especially marked is the increased integration of the Chinese economy. However, the African nations do not seem to be integrated into the financial flows at all and they are only just starting to receive significant direct investment.

c) Negative figures illustrate the withdrawal of capital from nations e.g. the Asian crisis aftermath. This might significantly reduce AD and AS in the nations concerned.

d) *For:*

Employment
Multiplier income gains
Transfer of technology and skills
Tax revenue
Provision of infrastructure.

Against:

Environmental problems
Growing inequality
Exploitation of workforce
Monopoly power
Political interference.

Activity 4

a) The real effective exchange rate is a trade-weighted average of the pound's value against other currencies adjusted to remove differences in inflation between nations. It compares the unit labour costs of the UK manufacturing sector to a trade-weighted average of those of its industrial trading partners.

b) Increased demand for sterling or decreased supply of sterling.
   Causes:
   - Higher UK real interest rates than abroad.
   - Current Account surpluses.

c) The appreciation of the currency may have caused an inverse J-curve effect. In 1996-7, in the short run, when the Marshall-Lerner condition failed the UK current account improved. However, by 1998-9 the demand for UK exports may have become more elastic and the strength of sterling might have severely damaged our competitiveness.

Exam guidance and practice

Exam guidance

Unit 6 comprises 20% of the total A-level mark (or 40% of the A2 mark).

This is the synoptic unit allowing you to bring in economic theory and ideas from anywhere in the course, if you feel that it is relevant to the question. However, the syllabus content is concentrated in the area of international economics. You must answer ONE of three structured essay questions and ONE of the two data response questions. The time limit is one hour and forty-five minutes.

This time allowance gives you sufficient time to consider carefully which questions you are going to attempt and to plan out your essay answer. You may answer either section first, and some candidates may find that the data response passages provide some useful material that might generate ideas for the essays.

Section A: the structured essay questions

It is obviously crucial that you select the essay that you can perform best on. An essay plan is a useful way to draw together your ideas and lend coherence to the structure of the essay, but it is also a good tool to confirm that you can write at length in response to that question. You should spend about 5-10 minutes choosing and planning your essay and 40–45 minutes writing. The plan should identify the main points that you intend to expand on, but should not be too long. Each essay will be split into two parts and you should allocate your time in proportion to the marks available, for example if part a) is worth 40, you should spend 16–18 minutes on it.

If your essay appears one-sided it is likely that you have missed the evaluation element of the question, which is worth 30% of the total marks on unit 6. You should respond directly to the specific question set and not write the essay in response to a title that you have prepared. It is a good idea to bring the wording of the title back into your essay frequently to ensure that your argument is always kept relevant.

Section B: the data response questions

Question selection is again vital so 5–10 minutes should be spent reading the passages thoroughly. Read the questions first to make the initial reading of the passages more profitable. Note that the marks tend to be higher in the later questions so make sure that you get through to answer them. You should have at least 40 minutes for writing, so if a question is only worth 4 marks out of the 50 you should only be spending 2-3 minutes answering it and move on. Remember to quote the passage and manipulate the data (for example, calculate percentage changes). The passages are based around contemporary economic articles and so it is a good idea to read widely around economic affairs throughout the course to gain a prior working knowledge of the issues that are raised.

Pitfalls to avoid

Although the essay (section A) appears to be marked out of 100 and worth twice as much as the data response (section B) the mark is then halved. Therefore both sections are equally weighted and you should allocate your time accordingly.

Exam hint

Do not rush into answering an essay question because you like the topic area. Make sure that you understand what *both* parts of the question are about. If you rush into doing the wrong essay and then start another you will experience real time difficulties.

Exam practice

1) a) What impact might an appreciating exchange rate have on the rate of inflation and unemployment in the UK? (40)
   b) Examine the factors other than the exchange rate that might influence the competitiveness of UK goods and services? (60)

2) a) Why has the UK moved back into a budget deficit in 2002? (40)
   b) Evaluate the desirability of a government running a budget deficit. (60)

3) In 2002 the United States ran a $503.4 billion current account deficit on the balance of payments while Japan had a $113 billion surplus.
   a) Examine the factors that might explain these figures. (40)
   b) Examine the effects that this might have on the US and Japanese economies? (60)

4) a) Examine the arguments for reducing the tariffs that the EU places on imported agricultural products. (40)
   b) To what extent are there still justifications for protectionism in the modern global economy? (60)

5) a) Assess the case against raising the higher rate of income tax in the UK. (40)
   b) Examine the effects of raising tax revenue through higher levels of indirect taxation. (60)

6) a) What constraints would membership of the Euro place on UK macroeconomic policy? (40)
   b) Evaluate the effectiveness of the policy tools that would remain to control the rate of unemployment and inflation if the UK joined the Euro? (60)

Boost your grade

The higher rate of income tax is 40% on all income earned above £35,115 in 2003–4 (for a single under–65 year old). This is the lowest higher rate in the European Union although other nations' tax systems may have very different tax thresholds where the higher rate becomes applicable.

Further reading

6.24

6.2
C. Bamford and S. Grant, *The UK Economy in a Global Context*, Heinemann, 2000, Chapters 4 and 5.

6.3, 6.4, 6.5 and 6.6
C. Bamford and S. Grant, *The UK Economy in a Global Context*, Heinemann, 2000, Chapter 5.

6.7
C. Bamford and S. Grant, *The UK Economy in a Global Context*, Heinemann, 2000, Chapter 2.

6.8
C. Bamford and S. Grant, *The UK Economy in a Global Context*, Heinemann, 2000, Chapter 5.

6.9
C. Bamford and S. Munday, *Markets*, Heinemann, 2002, Chapter 6.

6.10
C. Bamford and S. Grant, *The UK Economy in a Global Context*, Heinemann, 2000, Chapter 5.
B. Hill, *The European Union*, 4th edn., Heinemann, 2001, Chapter 6.
M. Russell and D. Heathfield, *Inflation and UK Monetary Policy*, 3rd edn., Heinemann, 1999, Chapter 10.
D. Smith, *UK Current Economic Policy*, 3rd edn., Heinemann, 2003, Chapter 9.

6.11
C. Bamford and S. Grant, *The UK Economy in a Global Context*, Heinemann, 2000, Chapters 5 and 8.

6.12 and 6.13
C. Bamford and S. Grant, *The UK Economy in a Global Context*, Heinemann, 2000, Chapter 3.

6.14
C. Bamford and S. Grant, *The UK Economy in a Global Context*, Heinemann, 2000, Chapter 3.
D. Smith, *UK Current Economic Policy*, 3rd edn., Heinemann, 2003, Chapter 3.

6.15
C. Bamford and S. Grant, *The UK Economy in a Global Context*, Heinemann, 2000, Chapter 3.
D. Smith, *UK Current Economic Policy*, 3rd edn., Heinemann, 2003, Chapters 1–5.

6.16

C. Bamford and S. Grant, *The UK Economy in a Global Context*,
Heinemann, 2000, Chapters 2 and 7.

G. Hale, *Labour Markets*, Heinemann, 2001, Chapter 5.

D. Smith, *UK Current Economic Policy*, 3rd edn., Heinemann, 2003, Chapter 5.

6.17

C. Bamford and S. Grant, *The UK Economy in a Global Context*,
Heinemann, 2000, Chapter 6.

G. Hale, *Labour Markets*, Heinemann, 2001, Chapter 5.

6.18

C. Bamford and S. Grant, *The UK Economy in a Global Context*,
Heinemann, 2000, Chapters 2 and 6.

M. Russell and D. Heathfield, *Inflation and UK Monetary Policy*, 3rd edn.,
Heinemann, 1999, Chapters 2 and 4.

6.19

C. Bamford and S. Grant, *The UK Economy in a Global Context*,
Heinemann, 2000, Chapter 6.

M. Russell and D. Heathfield, *Inflation and UK Monetary Policy*, 3rd edn.,
Heinemann, 1999, Chapter 3.

6.20

C. Bamford and S. Grant, *The UK Economy in a Global Context*,
Heinemann, 2000, Chapter 6.

M. Russell and D. Heathfield, *Inflation and UK Monetary Policy*, 3rd edn.,
Heinemann, 1999, Chapters 4 and 5.

D. Smith, *UK Current Economic Policy*, 3rd edn., Heinemann, 2003, Chapter 5.

Glossary

Ability to pay principle the rule that people with higher incomes should pay more in tax

Absolute poverty the inability to purchase the basic necessities of life

Benefit principle the rule that the amount people pay in tax should be related to the benefit they derive from public expenditure

Bilateral monopoly a market with a single buyer and seller

Capital equipment man-made goods used to produce other goods and services

Cartel a group of producers who agree to fix price levels

Collectivisation forcing individual farmers to form larger agricultural holdings to gain economies of scale and other productivity gains

Contestable market a market that may appear to act as if it were competitive, even though the structure is oligopolistic

Cyclical unemployment unemployment arising from a lack of aggregate demand

Debt service the proportion of a country's foreign earnings required to pay interest and repay foreign loans

Deflationary fiscal policy decreases in public expenditure and increases in taxation designed to decrease aggregate demand

Dependency ratio measures the economically inactive population as a proportion of the total working population (employed + unemployed). Economically inactive dependents include children, the elderly/retired and housewives

Derived demand the demand for one item depending on the demand for another item

Devaluation the reduction of a fixed exchange rate from one value to a lower value by the government

Discouraged workers people who have given up looking for work

Dumping the sale of products at less than cost price

Economically inactive	people who are neither in employment nor unemployed, for example, children, the elderly/retired and housewives
Elasticity of demand for labour	the responsiveness of demand for labour to a change in the wage rate
Elasticity of supply of labour	the responsiveness of the supply of labour to a change in the wage rate
Euro area	the countries that have adopted the euro as their currency. The area currently consists of Austria, Belgium, Finland, France, Germany, Greece, the Republic of Ireland, Italy, Luxembourg, the Netherlands, Portugal and Spain
Female participation rate	the % of women that are either employed or unemployed using the International Labour Organisation's definition of unemployment calculated in the Labour Force Survey
Fiscal	the use of government spending and taxation to influence macroeconomic variables
Fixed exchange rate	an exchange rate fixed against other currencies that is maintained by the government
Floating exchange rate	an exchange rate determined by market forces
Foreign direct investment (FDI)	refers to the setting up of foreign subsidiaries or the acquisition of a lasting management interest in a foreign company (more than 10% of the voting shares in that company)
Frictional unemployment	unemployment arising because workers are in between jobs
Globalisation	the development of the world into one marketplace
Goodhart's law	the view that any measure of the money supply behaves differently when it is targeted
Hard currencies	those such as the $, £ and euro which are freely used for international trade. Many currencies of developing countries are not

	generally acceptable as a means of payment for international trade
Harrod-Domar model	suggests that the rate of economic growth of a nation will be equal to the savings ratio divided by the capital-output ratio. The savings ratio is the % of GDP that is saved. The capital-output ratio measures the efficiency of the capital in the nation
Horizontal integration	taking over or merging with businesses at similar stages of the distribution cycle, for example, supermarket retailers
Hostile acquisition	a takeover not accepted or welcomed by the current owners of a company
Human Development Index	calculated by the United Nations Development Programme. It measures longevity, knowledge and resources as components of living standards. One third of the index is given to real GDP per capita, one third to life expectancy and the final third to literacy rates and school enrolment
Import penetration	the ratio of imports to domestic consumption
Infant industry	a newly established industry that has not yet grown large enough to take full advantage of the available economies of scale
J curve effect	the tendency for a fall in the exchange rate to make the trade position worse before it gets better
Law of diminishing returns	applies to short run costs faced by a firm. It states that if a firm seeks to increase production in the short run, its marginal costs of production will first fall, then bottom out, then rise
Long run Phillips curve (LPC)	a curve that indicates that there is no long run trade off between unemployment and inflation
Managed exchange rate	an exchange rate system in which a government allows the exchange rate to move within margins

Marginal cost	the change in cost brought about by changing production by one unit
Marginal productivity theory	the view that demand for a factor of production depends on its marginal revenue product
Marginal revenue	the change in revenue brought about by changing production by one unit
Marginal revenue product of labour	the change in a firm's revenue resulting from employing one more worker
Marshall-Lerner condition	the view that for a fall in the exchange rate to be successful in improving a country's trade position, the combined elasticities of demand for exports and imports must be greater than one
Monetarists	a group of economists who believe that increases in the money supply in excess of increases in output will cause inflation
Monopoly	theoretically when one firm produces the whole output of a given industry
Monopsonist	a single buyer
Multinational companies (MNCs)	companies that produces products in several different countries
NAIRU (the non-accelerating inflation rate of unemployment)	the level of unemployment that exists when the labour market is in equilibrium
Newly industrialised countries (NICS)	countries that have experienced a rapid rate of growth of their manufacturing sector – most noticeably, the Asian tigers
Normal profits	includes (as a cost) the profit necessary to reward the entrepreneur with enough return to keep his capital/labour invested in the firm. This will be the opportunity cost, what that money/his time could have earned elsewhere
Oligopolistic firms	those operating in an industry with few competitors
Oligopsonist	one of a few dominant buyers
Parity	the price of one currency in terms of another currency or group of currencies

Participation rate	the proportion of those of working age in the working population (labour force)
Personal allowance	the amount of income earned before paying income tax (£4615 for a single person under 65 in 2003-4)
Phillips curve	a graph showing the relationship between unemployment and inflation
Pigouvian tax	a tax designed to correct a negative externality
Profit maximising level of employment	occurs when MRP = MC of labour
Protectionism	the restriction on the free movement of products between countries
Public limited companies (plcs)	companies that have limited liability and sell shares to the general public
Public sector net borrowing (PSNB)	the excess of public expenditure over revenue
Quota	a limit on the quantity of a product that can be imported
Reflationary fiscal policy	increases in public expenditure and cuts in taxation designed to increase aggregate demand
Regulatory capture	arises when regulators of industries become unduly influenced by the managers of the industries they are regulating
Relative poverty	a situation of being poor relative to others
Sales maximisation	a firm selling as much output as it can to maximise its market share, subject to the constraint of not making a loss. Thus the firm can lower its price to increase the quantity demanded, up to the point that the price (AR) is just equal to the AC
Social economy	the value of outputs not captured by GDP, such as childcare by other members of the family
Structural adjustment	the euphemistic term given to the act of forcing developing countries to adopt free market policies

Structural unemployment	unemployment arising from changes in demand and supply that cause a change in the structure of the economy's base and a change in demand for labour
Tariffs	tax on imports
Terms of trade	the ratio of export prices to import prices
The multiplier	the relationship between an initial change in aggregate demand and the final change in GDP
Trade union	an association of workers
Transfer payments	money transferred from one person or group to another not in return for any good or service
Transfer pricing	relates to internal trading within different parts of MNCs in which resource might be sold very cheaply from a developing to a developed country but thereafter they are traded internally at much higher prices
Trickle down	the argument that if the incomes of the better-off improve, the poor will also benefit
Vertical integration	taking over or merging with businesses at different stages of the distribution cycle, for example, manufacturers and distributors
Wage-price spiral	a rise in wages which triggers off rises in the price level and in turn leads to higher wage claims
Working population	those who are economically active, for example, in employment or unemployed

Index